Without This Ring

Surviving Divorce

Christ-centered
steps toward
hope and healing

Donna Pyle

This book is dedicated to Jesus.
His love never fails.

Published 2016 by Concordia Publishing House
3558 S. Jefferson Avenue, St. Louis, MO 63118-3968
1-800-325-3040 · www.cph.org

Manufactured in the United States of America

1 2 3 4 5 6 7 8 9 10   25 24 23 22 21 20 19 18 17 16

TABLE OF CONTENTS

Introduction 5

Chapter 1 What in the World Happened? 9

Chapter 2 Forgiveness: It's a Process, Not a Destination...........................25

Chapter 3 Anger: Releasing the Beast Instead of Caging It.....................53

Chapter 4 What Does the Bible Say about Divorce? 81

Chapter 5 Processing Grief: Surviving the Emotional F5 Tornado 95

Chapter 6 Using Kid Gloves to Walk Children through Divorce 119

Chapter 7 The Vital Roles of Counseling and Immersion in Scripture 141

Chapter 8 The Important Role of Your Church and Faith Family 165

Chapter 9 Repeat after Me: "I Cannot Change My Ex"
(Communication 101) 177

Chapter 10 How to Handle Family, Friends, and Nosy Neighbors.............195

Chapter 11 Sleeping Single in a Double Bed: Managing Loneliness
and Midnight Madness 207

Chapter 12 Practical Tips for Managing Your Home
and Finances Alone 221

Chapter 13 Handling Holidays, Wedding Photos,
and Your Wedding Ring...233

Chapter 14 Save the Date: Guarding Your Heart and Sexual Integrity......245

Chapter 15 When the Vow Breaks: Learning to Trust Again 263

Chapter 16 You Can Do It! 279

Chapter 17 Breathing the Fresh Air of Freedom
and Embracing Your Future 293

Acknowledgments 303

Expert Consultants 305

References 307

Introduction

You never thought divorce would happen to you. But it did. You may feel angry, vengeful, traumatized, relieved, hopeful, afraid—or all of the above. How can you ever heal from the trauma? How can you minimize the trauma for your kids? How can you possibly forgive such significant hurt? And where is God in all of this?

Following my divorce, one question haunted me: *If God hates divorce, does God hate me?* That may seem extreme, but for Christians experiencing divorce, that thought is very real. I felt as if the whole world were judging me or talking to me only to find out what happened or who did what. I trusted precious few people during the whole process.

Titling this book *Without This Ring: Surviving Divorce* may seem overly dramatic, but after experiencing the trauma of divorce—both internally and externally—I felt like I had survived a bloody war. The scariest part is that you don't know which side of the front line your friends fall behind until you step on a land mine. People I considered to be close friends simply backed into the shadows, and I've never heard from them again. Others stepped forward to become some of the most wonderful encouragers God could have ever provided.

Divorce affects every aspect of your life: emotional, spiritual, and physical. It feels like amputation without anesthetic. Probably the hardest part to grasp about the whole process is wondering what happened to the person you thought you married, the plans you made together, and the dreams you shared. You ride a mental roller coaster between desperation and revenge.

Without This Ring: Surviving Divorce provides clear steps for dealing with each stage of grief and transition from a biblical standpoint and from many people who have experienced it, as well as guidance for embracing and taking steps toward the new life God has already prepared for you.

When it's all said and done, *you* determine how well you get through divorce. I have seen some people turn angry and bitter, while others use their trauma to grow exponentially in every area of their life. The people I specifically chose to interview for this book fall into the second category, because I desperately desire everyone who experiences divorce to know that hope and healing are possible for everyone regardless of the circumstances. When we turn to God, He does not turn away. He reaches down into our pits and pulls us toward Him time and time again.

Without This Ring: Surviving Divorce is not a twelve-step process that guarantees life will work out exactly as you want. It's a heart-to-heart, been-there-done-that, faith-filled, and hope-fueled approach to topics such as forgiveness, anger, learning what the Bible says about divorce, regaining peace, walking children through divorce, counseling, communication, loneliness, finances, handling holidays, setting boundaries and goals, and embracing your future with hopeful expectation. Most of all, it's powerful reassurance from me and dozens of Christians who have experienced divorce that no matter what has happened or what may happen next, God still has His perfect plan for you.

Although it is true that God hates divorce, it's also true that *"[neither] height nor depth, nor anything else in all creation, will be able to separate us from the love of God in Christ Jesus our Lord"* (Romans 8:39).

You *will* learn to laugh and love again.

This book can help you do it.

What in the World Happened?

There comes a time when silence is betrayal.
—Martin Luther King Jr.

Christmas is my absolute favorite time of year, bar none. It's a special time of family, festivities, and fa-la-la-ing. Well, except for the Christmas of 2009. At a time when beauty and joy should have danced freely, darkness and heartbreak carried out a deadly home invasion.

MY STORY

My husband and I had made our usual Thanksgiving plans to spend the first half of the day with his family and the second half with mine. After a wonderful meal and visit, we left his parents' house around midafternoon and headed to my family's celebration.

Then, a few hours later, completely out of the blue, my husband informed me that he had made plans to go hunting with friends for the rest of the long holiday weekend. (As an aside, my husband had only begun to exhibit an interest in hunting that year.) Hurt and confused, I asked him why he hadn't told me earlier about his out-of-town plans. After all, I had thought we would decorate the house together, then snuggle on the couch under a blanket, sipping wine and chatting quietly, illuminated by our festive Christmas tree, like we did each year. Instead, he stumbled through an explanation, gave me a peck on the cheek, wished my family a happy Thanksgiving, and promptly left. I felt like the wind had been knocked out of me. I headed home alone a few hours later, upset and sad.

I felt like the wind had been knocked out of me.

The rest of the weekend, I moped around the house, not putting up a single decoration. My heart just wasn't in it. I was sad to start out the Christmas holidays alone. My husband returned on Sunday night with tales of fantastic hunting and good times. He also expressed surprise that the house wasn't all decked out for Christmas. When I told him how sad I felt, he apologized but ultimately just brushed the topic aside.

We both headed to work the next morning as usual. At around three o'clock that afternoon, my husband called to tell me that he and his hunting friends were getting together that night to clean their kills and divide the meat from the hunt. In that moment, I knew something wasn't right. Although I'm not a hunter, I am a native, lifelong Texan, and I had been around hunters my whole life. I knew that one of the cardinal rules is that you clean any kill immediately in order to preserve the meat.

My mind whirled the rest of the day as I slowly recalled similar stories my husband had relayed over the past year that didn't smell right. Normally, my mind would have not taken that train of thought, except for one important factor: seven years earlier (six years into our marriage), he had had an affair. Since he was the lifelong Christian and I was relatively new to the faith at the time, I thought perhaps I had done something wrong or was not acting like a proper Christian wife. Even though he said his affair was not my fault, I internalized all the blame.

We told no one about his affair. He promised to enroll us in counseling with the caveat that it occur at a different church so no one would find out. (That should have raised a red flag, but it didn't.)

The counseling never transpired, and I finally quit asking about it. I never brought up his affair again because I had always heard that once you forgive someone, you don't keep bringing up past sins. I realized too late that having no accountability provided my husband another seven years to master the art of hiding his extracurricular activities.

This time around I needed to know the whole truth and nothing but the truth, so help me God. Since I had found out about the first affair on his cell phone, I knew that would be the truth teller this time as well. I never saw his monthly bill since we held separate cell phone contracts. As a teacher, he arrived home each day much earlier than I did, so he always picked up the mail. The only way I had found out about his first affair was because I had stayed home from work one day and happened to pick up the mail first. His cell phone bill had arrived and I opened it, curious as to how much he paid compared to me. I never expected to find evidence of infidelity.

I knew this time would be no different. I needed to get his cell phone. When he returned home later that evening, I never brought up my suspicions. We retired as usual.

The next morning, Tuesday, December 1, 2009—the day that lives in infamy—we woke up at our usual 5:00 a.m. I made breakfast and coffee, then settled into my recliner with my Bible and notepad for my morning quiet time. I had slept poorly and felt a sobering sense of pending doom.

When he hopped into the shower to get ready for work, I knew my chance had arrived. Heart racing, I leaped out of my chair, found his car keys, and raced outside to search his car for his cell phone. I felt like such a thief. We respected each other's privacy, so it was completely out of my nature to rifle through his personal belongings. I located his cell

Even though he said his affair was not my fault, I internalized all the blame.

11

phone in the car's console, locked the doors, ran back into the house, and replaced his keys.

With a sigh of relief, I heard his shower still running, and I dove back into my recliner as if I had never left. Heart still pounding, I switched on his cell phone and began scrolling through his text messages. Less than thirty seconds of scrolling confirmed my suspicions.

I felt like bawling. Throwing things. Crumpling to the floor. Ripping off his head. Running away. Screaming until my throat hurt. So many emotions hit me in waves that I felt numb. I switched off his cell phone and waited.

I needed TIME.

He finished getting ready, kissed me good-bye, and left for work. That kiss was our last.

I switched on his cell phone again, turned to a new page in my notepad, and began writing names as I scrolled past them. Yes, names. *Plural.* Not just one woman. Several women. My mouth went dry. Then I noticed the time stamp on some of the texts started as early as 5:30 a.m. Right then, I heard the outside garage door raise. My husband rushed into the house in a panic, exclaiming that he believed his car had been burglarized since he was missing his cell phone and perhaps a couple of textbooks.

I looked him in the eye, held up his cell phone, and asked, "This cell phone?"

All the color drained from his face.

He sat on the arm of the chair across from me and said, "I'm so sorry." I asked if there was anything he wanted to tell me before I began digging. He said, "I'm having an affair."

I felt like bawling. Throwing things. Crumpling to the floor. Ripping off his head.

Devastated, I saw those four words float through the air in slow motion, then speed across the room and slam into my chest, sending my heart to the floor in a gazillion pieces. All that kept running through my mind in that moment was *But I gave you a second chance!*

Numb, I slowly told him that I needed to figure out some things, starting with uncovering the secrets his cell phone held. He didn't want to leave the house without it, but I told him that he could take my phone if he believed he would have an emergency. "I don't have anything to hide," I said.

He declined and started to argue about retrieving his phone. In the middle of listening to him build his case, it hit me: he was more concerned about hiding the evidence on his phone than doing everything he could to save our marriage.

It was too much.

I catapulted out of my recliner, sending my Bible and papers flying, and started shouting colorful, unsuitable phrases, ending with "JUST GET OUT!" At one point, I picked up something (I can't remember what) and aimed for his head, calling him ugly names with every jagged breath.

I'm not proud of that moment. I had never called him names like that before (or vice versa) and certainly had never thrown anything at him. Looking back, I'm torn between feeling bad about my behavior in those minutes and feeling like I didn't call him anything bad enough for the catastrophic pain he caused.

He left without his phone and drove to work. I couldn't even think straight. I called in sick to work then broke down in sobs.

Ten minutes later, I composed myself, picked up the scattered notepad and pen, switched on his phone, and began making calls. It was around 6:00 a.m. by then, and I woke up every woman who answered. I began each conversation with "Hi, my name is Donna Pyle. I think you know my husband."

Thirty minutes and half a dozen women later, I knew more than I ever wanted to know. I also knew in that moment that our marriage was over. My trust was irreparably shattered, and I realized that I could never believe any explanation he could offer.

A part of my heart died in that moment.

My Marriage

What you need to understand is that we had a loving marriage, as I saw it. I have so many more good memories than bad of our nineteen-year relationship (six years dating, thirteen years married). I don't know how to love in pieces, so he had my whole heart. We went on date nights, joyfully served our church together, took vacations together, had a large circle of friends, and enjoyed puttering around the house together in pajamas and slippers on lazy Saturday mornings. Yes, we argued over routine "married" issues, but we never called each other names or hit below the belt. Other than the usual busyness that keeps couples apart more often than they would like, I didn't feel any decline in our marriage.

"God, help me. I don't know what to do."

If you had asked me about my marriage before that morning, I would have stated emphatically that we were deeply in love and there was nothing that could destroy it. I thought we had already survived the worst following his first affair.

We didn't have children, so our time together was our own. We lived in a nice house and enjoyed a comfortable middle-class life together. I truly loved him, the relationship we shared, how we served God together, and the life God had given us. I was content and happy.

Seeking Help

One thing became crystal clear: I was not going to endure this trauma alone again. I made that mistake the first time. God had matured my faith enough to realize that I was in way over my head.

I sat motionless in my recliner for several minutes, trying to figure out what to do. I remember whispering a single prayer: *"God, help me. I don't know what to do."* In that instant, God brought to mind my friend Kristin. She is my senior pastor's wife and also a licensed Christian counselor (and an expert consultant for this book).

Kristin and I were scheduled to meet later that evening, so I called to cancel. I reached her voicemail and stumbled through a lame we-can't-meet-tonight-a-family-emergency-came-up message and hung up. She called back within ten minutes. From the tone of my voice, she admitted later, she knew something was terribly wrong. I broke down and told her what I had just discovered.

We arranged to meet together with one of my pastors that afternoon so that I could relay exactly what had transpired. I realized that the news would send ripple effects throughout our congregation since my husband was an elder and we served together as worship leaders. I knew it was important for one of my pastors to participate in our meeting to help us figure out how to walk through this together.

After hanging up, I slowly shuffled through each room in our home. Taking mental pictures. Trailing my fingers over photo frames. Remembering each moment captured. Cuddling with my two kitty cats. Staring out the living room windows, letting tears flow uninhibited. I knew in the depths of my soul that nothing would ever be the same again. I realized later that I was saying good-bye to the man and life that I had truly cherished.

I showered, dressed, and drove to my pastor's home for our meeting.

Kristin and my worship pastor, Doug, were waiting for me. The news hit them hard since they and their spouses were dear friends to both of us. For two hours, they listened, waited patiently when I needed time to compose myself, prayed with me, prayed for my husband, and provided much-needed wisdom. Looking back, I am thankful that God nudged me to take notes of my conversations with the women I had called earlier that day. Kristin and Doug never had to wonder whether or not they possessed the truth. I gave them a copy of my notes that included names, telephone numbers, and details about the relationships the women shared with my husband.

I felt completely numb after our meeting. I texted my best friend, who immediately met me at a local coffee shop. I told her all that had transpired since that morning. We cried together, and she prayed for me and my husband.

By that time, it was late afternoon, and I drove home to confront my husband. When he arrived home from work, I didn't shout or throw things. I felt very detached from the scene. I still couldn't believe what was happening. I asked him to tell me exactly what was going on, and he confessed to only some of what I had discovered. I told him that our marriage was over. I had given him a second chance and not only had he blown it, but he was actually living a double life that did not honor me, God, or our marriage covenant. He admitted that he had realized when he left our home that morning that our marriage was over. He told me that he loved me and that I didn't deserve what he had done.

Later, I would be grateful for those kind words. But not in that moment. I just felt lost, brokenhearted, and sad. We hugged for the last time, both of us in tears. He packed some personal items and left.

The sound of the door closing behind him felt like a two-by-four straight to my chest. I knew in that moment that life as I knew it would never be the same again. I sank into a puddle on the floor and sobbed uncontrollably.

I gave our pastors and church's elders several days to reach out to my husband. I simply couldn't. The emotional pain left me barely any strength to survive each day, much less try to discern between truth and lies. Four days later, my husband finally agreed to meet with my worship pastor. He made accountability promises to Doug that he never kept. In the days that followed, my husband continued to fabricate lies to his family and our mutual friends about what had transpired. I was heartbroken. I let him weave his web of lies that nailed the coffin lid on our marriage and then filed for divorce.

Four months later, dressed all in black, I stood in a courtroom. I signed the decree of divorce and left, a divorced woman.

Moving Forward

That's my personal account of what took place when my marriage exploded. I don't tell you this story to validate actions or point blame. I want you to realize that I understand the pain, doubt, and anger that you are experiencing. Our circumstances may vary, but I experienced the same feelings of loss, betrayal, broken trust, anger, sadness, grief, guilt, and so many other emotions. We will walk through them together in these chapters.

Over time, God will mend the pieces of your heart.

I am not a professional diagnosing a proposed scenario. I have wallowed in the muddy, bloody trenches of divorce, and I speak from hard-earned, heartbreaking experience.

Chances are you picked up this book because at some point, the same dirty bomb that leveled my marriage also leveled yours. You need to know how to walk through the spiritual, emotional, and physical shrapnel of divorce in order to experience God's healing.

You wonder how in the world God will ever bring good out of something so destructive.

You yearn to put the trauma to rest, once and for all.

You are tired of hurting and just want the pain to go away.

I understand.

Over time, God will mend the pieces of your heart. When you trust God wholeheartedly to heal your heart, soul, and mind, He always comes through. ALWAYS.

Although I still experience sadness when I remember certain things, God has removed their power to debilitate me into ineffectiveness.

If you experienced betrayal by the person who was supposed to love and cherish you above all, it is hard to recover. When trust is shattered, it affects every area of your life. Through Scripture, personal experience, and stories from dozens of others who have experienced divorce, we will walk together from victim to victor.

HOPE FOR YOU

Somewhere in these pages, you will find your story. You will also find the tools needed to turn this traumatic experience into opportunities for growth, change, and receiving God's ultimate healing. Although you may feel completely alone, God promises, *"I will not leave you nor forsake you"* (see Deuteronomy 31:8). If you think that your situation, actions, or words have driven God away, think again. His love for you is everlasting (Jeremiah 31:3).

You have experienced many sleepless, tear-filled nights, but remember: *"Weeping may tarry for the night, but joy comes with the morning"* (Psalm 30:5). Perhaps, like me, you have looked into the mirror and wondered, "How in the world did I miss the signs? How did I not see the reality?" My only response is that love is truly blind.

We don't want to see or believe the worst about those whom we love the most. But divorce forces us to hold up a magnifying glass. OUCH.

Through the pages of this book, we will work through these aspects of divorce:

- What the Bible says about divorce
- Receiving and extending forgiveness
- Surrendering anger and abdicating revenge
- The importance of counseling and immersion in God's Word
- Dealing with family and friends gently but firmly
- Walking children through divorce
- Managing your home and finances alone
- Sleeping single in a double bed (loneliness)
- Remaining connected with church and strong Christian friends
- Isolation and the importance of self-care
- Learning to trust again
- Setting healthy boundaries and goals
- Living in contentment
- Handling memories, wedding photos, and your wedding ring

- Allowing time to grieve the loss of your marriage before jumping into another relationship

- Embracing hope for your future

As you embark on this journey, God will never leave you for one moment. He will comfort you and provide exactly what you need in His perfect timing.

Every. Single. Need.

I wrote this book because I looked for such a Christian-based, hands-on resource to help me navigate the minefield of divorce, but no such book existed.

Now it does.

I want to be crystal clear about three important things:

1. This book does not show you how to get a divorce. It provides spiritual and emotional tools to help you heal if you are experiencing or have experienced divorce.

2. This book does not justify seeking a divorce simply because you fell out of love; that is not a biblical reason for divorce. But you will still find useful tools here if you are already divorced.

3. I do not advocate divorce. Some people have asked if I wrote this book to help people get divorced. Nothing could be further from the truth. This book is a survival guide for those experiencing divorce.

Walking through and moving past divorce is one of the hardest things you will ever do. You will need to re-read some of these chapters and spend extra time on others.

You will stumble and feel like giving up, but remember this: you do not operate in your own strength. Because you are God's child, His mighty strength resides in you through the power of the Holy Spirit. He has given you His mighty armor because you are one of His

This book does not show you how to get a divorce.

beloved soldiers. You have been wounded, but you are not defeated.

You may feel too weak to even get off the couch some days. That's okay. Just remember: *"The LORD is my shepherd. . . . He makes me lie down in green pastures. He leads me beside still waters. He restores my soul"* (Psalm 23:1–3).

I applaud you for getting this book. Your openness to devoting significant time, effort, and prayer toward healing speaks volumes about your desire to allow God to rebuild your life in order to step forward into the future that He has already prepared for you.

Keep reading.

Keep walking.

Keep praying.

God will hold you in the palm of His mighty hand every step of the way.

Every.

Single.

Step.

1: Pausing to Breathe, Pray, and Reflect

Relying on God and journeying with Him through the devastating hurt of divorce is not a suggestion—it's the only way you are going to emerge healed and whole when the storm is over. Admitting that you need God's help is not a weakness any more than admitting you need water to survive physically is a weakness.

Reaching the end of your rope is the beginning of hope.

God created you, and He has the perfect plan for your life. Your divorce was not a surprise to Him (though He weeps when you weep). He has already prepared the path to get you through it. Trusting Him and listening for His guidance are crucial.

You don't have to earn God's help—He provides His resources as a gift as we acknowledge our need for Him. He is ready to guide you through this and provide everything you need—yes, everything—to triumph over adversity and overcome even the most devastating circumstances.

Take your time walking through the following Bible passages, questions, prayer time, and journaling time before moving on to the next chapter.

SCRIPTURE TO READ, MEDITATE ON, AND MEMORIZE

Blessed are the poor in spirit. (Matthew 5:3)

He heals the brokenhearted and binds up their wounds. (Psalm 147:3)

Come to Me, all who labor and are heavy laden, and I will give you rest. (Matthew 11:28)

In left margin (handwritten): *That I took marriage vows "for better or worse"*

QUESTIONS FOR REFLECTION

At this point, you likely have many more questions than answers about how to survive the storm of divorce. As I mentioned in the introduction, one recurring question haunted me as I was going through the divorce process: *If God hates divorce, does God hate me?*

As we ease into the rest of this book, take a minute to answer these questions from the gut. No one is looking over your shoulder. It's just you and God. So get real and raw so that God can begin the healing process in your heart.

1. What recurring question haunts you most?

(handwritten) That divorce is not forgiven

2. What fear drives your question?

(handwritten) That I need God's forgiveness & to forgive myself

PAUSE FOR PRAYER

Beyond the shadow of a doubt, prayer is vital as you make life-changing decisions. God is the best guide for any path, so we need to take appropriate time to acknowledge His sovereignty, lay our hurts and frustrations before Him, and spend time listening to Him.

Now, I have never heard God audibly respond to my prayers. However, He speaks loud and clear through His Word and through godly people around me. The key is expectantly waiting for His response to your prayers. Throughout this book, we will use the **ACTS** acronym for our prayer time: Acknowledge, Confession, Thanksgiving, and Supplication (requests).

LET'S PRAY

A—Acknowledge God's sovereignty: You may not even have the brain bandwidth to know where to begin. I get that. So read Psalm 139:1–18 aloud to God with confidence.

C—Confession: You are experiencing hurt, confusion, fear, and perhaps anger right now (among a long list of other emotions). Even anger at God. Well, He can take it and turn you from it. Take this time to confess your feelings to God—the good, the bad, and the ugly. He already knows them, but believe me, when you verbally express those feelings, He begins to release that toxic brew from your heart, mind, and soul. Please pray aloud to God now to tell Him what you are feeling.

T—Thanksgiving: Expressing thanks in the middle of such pain may seem impossible. But pause the frantic race in your mind for a moment. You are breathing. Jesus still sacrificed His life to give you the certain hope of eternity with Him. He still has a specific purpose for you. Even in the storms, we have much to be thankful for, so we offer thanks to allow our mind to get past the pain pressing in and embrace God's love pouring in. List three things you are thankful for right now, and thank God for them.

1. *My family, their support*
2. *Priscilla and her honest Conversations*
3. *That I have had a faith in God*

S—Supplication (requests): God promises that when we pray, He faithfully hears us. One thing I remember clearly during those hard first days is asking God for His strength. Mine was gone. The emotional trauma of the divorce process left me feeling puny and incapable. Identify what you need from Him right now, and ask Him in faith to provide it.

Journal Prompt: Exhaling on the Page

One of the most helpful tools throughout my divorce process was faithfully keeping a journal (at the suggestion of my worship pastor). I confess that I did not journal regularly before then, but it turned out to be one of the most vital tools God used to get me through the divorce. Now, six years later, I read back over those pages and clearly see the hand of God at work when I could not see it then. I see times when I spewed ugly words and my writing was messy, hurried, and tear-stained. Then I see times when God struck me so deeply with His love and provision that I could not stop praising; there, my writing is beautiful and soothing.

If you have not started journaling through this process, begin TODAY. You don't need to have a fancy journal. Pick up the nearest yellow pad or some loose-leaf paper and start writing. God will use your journaling as another way to release toxic feelings and show how He is pouring His grace and mercy into you. You may not see it today, but you will one day. Trust me.

Here are some suggested questions to answer as you journal:

1. What happened today?

2. How do you feel?

3. What worried you or made you feel safe?

4. How did someone encourage you today or show kindness?

5. Where did you see God at work in your circumstances today?

You did it! Take a deep breath and exhale slowly. God is with you, dear one. He will NEVER leave you or forsake you. He will see you through each day and every circumstance.

Lean into Him. He is a safe place and our refuge.

2

Forgiveness:
It's a Process,
Not a Destination

It is easier to forgive an enemy than to forgive a friend.
—William Blake

My windshield wipers were useless as torrential rain turned the road into a murky blur. As I drove to my friend's house for the night, the tears cascading down my face did not make navigating any easier.

Thirty minutes earlier, my husband had left our home, closing the door on our marriage. In that moment, my heart experienced an excruciating tug-of-war. On one side, I felt like shouting and demanding to know if he was going to fight for our marriage. For me. For us. *Where was my knight in shining armor?* On the other side, I realized that there was nothing he could say or do to repair the catastrophic damage and shattered trust. So I let him leave without another word.

My cell phone rang, calling me back to reality from my sobbing puddle on the floor. My worship pastor, Doug, was calling to check on me and invite me to stay the night with him and his wife, Delo. They didn't want me to be alone.

I could not bear the crashing silence or the burden of the decision I had just made, so I left food for the cats, packed an overnight bag, and walked out the same door as my husband had.

I don't remember the drive to their house, only that it was pouring rain. It felt like God was crying with me. When I pulled into their driveway, Doug was waiting outside with an umbrella to shield me from the rain, and Delo waited at their front door with open arms. I cannot properly articulate what those simple, kindhearted, welcoming gestures meant to me when I felt so abandoned and utterly lost. A warm welcome, warm hugs, and a warm bed may seem ordinary, but not that night. They were lifelines.

Eventually, I retired and climbed into bed. I looked around their beautiful guest room but did not really see it. Too much had happened in the last fourteen hours. Exhaustion and emotional trauma had taken their toll. I cried. Slept fitfully. Journaled and cried. And cried some more. It felt like I was dying.

Over the following days, I wondered if actual death would have been easier. Although I never contemplated suicide, I acknowledged that at least you don't feel anything when you're dead.

In the darkness that night, I asked God endless questions and poured out unfiltered, raw pain and grief. *What am I supposed to do now? Why did he do this again? What's wrong with me that I wasn't enough for him? How in the world can I even think about forgiveness? I feel like a complete and utter failure. Please help me. I'm drowning.*

BEGINNING THE PROCESS OF FORGIVENESS

In our human nature, when someone hurts us deeply, feelings toward forgiveness seem counterintuitive. When my tears subsided, anger and self-righteous indignation invaded. The enemy launched debilitating ambushes, effectively turning my mind into a deadly battlefield. I remember those toxic, self-directed, and self-justifying conversations: *Who does he think he is, treating me like that? If lying gave out degrees, he'd have a double PhD. I hope God hurls lightning bolts at him until he's crispy-fried.* Not pretty, but real. And toxic.

It is difficult for others to see the war zone because the battle rages in our heart and mind. However, they can certainly feel the ravages and see the effects of our internal battlefield if they venture too close to Pain Central.

I learned over time that anger is a secondary emotion. It covers our initial emotions of hurt, sadness, and grief. Anger has its place, but staying there results in a bitter, hard heart. We will talk more about processing anger in a later chapter.

As my personal battle with forgiveness raged, I sought professional counseling for the first time in my life. God's Word tells us that we are forgiven and to extend forgiveness to others, but accomplishing such a feat myself seemed like scaling Mount Everest with no ropes. I felt overwhelmed by the enemy's onslaught, and I needed an objective, rational mind to effect a cease-fire.

From that first night when everything happened, I prayed for God to enable me to forgive. Before you think too highly of me, please know that I prayed through gritted teeth. Literally. In fact, I would grind my teeth as I prayed to forgive my husband, which always induced a pounding headache. Looking back, I am quite sure that during those prayer times, I looked like a petulant two-year-old sent to time-out.

Anger has its place, but staying there results in a bitter, hard heart.

I struggled to pray because the bottom line is that I didn't *want* to forgive my husband. Period. As far as I was concerned, he deserved the deepest pit in hell for the pain he had caused me and those I loved. I wanted him to hurt as much as I did. I allowed very few people to glimpse my struggle because holding on to grudges felt good.

Sigh. God had a long way to go with me.

YOUR STORY

Although we share similar pain, I cannot fully understand what you are going through. I do not know your divorce story. Divorce has many faces and causes numerous casualties. All things considered, my divorce experience may seem like a preschool playground compared to yours. There was no abuse. No children involved. No long, drawn-out, ugly court battle. That does not make the pain and trauma less, just different.

In my quest to ensure that this book might help the majority of people who have experienced or are experiencing divorce, I interviewed dozens of Christian women and men who have walked through it. I asked them to entrust me with their stories for the express purpose of providing help and hope to others enduring the heartbreak and chaos of divorce. Throughout these chapters, you will meet these friends with whom you may share a similar experience. I pray that you connect to their stories and that God provides you with insight and wisdom for your own journey.

Divorce has many faces and causes numerous casualties.

Meet Mae

Mae, mom of four sons, was married to an alcoholic husband and suffered both physical and mental abuse for more than two decades. As a practicing Catholic, Mae's fiancé joined the Catholic Church so that they could celebrate a Catholic wedding. However, her husband had joined only to please Mae's parents, and he stopped attending church after they married and moved away.

Over the years, their family life deteriorated due to her husband's alcoholism and inability to hold down a job. Mae shared this account:

> He was passed out on the family room floor by seven every evening, and we had to walk around him, throwing a cover on him when we turned down the furnace at bedtime. He shed all responsibility in helping with the

boys and taking care of usual household responsibilities, and he had difficulty keeping jobs. He was of no use for homework, transportation to Scout meetings, Little League ball practice, band concerts, etc. His alcoholism was destroying my family. Our family participated in several intervention sessions where we took bottles of booze from his hiding places and poured them down the drain, but he would simply replenish his supply. After visiting a marriage counselor, I asked my husband if he would choose me, our family, and our family home, or Jim Beam. He chose Jim Beam, so I requested that he move, and he moved out within ten days.

Since she did not want to give up on her marriage, Mae sought marriage counseling several times. However, her husband never attended. After exhausting all efforts to confront her husband and seek professional help, Mae filed for divorce. Five months before their twenty-fifth wedding anniversary, the divorce was granted. Looking back, Mae says:

I grieved some that the marriage failed. But it was a relief having him out of the house and no longer having to cook, clean up after him, and listen to his foul language when he was drinking. We had a peaceful household finally.

Perhaps you can relate to Mae's story of neglect and abuse. If you wonder how in the world God can possibly bring good out of such long-standing hurt, hang on. God wasn't finished writing her story. As Mae adjusted to life as a single mom of four boys, God completely changed her life:

I met three young ladies when I took bridge classes, and we formed nice friendships. We took turns meeting regularly at one another's homes to play bridge. One lady attended Bible Study Fellowship (BSF) and invited me to join her. The first two times she invited me, I was busy with prayer meetings at my church, but when she asked a third time, I went. I joined BSF, and it has been a life-changing experience for me. I truly felt I was born again and found my Savior, Jesus Christ. It was the first time I was aware that He was living within me to give me mercy, forgiveness, and many blessings. I attended BSF for fifteen years and gained much from the lessons and friendships formed in my classes. It was the best thing that had ever happened to me!

In the middle of hurt, Mae learned that God's forgiveness extends to all, regardless of our circumstances, for those who have faith in Jesus. How do you forgive nearly twenty-five years of emotional and physical abuse at the hands of an alcoholic? One step and one day at a time. When asked if she had forgiven her ex-husband, Mae candidly responded, *"Forgiveness is easy enough when it's good riddance of bad rubbish."*

I asked Mae what advice she would offer to you as you go through divorce, and she responded with these beautiful words:

Stay close to God, and He will help you through this turbulent time in your life. I have known many women who still hold a grudge or resent their ex-spouses even ten to twenty years after their divorce. I would tell them that when a window closes, other doors open in their future. Painful resentment only holds on and drags us down. We're best off to forgive, even though we don't need to forget.

Amen, Mae. Amen.

Meet Kole

For many years, Kole had been unhappy in a marriage to an abuser of alcohol. Even though he experienced episodes of physical abuse, Kole sought marital counseling to fight for his marriage. Kole's first Christian counselor told him he needed to help Kole find the courage to get out of his marriage. However, Kole was determined to salvage his twenty-year marriage. He left that counselor and sought another to help him develop coping skills so he could remain in his marriage:

> I honestly felt that I could not betray my marriage vows, and [I] believed that God never promised me happiness in marriage. I felt it was my job to be faithful to my vow and God would honor that. I knew there was a difference between happiness and joy, and I prayed I would still find joy even if I did not feel happiness. I also felt pressure (of my own creation) to not disappoint my parents and siblings by divorcing since nobody in my family had ever divorced.

Kole points out a necessary truth as we experience divorce: there is a vast spiritual difference between happiness and joy. While happiness is grounded on our circumstances, joy is grounded in Christ. Joy is one of the spiritual fruits God has already given to each and every believer, regardless of our circumstances: "*But the fruit of the Spirit is love, joy, peace, patience, kindness, goodness, faithfulness, gentleness, self-control*" (Galatians 5:22–23a).

His marriage, however, continued to deteriorate, so Kole eventually filed for divorce:

> It was an agonizing decision. It flew in the face of everything I believed as a Christian man and husband, but I filed for divorce.

Kole's divorce became a living nightmare. Although some people can act with class and grace toward each other while they are going through divorce proceedings, Kole had to accept that this would not be true for him:

Joy is grounded in Christ. Joy is one of the spiritual fruits God has already given.

> One of the hardest things was actually sitting across a table from my wife at court proceedings and feeling complete hatred directed toward me. It was difficult to sit and listen to lies under oath about me. I could not reconcile in my mind how

two people that had been married and shared children could feel so loathsome toward each other.

Perhaps Kole's story is your story, where ugly, scar-inducing battles rage and you don't believe forgiveness is possible. But remember that forgiveness is a process that takes time. Significant pain requires more time. Kole's insight lends clarity:

> I have forgiven my ex-wife, but she can still evoke a very visceral response in me when she attacks me verbally. I feel very certain that she has not forgiven me, as she has no problem swearing and berating me over the phone. It is tough not to sling words back, and I have often failed.

One of the most helpful truths to remember is that forgiveness is not a *destination* but a lifelong journey. Time doesn't heal all wounds; God does. So we use our time wisely to seek God through prayer and His Word. With faith in Christ, we confess our sins. God's forgiveness extends to us when we fail, and it extends to our ex-spouses when they fail as well. Clinging to God and His Word remains key. The Scripture passage that helped Kole most during his divorce was Jeremiah 29:11, *"For I know the plans I have for you, declares the Lord, plans for welfare and not for evil, to give you a future and a hope."*

After enduring such a heart-wrenching experience, Kole offers us this wisdom:

Forgiveness is not a destination *but a* lifelong journey.

As long as nobody is going to lose their life or go to jail, it will all be okay! You can survive this. Do not isolate yourself, but hold on to your family, your friends, and your faith.

God never tires of offering us hope and a future. Some days it is challenging to even imagine your next hour, much less your future. Take hope in this truth: God promises that He has your future in His loving, capable hands. I pray that you cling to that today.

Meet Whitney

As Whitney discovered, life as a military wife with two small children was harder than she could have possibly imagined.

Her husband served in a frequently deployed, rotating position in the military and was sent to Iraq shortly after the war started. Whitney waited at home with their first child. When her husband returned, he was an angry man. The stress of that assignment seemed to drastically change him and their relationship. Before long, her husband was deployed a second time. She acknowledges that neither of them handled the situation very well:

> Understanding the strain of constant deployment, we had a "don't ask, don't tell" policy when he was overseas. We thought it would help during the sometimes eighteen-month separations. For my part, I had been in and around the military long enough to know what happened during deployments anyway, so why pretend we would be any different? As long as another relationship did not continue once he returned home, we thought we could handle it. But it led to trust issues on both sides.

If you have been a part of the military community, perhaps this is your story. It may be easy for those of us outside of this community to criticize the open-policy mind-set about relationships, but criticizing is not our job. We are learning together how to survive and thrive following divorce in the midst of many different situations.

Perhaps you were the one who committed adultery. Whether you're in the military or not, maybe you are looking back with shame and guilt. Then Whitney's story holds special significance for you:

> I never asked about his end of the "deal," but he was always quick to say something offhanded about it when he wanted to hurt my feelings or make me jealous. And he was also quick to accuse. I think that's one of the reasons I had an affair. If I was going to be constantly accused, then I might as well be guilty. I knew it would

be the final straw for him. It would clearly signal to him that I was done with the marriage and wanted out.

When it comes to forgiveness, Whitney admits that receiving God's forgiveness for herself after committing adultery was extraordinarily difficult. She felt like she had failed her children, her parents, and her church:

> I went through a period of darkness when I felt that I was not worthy of church or forgiveness. But I wasn't angry with anyone other than myself. I emerged with a much deeper understanding of my faith and my relationship with God. At the end of the day, you are the one who ultimately struggles with your decisions—not your family (other than children), not your friends, not even your church.

The bottom line is that we are not worthy of forgiveness from God. We have all sinned and fallen short of His glory, yet He relentlessly extends His forgiveness—to us and to those who have hurt us. Even if you are the one who committed adultery, God's forgiveness can extend to you.

Bearing these stories and our experiences in mind, let's dig deep into the topic of forgiveness.

He relentlessly extends His forgiveness—to us and to those who have hurt us.

GETTING REAL ABOUT FORGIVENESS

One overarching truth in these heartbreaking situations is that Kole and Whitney trusted God to work forgiveness in them—and then *through* them—despite the depth of their pain and sorrow.

The dictionary defines *forgive* as "excuse a fault or offense; to stop feeling anger or resentment against; and to absolve from payment of."

God convicted me early on during my divorce that thoughts of hate and bitterness do not line up with His teaching to love as

He loves. Although I willfully walked away from God in my teenage years, He never gave up His pursuit of my heart. He loved me throughout my willful disobedience, terrible life choices, and accrual of cavernous debt. After I became a Christian in my early twenties, God even loved me despite the fact that my heart was far from Him. There's a vast difference between playing Christian and wholeheartedly seeking after God. Even today, He still has to remind me to love others as He does.

Since I tend to be positive and an encourager, the burden of unforgiveness during my divorce felt like I was wearing an ugly, suffocating coat in the desert. Consequently, I began searching Scripture for every passage I could find about forgiveness. Slowly but surely, God began turning my heart back to His. One passage hit me hard. Colossians 3:12–13 says:

> Put on then, as God's chosen ones, holy and beloved, compassionate hearts, kindness, humility, meekness, and patience, bearing with one another and, if one has a complaint against another, forgiving each other; as the Lord has forgiven you, so you also _must_ forgive. (Emphasis added.)

One word in particular stopped me: MUST. *Seriously? After what he did?* Yes, seriously. *"You also must forgive."* At that point, my heart and mind were far removed from any of those godly attributes. Those passages forced me to look in a spiritual mirror and own the fact that I was intentionally holding on to unforgiveness.

God convicts us when we are disobedient. This is especially evident when we remember Jesus' death on the cross and the life-changing forgiveness He extended in spite of it. Jesus loved those who hated and beat Him. And He did it for you and me. Keeping that gruesome image in my mind's forefront actually helped. God allowed me to understand that I did not have any hope of forgiving my ex-husband without diligent prayer and the power of the Holy Spirit working His forgiveness in me. That moment was the game changer in my prayer life.

Forgiving Your Ex-Spouse

It's amazing how easily we banter about forgiveness—until we are required to actually step forward and extend it. God convicted me that it was the necessary next step, so I kept praying strictly through obedience. I came to understand that true forgiveness was the only way I would survive, spiritually and emotionally.

A crucial truth God spoke clearly to me through His Word is that His command to forgive is for OUR benefit. Obeying His command to forgive freed my future from the burden and toxicity of unforgiveness. I was literally stepping into and embracing MY freedom. It has nothing to do with the other person. It doesn't matter if he or she asks for forgiveness or even apologizes for hurtful actions. It simply doesn't matter. That's right. IT. DOESN'T. MATTER.

His command to forgive is for OUR benefit.

Even if those who hurt us do not repent, we heed God's Word and offer them our forgiveness in order to release the anger and resentment we feel. God never said to wait until they apologize. Realizing how much God has forgiven me over the course of my life, I knew that I had no right to withhold forgiveness from my ex-husband. Forgiven people forgive people.

There is a distinct difference between God's forgiveness and man's forgiveness. Man's forgiveness—mine to my ex-husband—means extending forgiveness for what he did to me. I do not hold the power to extend God's forgiveness. In other words, my forgiveness does not pardon my ex-husband for breaking God's marriage covenant or commandment. My ex-husband must seek that forgiveness from God alone. God extends His forgiveness to a repentant person who confesses his or her sin to Him. That transaction takes place between God and the offender.

If you have ever held on to a grudge, you know full well that eventually the burden of that grudge will become too much to bear. It becomes a rock in our heart and soul, weighing us down until it destroys us. Forgiveness is not extending a gift to someone else; it

36

means embracing the gift of freedom for yourself.

Forgiveness released toxins from MY mind and softened MY heart to move freely into the future God has planned for me. The longer you clamp tightly on the nuclear waste of unforgiveness, the deeper the poison seeps into your soul. A friend once put it like this: "Unforgiveness is like swallowing poison and hoping the *other* person will die." Exactly.

God alone is our avenger. That power or responsibility does not lie with us. Scripture clearly states in Romans 12:17–19:

> Repay no one evil for evil, but give thought to do what is honorable in the sight of all. If possible, so far as it depends on you, live peaceably with all. Beloved, never avenge yourselves, but leave it to the wrath of God, for it is written, "Vengeance is Mine, I will repay, says the Lord."

Forgiveness is aggressive. It breaks chains. It moves us forward. It races toward your future and releases your past. It plows past the enemy's whispers to hold on to hurt and nurse the grudge because it feels good. Forgiveness embraces God's promises of peace and contentment. Our part in forgiveness is to obey God's command to extend it and leave the vengeance to Him.

Forgiveness is not God's suggestion to us. It is His command: "Put on then, as God's chosen ones, holy and beloved, compassionate hearts, kindness, humility, meekness, and patience, bearing with one another and, if one has a complaint against another, forgiving each other; as the Lord has forgiven you, so you also must forgive" (Colossians 3:12–13). Again, Scripture teaches that we must forgive. Our human nature rears up and tries to defend our choice to withhold forgiveness: "But you don't understand what he did to me. If you had to endure what I did, you wouldn't be so quick to forgive." God understands all, and He still commands us to forgive.

Forgiveness is not God's suggestion to us. It is His command.

We have two choices: forgive or hold a grudge. Romans 12:21 puts it this way: "Do not be overcome by evil, but overcome evil with good." *Overcome* is the key word. When we try to act as our own avenger, we don't overcome. We succumb. The grudge sticks around and adds to our burden. But when, with God's strength through the power of the Holy Spirit, we release our grudges and unforgiveness, God overcomes evil with His good.

God promises that when we obey, His blessings follow: *"If you faithfully obey the voice of the LORD your God, being careful to do all His commandments that I command you today, the LORD your God will set you high above all the nations of the earth"* (Deuteronomy 28:1).

As months went by, I noticed that I no longer hissed my prayers to forgive my ex-husband through gritted teeth. They had morphed into matter-of-fact checklist prayers that were not sincere. One of those was *God, please answer this prayer because you said I should pray it. Check. Off we go.* Hmm . . . not quite what God meant. As I look back, I am embarrassed by how immature I acted in my prayer life during that time.

But several months later, by God's grace alone, I found myself praying through tears of genuine sadness for my ex-husband. He chose to leave our church and people who loved him dearly. God's compassion flowed in to replace my anger. The hurt that numbed my heart and mind finally began to subside.

I wholeheartedly believe that forgiveness never would have happened outside of God's grace, relentless prayer, and the prayers of loved ones.

RECEIVING FORGIVENESS FOR YOURSELF

As I pondered which important topics to include in this book, I asked a trusted pastor friend what he thought should be included. His first response was forgiveness—both for my ex-husband and myself. On the outside, I took his comment in stride and nodded in somber agreement. On the inside, I was seething. *Wait a second. Forgiveness for me? Are you kidding? I didn't do anything wrong. What in the world do you mean that I need to ask for God's forgiveness?*

His comment troubled me for months, so during my prayer times, I began to ask God to reveal where I needed His forgiveness. He began to clearly convict me through His Word and leading of the Holy Spirit that I had not done everything I could to save my marriage. I did not suggest joint counseling or make any effort to meet with my ex-husband even though he asked. Although the continual untruths he told to mutual friends and his family confirmed that I never could have trusted him again, the fact remains that I am the one who filed for divorce.

Despite the fact that my ex-husband repeatedly violated our marriage covenant through adultery, I confessed and repented to God for my part in throwing in the towel. I have received God's forgiveness and I thank Him for it daily. That may sound presumptuous, but I am assured of God's forgiveness because He promises forgiveness to those who earnestly repent. I have confessed my sin of holding on to unforgiveness, losing my temper, and harboring hateful thoughts, and I have repented of those willful, harmful spiritual toxins to God. Therefore, according to God's promise, I have received His forgiveness.

He promises forgiveness to those who earnestly repent.

Like the old me, you may not believe that you need to seek God's forgiveness for yourself. The benefit of following my friend's advice is that now I have a clear conscience before God. I asked God to forgive my inaction to save my marriage but also to forgive any actions over our thirteen-year marriage that may have contributed to its dissolution. I realize full well that I am not the easiest person to live with. I am not excusing my ex-husband's actions, nor do I regret my decision to divorce. I am simply taking responsibility before the Lord for any part I willingly or unwillingly played.

The result is that I can face myself in the mirror, knowing that I have received God's forgiveness. It was a humbling process, and

I believe that it helped soften my heart toward my ex-husband. We were and are both sinners in need of God's grace and mercy.

There is a myth that we often hold as truth: "God has forgiven you; now you need to forgive yourself." That presupposes that God extends 80 percent of the forgiveness and it's up to you to muster the other 20 percent. That dangerous lie looks for healing in the last place we should look for it: ourselves. The truth is that you haven't believed and received God's complete forgiveness. We do not feel worthy of God's forgiveness, especially if our actions actively contributed to the divorce, but that is what God's amazing grace is all about.

I discovered how hard it is to receive God's forgiveness when I reached out to my ex-husband to let him know that I had forgiven him. He responded by thanking me, but he also confessed that he did not know if he could ever forgive himself. There's that dangerous lie again. We cannot forgive ourselves. The gift of forgiveness had been extended to my ex-husband, but he could not receive and open the gift. I hope in these six years since our divorce that he has been able to embrace God's forgiveness and mine.

Your hurt may be too fresh to move toward forgiveness today. That's okay. It takes time, moving forward step by step. Right now, revel in the fact that no matter what you have thought, done, or will do, God forgives you because of His Son's sacrifice on the cross. God forgives you. If the divorce was your idea, God forgives you. If you ranted at the one who hurt you until your neck veins bulged, God forgives you. If you're mad at God for your divorce, God forgives you.

God forgives you because of His Son's sacrifice on the cross.

Even though the hardest part about forgiveness is receiving it for ourselves, take a step back for a second. Almighty God, Maker of heaven and earth, Creator of all things has forgiven you, yet you cannot receive it for yourself? Again, we're trying to do God's job—and we stink at it. Forgiveness starts with embracing the truth and receiving God's forgiveness for yourself. If you have trouble receiving God's complete forgiveness, pray for God to increase your faith to believe that truth. That's exactly what I had to do. We cannot forgive ourselves—that's God's job.

The hardest thing I ever did was stand in front of the mirror and tell myself out loud, "God forgives you." I broke down crying. It reminds me of the hymn lyrics "What can wash away my sin?" Perhaps you started your faith journey as a child when you were taught to pray and ask God for forgiveness. Even back then, you probably learned that the pesky thing about Sin is that it brings along "friends," like Shame and Guilt. Those friends can cause significant harm in our lives.

Hang on to this important truth: *When you repent and ask God's forgiveness, He grants it. Period*. Lift your head and embrace the incredible future God has already planned for you.

Forgiving Others

I had arrived early to my first choir rehearsal following the news that I was going through a divorce. Even though I had been attending our Sunday church services, I purposely stepped back from the music ministry for several months. I did not want my presence up front to distract people's worship focus on Sunday mornings. My ex-husband and I had served as worship leaders, and we were an integral part of the ministry that we loved dearly.

My ex-husband had a powerful, rich tenor voice that God used time and again to accomplish incredible ministry. Although I can sing, he could have been a professional singer—he was simply that good. We often sang duets, and his strong voice made me brave. When we sang together, I belted confidently, whereas I was more timid on my own. Over the years, I would mourn the loss of our music ministry together. For a long time, every song was a reminder that he was gone.

I showed up at rehearsal sad and nervous that Wednesday evening. It felt as if half of me was missing that night—a feeling that continued for many months. I wanted to get situated, arrange my music, and make myself as small as possible to minimize the inevitable, uncomfortable attention. I purposefully kept my nose buried in the music and tried to blend into the carpet.

Before rehearsal, I had called two of my best friends who were also in the soprano section and asked them to sit on either side of me as a protective buffer. That may sound silly, and it's certainly not intended to reflect anything unkind about my fellow choir members. However, my heart was still tender and vulnerable, and I felt the need to operate in self-preservation mode.

My two friends jumped at the chance to help (true friends usually do), and they were fantastic. Because of their love and support, I did not spend breaks between songs in awkward conversations, or worse, the same conversation over and over. My fellow choir and worship team members were wonderfully supportive and kind, as I knew they would be. Yet it felt awkward for me, as I am sure it did for them. My ex-husband had been their friend as well.

The choir director prayed us out and people stood to leave. I thought I had survived the rehearsal relatively unscathed, but I was dead wrong. Without warning (and with several people still within earshot), a longtime fellow choir member hurried over to me with excitement on her face and asked in a loud whisper, "Was it adultery? Is that what he did?" No hello. No asking how I was doing. She just wanted the scoop. *Sigh. Really?*

I learned in that moment that I would need God's strength to extend forgiveness to others—not just myself and ex-husband. That evening was the first of countless occasions when I would need to forgive others for thoughtless comments. Most people are not intentionally thoughtless, but unfortunately some people are willfully unkind. I found it interesting to observe how easily people judge when they don't share our particular situation or struggles. I committed to memory the words that Jesus said when Peter asked Him how often forgiveness should be extended:

> If he sins against you seven times in the day, and turns to you seven times, saying, 'I repent,' you must forgive him. (Luke 17:4)

The thoughtless comments and intentional unkindness will likely happen to you if it hasn't already. Judgmental people can't resist a good jab. In a later chapter, we will dive deeper into how to handle people who are intentionally and continually unkind. Suffice it to say that while you are seeking after God to heal your heart, it is best to limit your exposure to such toxic people.

Forgiving others is a necessary component to allow God to rid your heart and mind of bitterness and anger before they have time to take root. Preparation ahead of time helps speed up the process. The beautiful words of forgiveness that Jesus spoke to those who participated in His crucifixion have also helped me tremendously:

> Jesus said, "Father, forgive them, for they know not what they do." (Luke 23:34)

Jesus prayed that for people who were causing Him more pain and suffering than you and I will ever experience. It helps put our hurt into perspective, and it helps us ask God to give us a heart like Jesus' to forgive others who hurt us.

WHEN YOU KNOW YOU HAVE FORGIVEN

Divorce is one of the most painful experiences anyone can face. It feels like an F5 tornado leveling your life and hurling flying debris without ceasing. Then, in the midst of the storm, you realize that the person you were invested in most deeply doesn't want you anymore. Ugh. Although it may not feel like it right now, there is life after divorce. In fact, thanks to God's promises, we can expect Him to bring something glorious out of the ruins. God brought this particular Scripture to my mind the morning after my divorce was final: "*It is the* LORD *who goes before you. He will be with you; He will not leave you or forsake you. Do not fear or be dismayed*" (Deuteronomy 31:8).

God goes before you and me. God never tells us in Scripture to walk this road alone. I am thankful, because you and I both know that it is a painful, sometimes scary journey.

God never tells us in Scripture to walk this road alone.

43

Let's face it, the process of forgiveness can feel like hot flashes: you are cool and calm one minute, then melt down into a ninja assassin the next. Hang in there. God goes before us, behind us, and beside us.

So, how do you know when you have arrived at forgiveness? As a card-carrying Type A personality, I value progress, and I look for markers of achievement in order to determine if my courses of action are legitimately working toward success. In my mind, success indicates arrival at a goal.

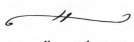

We will spend a lifetime forgiving our ex-spouses.

My pastor's words during a sermon after my divorce provided the answer: *"You know that you have forgiven when you are more sad at who that person has become than what they have done."* Read that last sentence once more. If you find that true of yourself, then God has already allowed you to forgive. If not, keep persisting in prayer.

I remember the tears flowing freely down my cheeks after he said it. Relief flooded my mind and heart because in that moment, I realized that God had allowed me to forgive my ex-husband. I didn't even realize it had happened. By God's amazing grace, I no longer held a grudge against him for the hurt he had caused. God softened my heart toward compassion instead of revenge. I understood immediately why I had recently begun to shed tears as I prayed for my ex-husband.

If you have been wondering how you will know if you have truly forgiven, that's it. When you are saddened more by who your ex-spouse has become than by what he or she has done, you have forgiven. Yes, we will spend a lifetime forgiving our ex-spouses when emotional shrapnel surfaces, but we are no longer incapacitated by the wounds.

Forgotten Equals Forgiven . . . Not

There's a lie that is so prevalent in our world today that people actually buy in to it, believing they have the power to erase their own memories. The lie says, "If I haven't forgotten, I haven't forgiven." That is a load of garbage. The enemy loves that lie because there is no solution. When someone deeply hurts us, we remember. Period.

For example, imagine a physical scar. If someone takes a knife and slashes you across the forearm, every time you see that scar for the rest of your life you will remember how it happened. Likewise, we remember when someone slashes our heart. The key is how we respond when we remember those hurts.

While interviewing dozens of people for this book, I discovered that we generally respond in one of four ways when we remember a past hurt:

1. We berate ourselves for remembering and try to make ourselves forget again.

2. We relive every detail of the hurt and end up angry or in a sobbing puddle.

3. We rehearse how we would like to verbally destroy that person if he or she should ever be so unlucky as to cross our path again.

4. We relentlessly surrender the hurt up to God in prayer before bitterness builds a permanent war bunker in our heart and mind.

Forgiving your spouse may not be the first thing that happens, but you have to get there at some point or your lack of forgiveness will consume you.

Now that you have heard my experiences, hard-earned lessons, and the stories of others, let's hear from the professionals. Next, Pastor Mike Mattil provides insight from Scripture about forgiveness, and licensed Christian counselor Kristin Niekerk provides practical steps we can put into use to walk toward forgiveness.

Pastoral Wisdom

"I'll never forgive him for what he did." Ever heard those words? Maybe you've said them or something very close to that. God could

have taken that attitude toward us. He had every right to do so. Not just for the first sin in the Garden of Eden, but for all our subsequent disobedience that continues down to this very day.

But God had a different plan. He let Someone take our place and our punishment so that we could be forgiven, even though we do not deserve it. That is what the life and death and resurrection of Jesus are all about. He endured all the temptations we have, but He never once sinned. Then He allowed Himself to be crucified even though He had done nothing wrong. He went through all that to accomplish your forgiveness.

As those who have been forgiven by God for Jesus' sake, we have been called to be forgiving people. In the prayer our Lord taught us, He said, "Forgive us our trespasses as we forgive those who trespass against us." And the Lord led Paul to write these passages:

> Be kind to one another, tenderhearted, forgiving one another, as God in Christ forgave you. (Ephesians 4:32)

> [Bear] with one another and, if one has a complaint against another, [forgive] each other; as the Lord has forgiven you, so you also must forgive. (Colossians 3:13)

We are called to be forgiving people. Yet we often have the completely opposite thought and attitude. We act as if not forgiving someone will hurt that person, when in fact the one you end up hurting is yourself. Lack of forgiveness is harboring a grudge, which is a sin on your part! And the longer you let it eat at you, the longer you remain in your sin.

Think of it this way: if you refuse to forgive someone who has already confessed his or her sin to God and has been forgiven by the Almighty, how much do you think your refusal to forgive will hurt that person in the grand scheme of things? All it will do is keep you angry and keep you from living the joy-filled life that God desires for His redeemed children.

However, when you forgive someone, the weight of anger and

resentment is lifted from you. You no longer have to carry it around and allow it to drag you down.

And let's be clear about something. Your forgiveness is not the same as God's forgiveness. We forgive because we have been forgiven by God, but your forgiveness does not equate to God's remission of sin. When you forgive someone, it is to keep you from sinning. It is still up to that other person to confess his or her sin to God and ask to be forgiven for Jesus' sake. That is the forgiveness that matters in the long run.

> If we confess our sins, [God] is faithful and just to forgive
> us our sins and to cleanse us from all unrighteousness.
> (1 John 1:9)

COUNSELOR'S CORNER

Practical steps to walk toward forgiveness

Donna bravely and lovingly shared her story of her struggle of forgiveness in her divorce. Her words may have ripped open a newly formed or thin scab on your heart. Go ahead . . . it's okay to scream OUCH!

I'm sorry to tell you this, but forgiveness is a foundational part of not just surviving your divorce but healing from it. For multiple decades, I have worked with individuals who are dealing with several different issues, and many of those people were currently going through a divorce or had divorced. Many of them have merely survived and are still walking through life with ugly, infected, gaping wounds that are not close to being healed. Unfortunately, this has painfully affected their lives and the lives of others.

Do you want to be one of those people? Are you already one? Well, healing your heart and forgiving is going to be a long process, so if you are an instant-results kind of person, take a HUGE deep breath and pray for sustaining patience.

This book and our time together will break down healing into a manageable process. So let's get started on our part together. Here are a few exercises you can do to move closer to healing and forgiveness. There is no step-by-step order. Do them as you feel ready or as God nudges you. Remember, He is right there with you!

1. Forgiveness means looking back but not getting stuck there. It also means looking forward toward healing that only God can bring about.

   a. List all the wrongs you feel your ex-spouse has done to you and your family. Write them down, feel them, and WEEP over them. Pray, asking God to help you release each one to Him and help you forgive your ex-spouse.

   b. List all the things you need to confess and forgive yourself for. Write them down, feel them, and WEEP over them. Pray, asking God to help you release each one to Him and help you forgive yourself for them. I love Donna's honesty in doing exactly this out loud to a mirror. There is something about saying things out loud and not just keeping them in our heads!

2. When we are hurt, it is easy to focus on the negative and lose the positive. We do this with life's situations, with those who are in our lives, and even ourselves. By focusing on the negative, the hurts lead to anger, which can lead to hate. Satan wants nothing more than for us to stay stuck and angry. Force yourself to look for the positives. No situation or person is 100 percent bad, and that includes you and your ex-spouse! In the thick of it, force yourself to look for and acknowledge the positive in the day and in others. Write these positive points in your journal and tell someone about them. Make a habit of doing this every day. If you have family, make it a habit at the dinner table to talk about the positives of the day and of those around you.

3. In that same fashion, in some personal time, ask God to help you remember the good in you, your ex-spouse, and your marriage. Again, WRITE THIS DOWN, (yup, three lists). You will need to refer back to it in difficult times when the pain returns.

Remember that God is right there next to you while you struggle through these exercises. He is there to weep with you, comfort you, strengthen you, and give you peace through His forgiveness.

Forgiveness releases you from being a hostage to emotions, others, and yourself.

Press on.

1) Used my fenancial success to his selfish needs.

2) Cursed and verbaly abused all of us. Be littled us.

3) Physically hurt us. Pulled Travis' hair, broke a ligiment in my knee. Shoved a ladder into my mouth.

4) Belittled our marriage continually by watching porn.

5) Hurt us socially by his actions.

2: Pausing to Breathe, Pray, and Reflect

I realize that this has probably been a very hard chapter to walk through. Take a moment to take a deep breath and sit back.

You may need to reread parts of this chapter several times. That's okay. The most important thing is to ask God to bring you to the point where you can wholeheartedly extend forgiveness without malice or reservation. There is no time limit. However, it is vital to your spiritual and emotional well-being to reach that point someday.

In the meantime, let's process this chapter personally. Take your time walking through the following Bible passages, questions, prayer time, and journaling time before moving to the next chapter.

Scripture to Read, Meditate on, and Memorize

Put on then, as God's chosen ones, holy and beloved, compassionate hearts, kindness, humility, meekness, and patience, bearing with one another and, if one has a complaint against another, forgiving each other; as the Lord has forgiven you, so you also must forgive. (Colossians 3:12–13)

Be kind to one another, tenderhearted, forgiving one another, as God in Christ forgave you. (Ephesians 4:32)

If we confess our sins, [God] is faithful and just to forgive us our sins and to cleanse us from all unrighteousness. (1 John 1:9)

Questions for Reflection

You may wrestle with anger at the thought of extending forgiveness to your ex-spouse. Forgiveness does not mean that you condone their actions or forget what they did. Forgiveness means living in obedience to God's command and reaping the benefit of an uncluttered heart afterward.

Answer these questions with complete honesty. No one is looking over your shoulder. It's just you and God. So get real and raw so that God can begin moving your heart and mind toward extending forgiveness.

1. What good will you reap if you decide to harbor unforgiveness? *No good, only bitterness, that will come through to others*

2. What fear lies at the root of your withholding forgiveness? *I don't fear forgiving. I WANT to forgive So I CAN release both Robert & myself from moreon.*

PAUSE FOR PRAYER

I cannot encourage you strongly enough to keep moving toward forgiveness. I know it's hard. At first, I didn't want to either. But I realized that unforgiveness was poisoning my mind and heart. I realized that living like that wasn't really living—it was merely existing. God has bigger plans for both of us beyond existence. He desires us to live fully in His love and joy. So let's pray:

A—Acknowledge God's sovereignty: God alone provides the strength and wisdom you need. So read Psalm 119:105–112 aloud to God with confidence.

C—Confession: Take this time to confess your feelings to God— the good, the bad, and the ugly. He already knows them, but when you verbally express those feelings, He begins to release that toxic brew from your heart, mind, and soul. Please pray aloud to God now.

T—Thanksgiving: From salvation to the air you breathe, you have much to be thankful for. List three things you are thankful for right now, and thank God for them.

1. *My resistance to COVID*
2. *My faith & reassurance from God*
3. *My financial position & pray God will help me protect it.*

Bible study group

S—Supplication (requests): God hears you when you pray, and He will work miraculous healing in your heart. Identify what you need from God right now, and ask Him in faith to provide it.

EXHALING ON THE PAGE

As stated at the end of chapter 1, if you have not started journaling through this process, begin TODAY. God will use your journaling as another way to release toxic feelings and show how He is pouring His love into you. You may not see it today, but you will one day. You don't need to have a fancy journal. Pick up the nearest yellow pad or some loose-leaf paper and start writing.

Here are some suggested questions to answer as you journal:

1. What happened today?

2. How do you feel?

3. What worried you or made you feel safe?

4. How did someone encourage you today or show kindness?

5. Where did you see God at work in your circumstances today?

ADDITIONAL EXERCISE

If you struggle receiving God's forgiveness for yourself, remember that God forgives those who earnestly repent. Take a minute to confess your sin to God and ask for His forgiveness. He faithfully extends it.

You did it! Take a deep breath and exhale slowly. God is with you, dear one. He will NEVER leave you or forsake you. He will see you through each day and every circumstance.

3

Anger: Releasing the Beast Instead of Caging It

The fiercest anger of all, the most incurable, is that which rages in the place of dearest love.
—Euripides

It was a chilly, bright December Thursday. Only a few days had passed since I discovered my ex-husband's secret double life. I took the rest of the week off from work since I was in no shape to focus past the pain. I decided to drive to my in-laws' house to talk with my mother-in-law. I had no idea if she was even aware of what had happened. I loved her dearly (and still do) and wanted her to hear from my own lips that I would always love her and hoped that we could one day remain friends.

When I pulled into their driveway, my mother-in-law was unloading groceries from her car trunk. I parked and walked up to their garage, waiting for her to come back out of the house. When she reappeared, her usual warm, welcoming hug had been replaced by a cold stare. She expressed her surprise that I had the nerve to show my face. Completely taken aback, I asked her what her son had told her about what had happened. I was not prepared for what came next. My husband had told his parents (and others, as time would reveal) that I had thrown him out of the house so that my mother could move in with me instead.

I was so stunned that I couldn't even get upset in that moment. I simply stared at my mother-in-law and said quietly, "No, that's not true. Your son had an affair, but there's much more to it than that. I believe he should be the one to tell you the rest." It broke my heart to see the look of complete shock and sadness on her face. I told her, "I know that you did not raise your son to act like that. I don't hold you responsible. I love you and don't hold any bad feelings toward you. I hope we can be friends again one day." She nodded slowly and said, "No, I didn't raise him like that. But he's my son." Those last four words let me know where things stood. I reassured her that I understood her position and was not asking her to choose between her son and me. Through tears running down my face, I expressed the hope that one day her son would tell her the truth. I apologized for her pain and suffering, climbed back into my car, and drove away.

I have not seen or talked with my ex-mother-in-law since that day. It still makes me sad. She is a truly kind, sweet lady, and I love her still. I was the daughter she never had. We had a special bond, and I miss her to this day. I hope one day that we will see each other again and begin repairing our relationship. But when I remember her last four words to me, I don't know if that will be possible in this lifetime.

Those last four words let me know where things stood.

As I drove away from my in-laws' house in tears, anger hit me so hard that

I needed to pull over and take several deep breaths to stop shaking. I was livid to discover the lie that my husband had told her about the reason for our split, but I was even angrier about the collateral damage his self-centered actions had caused. I was angry that people I cared about were hurting over more lies instead of the truth. I wondered if my ex-husband had ever considered the enormous hurt that his actions would cause so many.

When it comes to suffering, we tend to get angry and turn on God. We assume that He has no clue how much we're hurting or what we're going through. But God patiently turns our face once more toward the cross and reminds us that He knows *exactly* how much pain we are experiencing. Jesus absorbed our arguments, excuses, and accusations along with the nails. He understands every pain we will ever endure.

But in the midst of anger and hurt, sometimes we choose the Rambo route. The *Rambo* movie series struck a popular chord with our basic human nature. Rambo acted exactly as most people want to act when someone hurts us: give in to anger and seek revenge.

Experiencing the divorce process provides countless opportunities to give in to anger: when our children hurt, when we hurt, when we dwell on "This isn't fair!," or when our ex-spouse leaves us to clean up the mess he or she created, to name a few. When anger flares up, we need the hope, peace, and knowledge that God knows our troubles and has our back.

The soul-freeing, anger-releasing truth is this: God does not leave His children to fend for themselves—He fights for them.

One hundred percent of the people I interviewed for this book admitted that they struggled with anger at some point during the divorce process, and some struggled with it long afterward. The fear is that if we look anger in the eye, we will turn into raving lunatics and remain angry forever. Just because the divorce decree is signed all nice and neat does not mean that our emotions are also wrapped up in the same tidy envelope.

I struggled with anger as well. It is one of the stages of grief we experience when such trauma and loss occur. Anger is a bully; it grabs us by the throat and shakes us like a toy. But God excels at taking down bullies. Looking back, I am thankful that the only day I was able to vent anger at my ex-husband was the day I first discovered his betrayal. I have never seen him since. You may envy that, but it was extraordinarily hard to have him suddenly cut completely out of my life. It was almost like he died, but he was alive and well—just not with me.

My entire divorce process was handled through texts, emails, and our attorney. My ex-husband signed the divorce papers via courier and never even showed up in court. It felt surreal. One day everything was fine, and the next day a tornado leveled my marriage—and I have never seen my ex-husband again. In those early days, knowing that he was out there somewhere yet not with me added fuel to my anger.

Anger is a bully; it grabs us by the throat and shakes us like a toy.

The day when his adultery came to light was the only opportunity I had to throw something at him, which, shamefully, I did. My anger boiled over many times during my divorce. I have a feeling that if I had seen my ex-husband two months into the process, I would have reduced him to a bloody pulp for destroying the love, trust, and intimacy of our marriage. Over time, I learned how to cage the anger beast. Unfortunately, it would not sit docilely behind bars.

One day in particular comes to mind. I telephoned my television cable provider to switch the service from both our names to mine (since I was keeping the house). For some unknown reason, the customer service representative could not seem to understand that my husband was unavailable to approve my request. Even after telling her that my husband no longer lived in our home and would not be returning, she still could not get her mind around the fact that his name needed to be removed from the cable account. I reached the breaking point. I shouted something about her being too deaf to hear and too dense to understand, slammed down the phone's receiver, yanked the whole thing out of the wall, and threw it across the bedroom with all my might.

That was not a proud moment, on many levels. Here enters the old saying, "We don't know our own strength." The force with which I threw the phone made a perfect telephone-shaped hole through the drywall, and the phone promptly disappeared down into the wall. I stared openmouthed for a split second before bellowing at the top of my lungs, "THIS ISN'T MY FAULT! I'M NOT THE ONE WHO CHEATED! GIVE ME A BREAK!" Then I broke down in sobs. My anger was not directed at that poor customer service rep. It echoed through an empty house at my ex-husband for the pain he caused.

In that moment, my over-the-top anger brought two truths into sharp focus: one, my anger could cause damage; and two, I am terrible at repairing drywall. That incident made me realize that the razor-sharp shards of a shattered heart can slash innocent bystanders. I needed to ask God to remove those sharp, angry edges and begin the process of mending my heart. I prayed for that poor customer service rep whose hair I set aflame, and I asked God's forgiveness.

Although I tend to have a quick temper, I am not a violent person. However, I was very glad that my ex-husband was not within swinging range right then. My anger level raised a six-foot red flag, and God convicted me that I did not possess the strength to cage my anger. I needed to release it to Him for disposal. Christians tend to suppress negative responses like anger, which can smolder and cause us to seek revenge unless dealt with properly.

I knew that I desperately needed God's intervention to eradicate every root of resentment or bitterness before it became a permanent fixture in my heart and mind.

ROOTS OF BITTERNESS

By definition, bitterness is usually associated with anger and grudges that we allow to take root. God's Word provides clear insight and instruction about such roots in both the Old and New Testaments. Deuteronomy 29:18 says:

> Beware lest there be among you a man or woman or
> clan or tribe whose heart is turning away today from
> the LORD our God to go and serve the gods of those

nations. Beware lest there be among you a root bearing poisonous and bitter fruit.

This passage tells us that the root itself is not bitterness, but rather that it bears the poisonous fruit of bitterness. Scripture does not specify if the bitter fruit is festering anger or something else, but it points to the fact that it is deadly. In the New Testament, Hebrews 12:15 reminds us:

> See to it that no one fails to obtain the grace of God; that no "root of bitterness" springs up and causes trouble, and by it many become defiled.

Bitterness digs dark bunkers of anger far removed from the light and love of Christ. It begins as a seed planted in the soil of pain that takes root and bears deadly fruit. Since roots form underground, they are easy to hide and camouflage. People who allow bitterness to take root may say that they are fine on the surface, but their actions tell a different story. As I travel to speak and teach from God's Word, I occasionally encounter people who have allowed old hurts to morph into roots of bitterness. It becomes evident in their callous tone, guarded conversation, and defensive words.

After I spoke about forgiveness at a retreat last fall, a lady in her seventies sought me out privately during a break. She confessed that she had struggled with anger and unforgiveness against her ex-husband for fifty-two years. *Fifty-two years.* Although I felt joy that God had allowed her to finally recognize the need to release her toxic feelings, I also felt grief that she had carried that staggering burden for more than five decades.

Hebrews 12:14 lends insight about roots of bitterness:

> Strive for peace with everyone, and for the holiness without which no one will see the Lord.

Striving for peace becomes difficult when we are preoccupied with policing our anger beast to ensure that it remains caged. Since divorce is a volatile emotional roller coaster, the anger beast easily blasts through the bars at the slightest provocation and roars to the surface, belching fire and scorching everything in its path.

LESSONS FROM HURRICANES

Thanks to Hurricane Ike, God provided me with an unforgettable mental picture of a root of bitterness. When Hurricane Ike carved a path of destruction straight through Houston a few years ago, the huge, beautiful tree in my backyard ended up on my roof. Friends came to the rescue with a chainsaw to remove as many limbs as they could and then covered the damaged roof with a waterproof tarp. Later, my homeowner's insurance covered the cost to replace the roof and a few broken windows and to rebuild all of the fences that the storm had scattered. It also covered the cost of cutting down what was left of the tree, which left a nice, neat stump to sit on.

However, not long after the contractors reduced the tree remains to a stump, mini-trees began sprouting all over the backyard. Each week, I ran over newly sprouted mini-trees with the lawn mower. I could not figure out what was happening, so I asked a neighbor to take a look. He immediately identified the problem. He said that as long as the old tree stump remained, those mini-trees would continue to sprout from the live roots in a last-ditch effort to survive.

He referred me to a tree-grinding service that spent all day grinding down the tree stump, as well as all of the larger visible surface roots. The mini-trees never reappeared.

The life lesson learned from that experience became vital to me. Despite the pain and hurt, I did not want anger and bitterness to sprout from the stump of a failed marriage and take root in my heart. I called upon God through prayer and His Word to grind out those deep-seated roots. I did not want anger to sprout in other areas of my life and cause damage in other important relationships. Mark Twain once wisely observed, "Anger is an acid that can do more harm to the vessel in which it is stored than to anything on which it is poured."

The tree-grinding service left instructions that I needed to add fill dirt and grass seeds where the tree stood so the ground in that area would not collapse over time. It was a very large tree, so the enormous roots consumed a significant amount of underground space. As years went by, the rest of the roots eventually decayed. The tree grinder's wise advice came to fruition as the area where the tree once stood slowly began to sink. Left unchecked, it would have eventually created a dangerous pit.

As instructed, I continued adding fill dirt and grass seeds every six to eight months. Eventually, the root space consumed by the old tree absorbed enough fill dirt to level out. My backyard is now a peaceful, even landscape once again.

LESSONS FROM PITS AND PRISONS

As I look out my window into the backyard today, I realize that the tree grinder's advice translates into a vital spiritual truth regarding divorce: brokenness leaves pits that need to be filled before they swallow us whole. Whether other people's actions hurl us into pits or whether they are pits of our own making, getting out is imperative if we are to fully live the life that God has planned for each of us.

In the Old Testament, Joseph understood pits. He was his father's favorite and lived a blessed life until the day his angry, jealous brothers threw him in a pit:

Despite the pain and hurt, I did not want anger and bitterness to . . . take root in my heart.

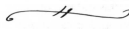

So when Joseph came to his brothers, they stripped him of his robe, the robe of many colors that he wore. And they took him and threw him into a pit. The pit was empty; there was no water in it. (Genesis 37:23–24)

Pits offer no easy exits. Dark, unfamiliar, waterless, and scary, they expose decaying roots of what might have been. Their steep walls strike fear in our hearts that our depression will never lift and our pain will never leave. Pits hold tearstains, bloodstains, and shattered dreams.

Joseph could have wallowed in despair and turned bitter. He could have abandoned hope and sat motionless or allowed his anger to metastasize into bitter hatred. I believe most of us can agree that he had the right to get angry. Instead, Scripture reveals that Joseph kept using his God-given gifts to serve others. In fact, he served in such extraordinary ways that people recognized that God was working through him.

Did you catch that last line? Joseph not only survived, he *thrived*. God gives us the free will to fill our pits with whatever we want. We can fill them with unforgiveness, anger, and plots for revenge. But through the power of the Holy Spirit, we cry out to our Savior to throw down His rescue ladder of love, forgiveness, and restoration.

Eventually, Midianite traders pulled Joseph out of the pit, transported him to Egypt, and sold him into slavery to Potiphar's house for twenty shekels of silver (see Genesis 37:28). I don't know about you, but that doesn't sound like an ideal rescue. However, Joseph's story was far from over:

> The LORD was with Joseph, and he became a successful man, and he was in the house of his Egyptian master. His master saw that the LORD was with him and that the LORD caused all that he did to succeed in his hands. So Joseph found favor in his sight and attended him, and he made him overseer of his house and put him in charge of all that he had. (Genesis 39:2–4)

When the Lord rescues us out of the pit, the journey may not progress as we envisioned it would. However, the Lord is with us through the Holy Spirit. Whatever He is working through our rescue will work out for our good and His glory in the end.

Just as Joseph's situation improved, he landed in another pit. Joseph honorably refused amorous advances from Potiphar's wife. Stung by his rejection, she accused Joseph of attacking her. When Potiphar heard his wife's tale, he threw Joseph into prison. Yet again, God did not abandon Joseph:

> But the LORD was with Joseph and showed him steadfast love and gave him favor in the sight of the keeper of the prison. And the keeper of the prison put Joseph in charge of all the prisoners who were in the prison. . . . And whatever [Joseph] did, the LORD made it succeed. (Genesis 39:21–23)

Even in prison, a place where success seems counterintuitive, the Lord never left Joseph to fend for himself. God still shows us His steadfast love, even in our pits and prisons. If you have ever visited a prison, you know that the sun does not shine inside. However, Jesus can shine in any circumstance when we look with eyes of faith.

Before God called one of my pastors, Tim Carter, into the ministry, he worked for the Texas Department of Criminal Justice for twenty years. At the culmination of his career, he was a member of the Texas "death squad," the exclusive group responsible for carrying out executions of condemned inmates. Before his penal career ended, Tim personally assisted in the legal deaths of more than 150 human beings.

In his remarkable book, *The Executioner's Redemption*, Tim vividly describes how the light of Jesus shines even in prisons:

> The world of the penitentiary is filled with pits and pain and darkness. I saw nothing but complete darkness in the beginning of the journey. I vividly recall my first trip [with the sergeant] to the Walls [execution building]. As one crash gate after another slammed shut behind my back . . . I felt like a lamb being led to the slaughter. . . . Each dimension of the capital punishment process is steeped in sad, gloomy darkness and I was shown that there is a serious need for servants of the Lord to serve Him in the middle of that darkness, pointing people to His light.

Tim's book profoundly affected my spiritual walk. God used his words to help me understand that for several weeks during the divorce process, anger had become my prison. Some days, I willfully turned my face away from the sun. It felt good to be mad. Eventually, however, I realized that anger accomplished nothing except exhaustion and deeper frown lines. Tim continues:

> God allowed for me to remain on that duty and keep walking through that valley for more executions than anyone else at that time. I regularly reminded myself

that God's ways are not our ways (Isaiah 55:8) and that in His wisdom, He has His reasons for allowing us to endure challenges and travel paths we would have never chosen for ourselves.

Perhaps you are looking up from your divorce pit, wondering about God's reasons for allowing it. The answer is different for each of us. During my divorce, God illuminated my dark pit with His light of hope through one particular set of Scripture verses:

> He sent from on high, He took me; He drew me out of many waters. He rescued me from my strong enemy and from those who hated me, for they were too mighty for me. They confronted me in the day of my calamity, but the LORD was my support. He brought me out into a broad place; He rescued me, because He delighted in me. (Psalm 18:16–19)

Jesus delights in me. He delights in you. Sometimes our pit experiences seem cold and bottomless. We cannot remember the last time we felt the warm sunshine of hope. Yet even in our pits, God reaches down and rescues us in His perfect timing. His Word is living and active and continues to work in us despite our pits.

As for Joseph, God used his pit time as uninterrupted classroom time. In those pits and prisons, God humbled Joseph, developed his people skills, used him to interpret people's dreams, and taught him valuable leadership tools. Over time, God molded Joseph into the second most powerful person in all of Egypt:

> Then Pharaoh said to Joseph, "Since God has shown you all this, there is none so discerning and wise as you are. You shall be over my house, and all my people shall order themselves as you command. Only as regards the throne will I be greater than you." (Genesis 41:39–40)

I would not have chosen the pit of divorce to appear in my life any more than you would. When I said "I do" on my wedding day, I meant it. I never sought to trade up or trade in my ex-husband. I was happy. But my ex-husband's pit of waywardness spawned my pit of abandonment. In order to survive and thrive like Joseph, I searched God's Word and prayed relentlessly for His guidance. Some days felt like a week. Some weeks felt like a lifetime. But God rescued me.

And He will rescue you as well.

Meet Tiffany

Even in our pits, God reaches down and rescues us.

Tiffany was born, baptized, raised, and confirmed as a member of The Lutheran Church—Missouri Synod (LCMS). However, she married a police officer who was unaffiliated with any church. She could never persuade her husband to attend a Lutheran church, so they attended different denominational churches.

They began experiencing marital problems early on, which led to continuous fighting. He became extremely controlling, and soon her situation became a living nightmare. He began emotionally abusing Tiffany by regularly accusing her of infidelity (which was untrue). He decided to pull their children out of school and move their family closer to Tiffany's parents. When Tiffany took the kids to visit her parents, her husband would drive by her parents' home to ensure they were there. He enlisted other deputy friends to do likewise. Eventually, Tiffany's husband placed a tracker on her cell phone so that he could pinpoint her exact location, day or night. She remembers:

> I began to hate being with him more and more. I became very short-tempered with my children. I was beginning to hate myself for allowing someone to treat me that way. We fought all the time, and the kids were seeing all that was happening.

Emotional abuse eventually led to sexual abuse:

> He would get off from work around 2:00 a.m. and expected me to get up and make him happy and apologize for my actions. If I wasn't awake or wouldn't wake

up, he would take advantage of me. When I told him that I didn't want to have sex with him, he would tell me that it was my job as his wife whether I wanted to or not. He forced himself on me on a regular basis, but he never hit me. There were days when I would beg him to hit me instead of having sex with me, but he never did.

After seven months of emotional and sexual abuse, Tiffany packed up their children and moved out. During their separation, she and her husband sought counseling together, but it only served as a forum for her husband to yell and blame all of their marital problems on her. Tiffany emotionally shut down in those sessions and individually sought advice from her pastor. Despite her exhaustive efforts, she and her husband eventually divorced. But her nightmare continued:

The judgment from my ex-husband and some of the people within my small hometown community was awful. I tried carrying on and moving on with my life for myself and my kids. My ex still tried to control everything by telling me who I could and could not be around when I had the kids. He still drove by and kept records of where I was and how long I was there. He asked other deputies to do likewise. Now, two years later, I still get monthly threats that he can arrest me at any time he wants for contempt of court if I don't abide by the divorce decree 100 percent.

Tiffany wrestled with pain and anger every time she faced her ex-husband to drop off or pick up their children. She often wondered how in the world her emotional wounds would ever heal when each encounter tore the scab open once again.

Perhaps Tiffany's story is your story. You have suffered abuse. You cannot see the sunlight from the bottom of your pit. Take heart, dear friend. Like Joseph, God will bring good from your pain, if you let Him. When all we can see is a desert, God has already made plans for your oasis in Him.

The gift of faith that God gave Tiffany in her early years continues to strengthen her every day. Specifically, Tiffany's confirmation verse from Isaiah 26:4 helped her the most during those dark, abusive days: *"Trust in the LORD forever, for the LORD GOD is an everlasting rock."* She recalls:

> My mentor and I looked up the wrong verse during one of our meetings together during my confirmation year. I fell in love with Isaiah 26:4, not knowing how much it would mean to me now, so many years later. I now have a beautifully painted sign hanging in my office with the Scripture verse on it so that I can look at it every day and remember to trust in God no matter what road I'm going down.

Tiffany's beautiful words remind us that even though our pits may feel far from God, He is as close as our next breath and heartbeat. We will not survive when we dig deeper into ourselves; we thrive when our solutions come from our faith in Christ alone.

Meet Gertrude

Gertrude and her husband were married for ten years before they divorced. Gertrude battled significant emptiness and loneliness after her divorce because she still believed that her husband was her best friend.

It was only a matter of time before the anger beast reared its ugly head in Gertrude's life—especially when people talked well of her ex-husband:

> My husband coached our son's soccer team and was involved with our kids' school. It was really hard when people would comment on how great a guy he was. I was so mad and hurt that I wanted to tell everyone how awful he was for leaving me. I wanted him to hurt as much as I was hurting, but I did not say anything. I sought anger management counseling from the student counseling center on the college campus we attended

at the time, but it didn't help much. I went from being extremely sad and depressed to being really angry.

Neither Gertrude nor her husband was walking with Christ at the time of their divorce, and Gertrude admits that she had expected her husband to fill that void. However, God was not done with them. Several years after the divorce, they began attending church together and worked through their old relationship difficulties. They responded to God's call to faith and were both baptized into the family of God. They began a life-changing relationship with Christ, and six months after their Baptism, they remarried.

Everything looked rosy in their marriage garden. Then, one devastating day a few months later, Gertrude discovered that her husband was having an affair:

> Although I was deeply upset and heartbroken, I did not have the same hopeless feeling that I did when he and I had divorced. I decided that I was not going to stay married, and he began drawing up divorce papers for a second and final time. God-fearing friends of mine encouraged me to ask God what He thought . . . and His answer was NO! I told my husband that we were not getting divorced, that I believed God did not want me to leave him. My husband did not think it was possible because I had never been able to get over past hurts, and [I] brought the past into current situations in order to magnify the problem. God helped me forgive my husband and the woman he had been in a relationship with. He helped me to let go of the hurt; I left it at the cross. God enabled me to love my husband, and in return, my husband has learned how to love me.

Gertrude now enjoys a marriage where she and her husband are devoted to each other. Their eyes are on God together, and she knows that even though people may disappoint her, placing her trust in God gives her the confidence to walk according to His plans.

It is uncommon for a person to remarry an ex-spouse, especially after infidelity. However, Gertrude's story proves that nothing is impossible for God. She candidly admits that it was not an easy road:

> God strengthened my faith and trust in Him by healing my heart. He truly turned my heartache to joy. This did not happen overnight, and I have good, God-fearing friends who helped guide me in Scripture and prayer.

I wanted you to read Gertrude's story for one particular reason: if you are not yet divorced, there may still be hope for your marriage. After discovering my husband's first affair six years into our marriage, I prayed and asked God for direction and wisdom. God's clear response at that time was for me to remain married and work through our difficulties with His help. Although my husband relapsed and we were eventually divorced seven years later, that does not mean that there is no hope for your marriage. With Jesus, there is *always* hope. And even if you are looking back on divorce, like me, God still has bright plans for your future.

Meet Louise

Sheer terror arrived late one evening dressed in two nice suits and police badges. After the two men identified themselves as detectives from the Houston Police Department's homicide division, they insisted on coming inside for safety reasons. Alarmed, Louise let them in. They began interrogating her about her relationship with her husband, who was a deputy with the Harris County Sheriff's Department. Specifically, they wanted to know if she had done anything to upset him. Completely confused, Louise told them that she and her husband were going through an ugly divorce. She never expected their terrifying response.

The detectives informed her that her husband had hired a violent gang to execute her and their three daughters. The HPD had obtained proof that her husband had provided the gang with money and a diagram of the home they had once built together; the diagram pinpointed where each of them slept. Louise remembers vividly:

I couldn't breathe. This was the type of thing I watched on *Dateline*. I was sobbing uncontrollably. How was I supposed to get through the next minute, hour, day? Is this really the kind of person I married? Hesitation, fear, sheer terror, trepidation, shock, horror, sadness, feeling sick . . . all of these emotions ravaged through me as I sobbed and sobbed. I didn't want [the detectives] to leave because then what?

With Jesus, there is always hope.

The detectives told Louise that the only reason they were at her home that night was because one of the gang members assigned to perform the executions apparently had a change of heart when he saw a picture of Louise and her daughters. Anonymously, he turned her husband in to the HPD, who immediately intervened. The HPD then contacted the sheriff's department—her husband's employer—and opened an internal investigation. They brought in her husband for questioning and relieved him of his badge and gun until the investigation concluded. But Louise's nightmare had only just begun.

The two detectives eventually left her home, but they stayed outside and guarded her and her daughters until they believed her family was safe. Louise immediately called a friend whose husband worked for the Texas Highway Patrol. They arrived within five minutes, and he spoke with the two HPD detectives outside to ascertain the situation while Louise's friend consoled her inside. She remembers:

> I wanted to go to sleep and when I woke up it was all just going to be a dream. [My friends] stayed most of the night. When I went into my room, I saw the three precious jewels in my crown sleeping peacefully on my bed. I wept through the rest of the night. I was crying out to the Lord, asking Him once again to please lift me from the miry pit I was in. I wanted Him to hold me, to show His face to me, to weep with me. I prayed without ceasing and talked to Him all night long. It was the longest night of my entire life.

The next day, a sheriff's office detective informed her that she and her daughters needed to go into hiding for their safety. The divorce had been granted. But local women's shelters refused them entrance when they discovered that their presence could endanger other residents. She emailed her boss, family, and friends, informing everyone that she and her daughters were getting away on a sabbatical together to regroup, pray, and seek God's guidance. None of them knew what was really happening. Eventually, Louise and her daughters packed only their essentials and literally ran for their lives.

Louise and her daughters went into hiding for several weeks at an anonymous country home far away, leaving all computers and phones behind since they could be tracked via GPS. With the help of the police department, Louise and one of her daughters were escorted back and forth to court, where the court eventually granted Louise a two-year protective order against her husband.

Eventually, Louise had to face her ex-husband in court as the Texas Rangers testified about her ex-husband's plans to execute her and their daughters. The gang member who had turned in her ex-husband refused to testify in front of a grand jury, so her ex-husband was a free man.

Let me pause here and ask, would you be angry in Louise's situation? As a personal friend of Louise's, I can tell you straight-up that I was angry at the unnecessary and cruel terror that her ex-husband put her and their daughters through. They were high school sweethearts, and she thought that he was her knight in shining armor. I didn't know most of Louise's story until I interviewed her for this book. I was appalled and angry on her behalf. But Louise had found peace from the Lord a long time ago. She said:

> I have forgiven [my ex-husband]. I forgave him instantly for the adultery. I pity him. I'm not sure if that's a good thing or not, but I feel sorry for him because he's missing out on three jewels that God gave us.

Perhaps your story resembles Louise's. How do you work past anger to embrace the peace of the Lord, extend forgiveness, and move forward? Louise is an incredible woman of faith. Even after enduring such a nightmare, the Lord's peace and forgiveness flow from her:

> I learned to rely on God 100 percent for the first time in my life. I didn't know what to do so I had no choice. God showed me His love and beauty through my pain. He showed me how to "be still" and know that He was taking care of everything. And He did. I was able to thank God for every trial He has given me. I was humbled, as crazy as that sounds, that He trusts me enough to get through this new temporary phase of life. I learned to let the Lord fill my cup.

Amen.

Hope Past Anger

> Hope has two beautiful daughters; their names are Anger and Courage. Anger at the way things are, and Courage to see that they do not remain as they are.
> —Augustine of Hippo

As I researched anger in various sources for this section, I was amazed (not in a good way) at how many magazine articles and secular experts suggested that remaining angry is a good idea. Some went so far as to make a top ten list of benefits for remaining angry, such as you receive attention, anger punishes your ex, anger motivates you, and anger enables you to avoid pain. Suffice it to say, I agree to disagree.

Let's answer their reasoning with some practical questions. Yes, angry people receive attention, but does anger shine a positive light? Yes, in certain circumstances anger punishes your ex, but who else is punished as well? I would agree that anger motivates, but how can we maintain such exhausting motivation? Yes, anger enables us to avoid pain, but then how do we properly identify it and surrender it to God for healing? Let's face it, anger hurts, and it makes us a grumpy,

How do you work past anger to embrace the peace of the Lord, extend forgiveness, and move forward?

71

stressed-out shell of a person. Anger inhibits our relationship with God and others and creates unnecessary fear that destroys intimacy.

Anger is referred to as a secondary emotion. A primary feeling is what we feel immediately before we feel anger. We almost always feel something first before we get angry. If you have experienced anger recently, think on it for a moment. What sparked it? You might first have felt afraid, attacked, hurt, humiliated, offended, disrespected, forced, trapped, or pressured. If any of those feelings is intense enough, we identify the emotion as anger. Benjamin Franklin once said, "*Whatever is begun in anger ends in shame.*" I don't know about you, but I have certainly felt ashamed after giving in to anger, especially if there was someone else on the receiving end of it.

However, anger represents the tip of the iceberg. Other emotions exist below the waterline, where they are not immediately obvious. Identifying those primary emotions holds the key to dealing with anger, and it opens our heart to God's healing.

Anger itself is not wrong. It's what we do with our anger that can be wrong. When I get angry, I ball up like a porcupine so that no one can get close enough to hurt me again. But the problem is that I am not open to receive God's comfort or healing in such a toxic, defensive position.

Anger inhibits our relationship with God and others.

Surrendering our anger to God removes that toxic barrier that prevents us from living fully and completely in His love, healing, and hope. Norman Vincent Peale put it like this:

Forget the mistakes of the past and press on to the greater achievements of the future. Give everyone a smile. Spend so much time improving yourself that you have no time left to criticize others. Be too big for worry and too noble for anger.

Anger and even hate can come about as a result of feeling that your ex-spouse "ruined" your life. When you are a child of God, your life is never ruined, because His plans are for your ultimate good.

His plans do not hinge on how your ex-spouse treated you. God's plans hinge on His great love for you, which always brings beauty out of ashes.

Wallowing in anger traps us in dark pits and prisons. A hard heart never heals. We need to feel it and then allow God to rescue us, to heal it. Cast the burden of past mistakes to the Lord and pursue Him relentlessly with your every breath. In that pursuit, we no longer seek revenge or hiss criticism; we stand tall in the strength of His might.

Pastoral Wisdom

What does the Bible say about anger?

Recently, someone was talking about the question "What Would Jesus Do?" and said this: "Grabbing a whip and turning over tables is within the realm of possibility." This comes from the cleansing of the temple, when Jesus was angry that they had corrupted true worship by making the temple a marketplace (Matthew 21:12–13). Jesus was also angry with the unbelief and "hardness of heart" of the Jewish leaders (Mark 3:5).

Some use these passages to try to justify their own anger. They try to identify their anger as "righteous," especially if they feel victimized or are an innocent party in a divorce. While it is possible to have righteous anger over sin, righteous anger is seldom what we mortals feel. Instead, our anger is more like what Cain felt against his brother, Abel (Genesis 4), and that led to murder!

The apostle James reminds us, "*The anger of man does not produce the righteousness of God*" (James 1:20).

Human anger comes from hurt, feeling as though we have been discounted or ignored or wronged. It is a selfish thing. It is the antithesis of the life to which God has called us in Christ. So Scripture warns us, "*Refrain from anger, and forsake wrath! Fret not yourself; it tends only to evil*" (Psalm 37:8).

Most often we deal with anger in a way that leads to sin. But it does not have to be that way. It is possible to experience anger without sin. It has to do with the way in which we deal with our anger.

Trying to bury it, bottle it up, or pretend it is not there is NOT a solution. That is like using a pressure cooker without a relief valve. A pressure cooker has to have a release, or there will be a violent explosion. Search the Internet for "pressure cooker explosion" and you will find a lot of pictures. I saw one where the pot pushed the top of the stove down into the oven, the hood vent is wrapped around the cabinet doors above, and the lid of the cooker is embedded in the ceiling.

Anger will do the same thing if you do not deal with it and find a way to release it. A violent release of your anger might give you a brief feeling of contentment, but it will most likely be the cause of further pain and guilt because it will lead you to sin. Simply venting is not a God-pleasing solution:

> A fool gives full vent to his spirit, but a wise man quietly holds it back. (Proverbs 29:11)

How can you keep your anger under control? Find a healthy and constructive way to let it go. For some, physical exercise is a release, even if it is just going for a walk to give yourself a chance to cool off and calm down. If possible, try to talk things out with the other person (Matthew 18:15; 5:21–24).

You may also need to talk it through with a trusted Christian friend or counselor. And do not neglect talking to God directly. Pray about your anger. Ask the Lord to help you let it go. You have not because you ask not. Don't try to hold on to your anger. That will just lead you to sin:

> Be angry and do not sin; do not let the sun go down on your anger, and give no opportunity to the devil. (Ephesians 4:26–27)

Instead, remember that your sinful anger was one of the things for which Jesus died. He wants you to be free of it, to have a full life here and now:

> Let all bitterness and wrath and anger and clamor and slander be put away from you, along with all malice.

Be kind to one another, tenderhearted, forgiving one another, just as God in Christ forgave you. (Ephesians 4:31–32)

COUNSELOR'S CORNER

Practical steps to resolve anger issues

Anger comes in two types: passive anger and aggressive anger. We generally experience both at different times. Here's a quick look at the difference:

1. **Passive anger:** It can look like depression, anxiety, silent treatment, withdrawal, negativity, resentfulness, criticalness, words under breath, unhealthy conflict avoidance, and addictions, to name a few.

2. **Aggressive anger:** It can look like yelling, swearing, all types of abuse, direct threats and threatening behaviors, bullying, replaying the past for purpose of hurt, violence toward people or objects, etc.

Know which type of anger you are most prone to. Take time to analyze what situations or people trigger your anger. Make a list, if necessary. It's important to anticipate when you will be in those situations and plan for how to keep control of your emotions. And never underestimate the power of prayer!

Here are some helpful techniques to diffuse emotions:

- Take a time-out, walking away if possible.

- Practice deep breathing and progressive muscle relaxation: Start at your feet, tense muscles for few seconds, take two deep breaths and release tension, and then move up body slowly, ending at your head.

Do these while praying, saying a short, calming phrase, or reciting Scripture. You can do deep breathing and muscle relaxation without anyone seeing!

3: Pausing to Breathe, Pray, and Reflect

Even in the midst of our anger, God is not offended when our heart bleeds ugly questions. When we seek God's wisdom, answers will come. We can be thankful that our compassionate, loving God is slow to anger.

Anger is simply an emotion; it is neither good nor bad. We have a tendency to compare our emotions and deem them good or bad. For example, we say peacefulness is best, but loneliness is the worst. Some say happiness is good but anger is bad. However, many have used their anger to inspire them to change the world in some way by fighting to right wrongs. Sometimes anger provides courage to speak up or reach out with positive results.

The emotion itself is neither good nor bad; it's how we process it and react through it that makes the difference. It is important to remember to be patient. Anger does not lend itself to patience, so it will be a struggle. It was for me, anyway.

Through the exercises below, cling with confidence to this hope-filled truth: although your feelings come and go, God's love for you does not. Take your time walking through the following Bible passages, questions, prayer time, and journaling time before moving to the next chapter.

SCRIPTURE TO READ, MEDITATE ON, AND MEMORIZE

He sent from on high, He took me; He drew me out of many waters. He rescued me from my strong enemy and from those who hated me, for they were too mighty for me. They confronted me in the day of my calamity, but the LORD was my support. He *brought me out into a broad place; He rescued me, **because He delighted in me**. (Psalm 18:16–19, emphasis added)*

Be angry and do not sin; do not let the sun go down on your anger, and give no opportunity to the devil. . . . Let all bitterness and wrath and anger and clamor and slander be put away from you, along with malice. (Ephesians 4:26–27, 31)

But you, O Lord, are a God merciful and gracious, slow to anger and abounding in steadfast love and faithfulness. (Psalm 86:15)

QUESTIONS FOR REFLECTION

When you are not in the throes of anger, there are several questions that, with God's guidance, can help you to release the anger beast. As I stated in the previous chapter's pause time, be sure to take a minute to answer these questions from the gut. No one is looking over your shoulder. It's just you and God. So get real and raw so that God can continue the healing process in your heart.

1. What are you really angry about? Don't just talk about the divorce process in general, or your ex-spouse, but narrow it down and get specific.

2. How would you feel and be different if you surrendered your anger to God? More self confidence, more sure

3. Without anger, how would you react the next time a similar hurtful situation arises? dig a hole; retreat

PAUSE FOR PRAYER

No matter how fierce your anger, God promises that when we submit all things to Him, He will bring about good. Yes, He will. Although my anger did not drag on for years, it certainly affected my life for several months.

Can I just talk real with you from the viewpoint of someone who has struggled through anger during divorce? STOP AND THINK

[handwritten margin note: That I lost mom; your thinking that Robert loved me and I don't believe he did]

BEFORE YOU VENT to anyone other than God. If you are seeing a licensed counselor or pastor, then by all means, vent. God has put those gifted people in our paths to navigate highly charged emotions. However, venting to family, friends, or the person in the grocery line will land you back in the same place: ANGRY. In fact, the more we dwell on what our ex-spouse has or hasn't done, the angrier we get.

Take this time to pour out your anger to God. His big shoulders can take it. And little by little, piece by piece, He will restore you. He never abandons you. He will make you new. Those are His promises, not mine. Thank You, Lord.

LET'S PRAY

A—Acknowledge God's sovereignty: Sometimes we dwell on our situation, forgetting in our anger that God is still in control of everything. Even your situation. Read Psalm 103:15–19 aloud with confidence.

C—Confession: Working through anger and emerging healed by God on the other side takes time and diligence. Take this time to confess what you are angry about to God; narrow it down and get specific. He already knows each circumstance, but verbally expressing those feelings ejects them from your heart, mind, and soul so that He can begin the healing process. Please pray aloud to God now.

T—Thanksgiving: It is hard to express thanks when anger rages. Yet even in the midst of your circumstances, God has blessed you with people and/or things for which you owe Him thanks. It may sound silly, but when I struggled with anger I thanked God for the vocal cords to let it out. Afterward, I thanked God for absorbing those toxic feelings so that I didn't inflict them on someone I loved. List three things you are thankful for right now, and thank God for them.

1.

2.

3.

S—**Supplication (requests):** God promises that when we pray, He faithfully hears us. Anger saps us of vital strength that we need to survive and thrive following divorce. Identify what you need from God right now, and ask in faith for Him to provide it.

EXHALING ON THE PAGE

If you have not started our journaling process, begin TODAY. You don't need to have a fancy journal. Pick up the nearest yellow pad or some loose-leaf paper and start writing. God will use your journaling as another way to release toxic feelings and show how He is pouring His love into you. You may not see the benefit today, but you will one day. Trust Him.

Here are some suggested questions to answer as you journal:

1. What happened today?

2. How do you feel?

3. What made you angry or made you grateful?

4. How did someone encourage you today or show kindness?

5. Where did you see God at work in your circumstances today?

You did it! Take a deep breath and exhale slowly. God is with you, dear one. He will NEVER leave you or forsake you. He will see you through each day and every circumstance.

4

What Does the Bible Say about Divorce?

Even though I walk through the valley of the shadow of death, I will fear no evil, for You are with me.

—Psalm 23:4

Through movies and television, Hollywood places personal happiness at the center of life. Affairs, love triangles, and divorce are great for Nielsen ratings. Unfortunately, in real life they make for shattered hearts and broken homes that aren't resolved in one-hour segments.

In this chapter, we will dive into Scripture to understand the truth about divorce and remarriage. We will look at the teachings about divorce from Jesus, Moses, and the apostle Paul and walk through how to interpret them today. Until we understand how much God hates divorce, we cannot fully appreciate the grace, love, and sacrifice of Jesus, who restored us under the new covenant.

Pastors usually hear about divorce after the fact or when the marriage relationship is so far gone that the couple already determined to divorce. People today turn to the media, friends, and the Internet instead of the Church for counsel and wisdom. The Church is affected by divorce, especially when children are involved. Churches can be an invaluable resource when they take a proactive approach to provide counseling and workers trained to handle such emotional trauma.

Divorce is a process, not an event.

An important truth we need to remember is that divorce is a process, not an event. It is a negotiated settlement affecting relationships, lifestyle changes, and finances that requires years of readjustments. Fortunately for Christians, divorce does not define our identity. God's negotiated settlement happened at Calvary. He negotiated with Himself and settled our eternity. Our identity is found in Christ alone.

UNDERSTANDING THE MARRIAGE COVENANT

In Genesis 2, we learn that marriage is intended to be monogamous, between one man and one woman, and permanent until death. Well, now you're divorced. Like me, you probably have questions about the spiritual ramifications from a biblical standpoint.

In order to aid comprehension, we must begin with what marriage means. God gave marriage as a picture of the relationship between Christ and His Bride, the Church (Ephesians 5:32). Marriage is an unbreakable, God-made covenant, not a breakable, man-made contract:

> Therefore a man shall leave his father and his mother
> and hold fast ["cleave" (KJV)] to his wife, and they shall
> become one flesh. (Genesis 2:24)

The Hebrew word for *cleave* means "glue." In other words, we are bonded with our spouse for life. Significantly, the word is a covenant term in the Old Testament, denoting the affection and loyalty with which the Israelites are to cleave to the Lord (Deuteronomy

10:20; 11:22; 13:4; 30:20; Joshua 22:5; 23:8). Two have become "one flesh." The term *flesh* references our entire being in both physical and psychological dimensions.

When the apostle Paul discussed sexual intercourse in light of the "one flesh" union in marriage (1 Corinthians 6:12–20; Ephesians 5:21–43), he stated:

> Do you not know that he who is joined with a prostitute becomes one body with her? For, as it is written, "The two will become one flesh." (1 Corinthians 6:16)

Therefore, a merely physical, transient relationship is not possible. It is not something "in" a husband and wife that unites them; they have become one. A divorce does not break God's covenant. In God's eyes, we are united with our first spouse until death parts us. Legal justification in court does not translate to divine approval.

It is important to understand that marriage is strictly an earthly relationship. We will not be married to each other in heaven, and we will not be reunited with lost spouses in heaven in the same way. For example, Jesus tells the story of the woman who had lost seven husbands:

> "Now there were seven brothers among us. The first married and died, and having no offspring left his wife to his brother. So too the second and third, down to the seventh. After them all, the woman died. In the resurrection, therefore, of the seven, whose wife will she be? For they all had her." But Jesus answered them, "You are wrong, because you know neither the Scriptures nor the power of God. For in the resurrection they neither marry nor are given in marriage, but are like angels in heaven." (Matthew 22:25–30)

We are united in heaven only as brothers and sisters in Christ, not as husbands and wives.

Divorce first comes to light in Deuteronomy 24. Husbands were dismissing their wives over trivial matters (like burned food). The discarded wives had no way to prove they were no longer married and faced dire survival circumstances. To alleviate the problem, Moses commanded that the men issue certificates of divorce so that the women could find other husbands to care for them. Thus, divorce was born.

However, even in Jesus' day when divorce was commonplace and legitimized on biblical grounds, Jesus taught, *"But from the beginning it was not so"* (Matthew 19:8).

As New Testament believers, we are guided today by Jesus' teachings in the Gospels. When it comes to divorce, Scripture mentions only two acceptable reasons to seek it: adultery and abandonment.

ADULTERY

Following God's original teaching about marriage, the second thing God mentions related to marriage appears in the Sixth Commandment: *"You shall not commit adultery"* (Exodus 20:14). This is known as a categorical imperative, or unconditional command, which upholds the sacredness of marriage.

All of God's Commandments involve upholding the sacredness of things. In today's terminology, it translates as respect. We are to respect God's name, His day, our parents, life, marriage, property, and reputation. When we lose respect or fail to uphold the sacredness of things, they begin to crumble.

All of God's Commandments involve upholding the sacredness of things.

When it comes to adultery, Scripture classifies it in a category all its own because it betrays a covenant made in God's sight. Consequently, when my ex-husband chose to commit adultery, he betrayed God's covenant. One day, my ex-husband will answer to God—not me—for that violation.

In Matthew 5:31–32, Jesus references the term *divorce* (as well as in Matthew 19:3, 7–9; Mark 10:2, 4, 11–12; and Luke 16:18) as the act of dismissing or "putting away" (KJV) one's spouse by issuing a bill of divorce and sending her away from his house. In this context, if she has committed no moral wrong, the husband makes his wife an adulteress.

In Matthew 19:9, Jesus does not classify the victim of adultery as an adulteress; therefore we cannot judge differently. Jesus says:

> "And I say to you: whoever divorces his wife, except for sexual immorality, and marries another, commits adultery."

In other words, if your spouse committed adultery in your marriage, you have the right (though you certainly are not commanded) to obtain a legal divorce and remarry without earning the label of adulterer.

That being said, whenever reconciliation is possible and both spouses desire to remain married, then reconciliation should be the goal. When my ex-husband first committed adultery six years into our marriage, I could have easily thrown in the towel. And I certainly considered it. However, even though it was a daily challenge, I chose at the time to walk toward reconciliation.

ABANDONMENT

The apostle Paul later addresses divorce and remarriage by discussing the second reason Scripture gives for divorce: abandonment.

> To the married I give this charge (not I, but the Lord): the wife should not separate from her husband (but if she does, she should remain unmarried or else be reconciled to her husband), and the husband should not divorce his wife. To the rest I say (I, not the Lord) that if any brother has a wife who is an unbeliever, and she consents to live with him, he should not divorce her. If any woman has a husband who is an unbeliever, and he consents to live with her, she should not divorce him. For the unbelieving husband is made holy because of his wife, and the unbelieving wife is made holy because of her husband. Otherwise your children would be unclean, but as it is, they are holy. But if the unbelieving partner separates, let it be so. In such cases the brother or sister is not enslaved. God has called you to peace. (1 Corinthians 7:10–15)

85

Here, Paul specifically teaches about when a believer marries an unbeliever. When an unbeliever refuses to continue the marriage and departs, the believer is free to secure a legal divorce and subsequently remarry.

Paul recognizes that when one spouse does not submit to Christ's teaching and leaves, the marriage is terminated. The believer is not bound to preserve a union that has suffered dissolution by the unbelieving spouse, who does not recognize the authority of Christ's Word. Therefore, the Christian spouse is no longer bound, but is free to file for divorce and remarry.

Perhaps for this very reason, Scripture teaches that believers should not marry unbelievers: *"Do not be unequally yoked"* (2 Corinthians 6:14). If you are married to an unbeliever, you have likely experienced in real time the difficulties associated with such a union.

If you intend to remarry one day, this is a vital Scripture passage to follow. Our most important relationship is the one with our Lord and Savior, Jesus Christ. Disregarding what God says about being unequally yoked is a recipe for heartache in a matter as foundational as marriage.

THE RESULT

After researching and studying Scripture about marriage, I felt a sense of failure and hopelessness. I am divorced, so does that translate into a life of singleness? In treating God's covenant like an earthly contract, did I commit an unforgivable sin? Maybe those questions sound silly, but I struggled with them for years. Perhaps you have struggled as well. Divorce is not an unforgivable sin because we are loved by a grace-dispensing God who listens to repentant sinners and grants forgiveness.

I chose divorce only after my ex-husband did not follow through with counseling and then later committed further acts of adultery. The final straw was the fact that when I took into consideration the variety of women he was involved with, I realized that I stood a very real chance of contracting HIV or another sexually transmitted infection each time my ex-husband and I made love. It may sound shallow, but I was not willing to die for a marriage that my ex-husband could not commit to honor with faithfulness.

CONCLUSION

Whether adulterer or victim, abandoner or abandoned, we are all invited to place our hope for restoration in Christ alone: *"There is therefore now no condemnation for those who are in Christ Jesus"* (Romans 8:1). What a beautiful label to wear: Not Condemned.

We all wear labels, which can vary by the hour. Some labels we like: Smart, Beautiful, Rich, Skinny, Successful. Some labels we don't like: Ugly, Needy, Fat, Lacking. Some labels go deeper and deposit adhesive marks on our heart: Abused, Abandoned, Failure, Childless, Widowed, Divorced.

Those cruel labels cause us to lower our heads and avoid eye contact. They strike something so deep in us that we just want to run from the stigma and memories. We are not alone. People in the Bible wore labels too:

King David—Adulterer
Moses—Murderer
Solomon—Idolater
Judas—Betrayer
Noah—Drunk

It's easy to label others because it doesn't cost us anything. Perhaps you have some labels for your ex-spouse that cost you dearly. But you and I wear a label that trumps the rest. It was made before the beginning of time by God Himself: **LOVED.** *"I have loved you with an everlasting love"* (Jeremiah 31:3).

God labeled us first—He gave us His manufacturer's stamp, so to speak. But we have allowed it to be covered over, or we have allowed others to deface it with a mustache and beard. Perhaps you covered it yourself or even tried to peel it off because you just don't feel worthy of His love. But we can't erase it. God's love STICKS.

As you read through God's transforming Word, He offers us these life-restoring labels:

Forgiven—Psalm 86:5

Redeemed—Job 19:25

Pardoned—Psalm 103:3

Renewed—Isaiah 40:31

God's labels don't change. You are always loved by Him—regardless of what you have told yourself or heard from others during your divorce process.

You are God's priceless treasure and dearly loved child. Worth creating. Worth dying for. Worth spending eternity with Him. Wholly and completely loved.

As you walk through the aftermath of divorce, look to God and remember His label of love. Lift your head and search the horizon with the eyes of faith. God has a plan for your life. Trust Him.

PASTORAL WISDOM

> "So they are no longer two but one flesh. What therefore God has joined together, let not man separate." (Matthew 19:6)

Divorce is contrary to the will of God. Divorce always involves sin. Those are hard statements, but they are the truth of God's Word. While it is true there may be an "innocent party," sin is still involved when there is a divorce. It is outside of God's will, but sometimes it is inevitable and beyond your control. It does no good to try to deny sin in this situation, because it is there.

That is why there needs to be repentance and forgiveness. Even if you are an "innocent party" and did not want the divorce, no one is ever completely innocent. I am not saying you willfully or intentionally caused the divorce, or that you should try to invent something you might have done that contributed to it. You don't need any more guilt than you already have. What I am suggesting is that you admit to yourself and to God your sins in the marriage relationship and receive the forgiveness He offers you through Christ. That will enable you to move forward covered with God's grace.

> Surely there is not a righteous man on earth who does good and never sins. (Ecclesiastes 7:20)

> Repent therefore, and turn back, that your sins may be blotted out, that times of refreshing may come from the presence of the Lord. (Acts 3:19–20)

(By the way, this is good advice for couples who are *not* divorced: admit your sins in the marriage relationship to yourself, your spouse, and to God, and hear His assurance of forgiveness for Jesus' sake.)

The first step to getting on with your life is to look to Jesus. He loves you and wants to help you through the days ahead. You take each step knowing that His perfect life and His death for sin covered any and every sin that contributed to your divorce. Those sins will not be held against you! Grab hold of that forgiveness. Let it fill you up and comfort you.

Even when you accept this gift from God, there will be difficult days ahead. The implications of divorce are varied and manifold. You cannot be prepared for all of them or even when they occur. But you can face them with the confidence that you are a redeemed, loved, forgiven child of God. And He wants to help you.

The first step to getting on with your life is to look to Jesus.

Philippians 4 is a powerful chapter. It speaks of the joy we have in Christ, which you might find lacking in your life in the aftermath of a divorce. But I encourage people in your situation to read this chapter. Did you know this chapter begins by addressing people involved in a dispute? Paul tells them to get past it. Move on. And it is in that context that Paul points them to the joy that we have for Jesus' sake. Rejoice! Don't let conflict in this world steal the joy God has given you in Christ.

Paul was having some struggles of his own, and he mentions some of them in verse 12. But then he shares that phrase that we all need to be reminded of:

> I can do all things through Him who strengthens me. (Philippians 4:13)

You don't have to face this alone. Draw on the strength God gives you. These are awesome words of comfort.

But wait—there's more. Before this chapter ends, Paul wrote some words that my father shared with me at the end of each of his letters to me, words that have stuck with me and strengthened me in a variety of situations:

> And my God will supply every need of yours according
> to His riches in glory in Christ Jesus. (Philippians 4:19)

 You have all kinds of needs in your life right now. God says to you, "I've got this." More important, He says, "I've got you!" The riches provided by Jesus will meet your needs.

4: Pausing to Breathe, Pray, and Reflect

One of the heartbreaking results of divorce is that we often feel unloved. However, the theme of love permeates Scripture. Now that we understand what divorce means from a biblical standpoint, it's time to remind you of how much God still loves you. He has not abandoned you.

Through the following exercises, cling with confidence to this hope-filled truth: though your feelings come and go, God's love for you does not. Take your time walking through the following Bible passages, questions, prayer time, and journaling time before moving to the next chapter.

Scripture to Read, Meditate on, and Memorize

I have been crucified with Christ. It is no longer I who live, but Christ who lives in me. And the life I now live in the flesh I live by faith in the Son of God, who loved me and gave Himself for me. (Galatians 2:20)

But God, being rich in mercy, because of the great love with which He loved us, even when we were dead in our trespasses, made us alive together with Christ—by grace you have been saved. (Ephesians 2:4–5)

But God shows His love for us in that while we were still sinners, Christ died for us. (Romans 5:8)

[handwritten margin note, left side: If God forgives, then we both need that forgiveness to move forward]

QUESTIONS FOR REFLECTION

Realizing that God hates divorce is hard when that is part of your experience now. Divorce destroys relationships, and God is love. Love is not only who God is; it is what He does. And you are still loved by God. Take a minute to answer these questions honestly in order to assess how you feel:

1. Do you have trouble believing that God loves you in spite of what has happened? *yes*

2. Knowing how much God loves you, realize that He also loves your ex-spouse, regardless of what he or she has done. Does that make you mad or glad? Why?

PAUSE FOR PRAYER

Take this important time to be still before the Lord and pray.

A—Acknowledge God's sovereignty: Despite how much you may want to manipulate your situation, God alone is in control. He promises to work out your situation for your good and His glory. Read Psalm 121 aloud with confidence.

C—Confession: Take this time to confess what you're struggling with to God; narrow it down and get specific. He already knows each circumstance, but verbally expressing those feelings ejects them from your heart, mind, and soul so that He can begin the healing process. Please pray aloud to God now.

T—Thanksgiving: It is hard to express thanks when so much hurt has happened. Yet even in the midst of your circumstances, God has blessed you with people and/or things for which you owe Him thanks. List three things you are thankful for right now—no matter how big or small—and thank God for them.

1.

2.

3.

S—Supplication (requests): God promises that when we pray, He faithfully hears us. Identify what you need from Him right now, and ask Him in faith to provide it.

EXHALING ON THE PAGE

If you have not started our journaling process, begin TODAY. God will use your journaling as another way to work out your feelings and show how He is pouring His love into you. You may not see the benefit today, but you will one day.

Here are some suggested questions to answer as you journal:

1. What happened today?

2. How do you feel?

3. What made you sad or grateful today?

4. How did someone encourage you today or show kindness?

5. Where did you see God at work in your circumstances today?

You did it! Take a deep breath and exhale slowly. God is with you, dear one. He will NEVER leave you or forsake you. He will see you through each day and every circumstance.

5

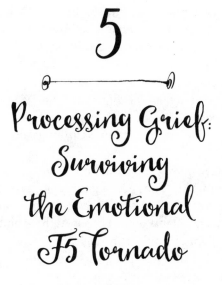

Processing Grief: Surviving the Emotional F5 Tornado

Though He cause grief, He will have compassion according to the abundance of His steadfast love.
—Lamentations 3:32

I slowly walked into my house, dreading turning on any lights. I wasn't afraid that someone lurked within. I simply knew what awaited. *Holes.* It was December 21 and my husband and I should have been celebrating our thirteenth wedding anniversary. Instead, he moved the rest of his belongings out of our home that day.

It had been three weeks since I discovered my husband's unfaithfulness. At the time, he had moved his clothes and personal items into a friend's guesthouse. Now it was time to divide the rest and move forward apart.

We owned a nice, four-bedroom home, and since we did not have children, each of us enjoyed our own study, plus there was a spare guest room for overnight visitors. Earlier in the week, I methodically went through the house to tag the items for him to take: contents of the entire guest room, the kitchen dining set, his entire study, his favorite recliner and side table, a bedroom chest of drawers and linens, lamps, kitchen supplies, and odds and ends. Everything he needed to furnish a new place.

While my ex-husband moved out, dear friends of ours called me at work and invited me out for dinner and a movie. They knew that it was our thirteenth wedding anniversary, and they wanted to cheer me up. I was thankful for their friendship, especially at such a heartbreaking time.

However, staying away longer did not change what greeted me at home that evening. The light peeking through the open garage door illuminated the kitchen. The kitchen table where I usually deposited my purse and workbag was gone. I dropped them onto the floor and turned on the lights. I walked through the kitchen straight ahead into my husband's study. Except for scattered loose papers and trash, it was completely empty. Tears began to flow.

I shuffled through the connecting bathroom and into the now-empty guest room, openly sobbing. The holes where furniture once stood served as stark reminders of the holes in my heart.

I walked into the living room and stopped dead. It looked like the house had been ransacked. Whatever my husband didn't want to take had been thrown haphazardly into piles. Shoes. Clothes. Contents of drawers. The same scenario greeted me in our bedroom. I couldn't even see the bed for piles of his unwanted clothes, ties, belts, shoes, and hangers.

The holes where furniture stood served as stark reminders of the holes in my heart.

That moment was a visual translation of the trash that his actions had created. He trashed our marriage vows, trashed my heart, and as if that weren't enough, he trashed our home. Hurt and anger hit me so hard in that moment that I thought I would be physically ill. I screamed through angry tears, *"WHO GAVE YOU THE RIGHT TO DESTROY US?! WHO DO YOU THINK YOU ARE?! I HATE YOU!"*

As those last three words echoed off the walls, they stopped me short. Did I actually hate him? It was the first time those words had spewed out since the whole mess started three weeks before. They sobered me instantly, stopping the tears. I sat down in the middle of the mess and quietly asked God, *"Do I really hate him?"*

STAGES OF GRIEF

That day I felt the shifting effects of the grieving process. Professionals generally agree that there are five main stages of grief, though some have extended the list to as many as twelve. The grief stages are denial (isolation), anger, bargaining, depression, and, finally, acceptance. We experience grief when we experience loss, whether that loss is through death, divorce, job change, or a cross-country move.

I experienced the stages of grief after my dad passed away from cancer thirteen years ago. Even though I missed Dad terribly, I ultimately thanked God that he no longer suffered. With divorce, it was much more difficult to embrace a state of thankfulness, especially since I never saw it coming.

I lingered in some grief stages longer than others, and you may find that true as well. At first, I saw only the unnecessary destruction from one person's thoughtless actions. Eventually, I experienced each grief stage and emerged on the other side stronger by the grace of God. God grew my faith, trust, and love for Him, which nurtured the confidence to keep walking into the new future He already had planned for me. That is my fervent prayer for you.

GRIEF STAGE ONE: DENIAL

The first reaction to learning about or deciding to divorce is to deny the reality of the situation. Rationalizing overwhelming emotions serves as a defense mechanism to buffer shock. We block out words or actions and hide from the ugly facts. This temporary shock and numbness carries us through the first wave of pain.

I experienced denial when I hung up the phone after talking with the last woman on the list of the women my husband was seeing. I kept looking at each of those names thinking that it just couldn't be possible for my husband to be involved with so many women. Where did he find the time? Had it been so easy to dismiss his wife and a good life? How could he so thoroughly destroy our marriage covenant without even saying a word? My denial stage did not last long because the evidence was written in black and white on the page in my lap. Even to this day, I still feel incredulous that all of his relationship rendezvous happened without my knowledge.

As the divorce process moved forward, I experienced denial each time another of his unpleasant actions surfaced. Each incident restarted the grieving process to the point that some days I felt like a caged hamster running mindlessly on a wheel. It didn't take long for me to zip right past denial to anger, the next grief stage.

GRIEF STAGE TWO: ANGER

Anger usually occurs when we feel helpless or powerless. In order to cope, intense emotions of hurt and pain are redirected and expressed as anger. People process anger differently: some verbalize and others internalize. Those who verbalize think it's a great idea to tell anyone and everyone that their ex is the biggest jerk on the planet. Those who internalize grieve and process difficulties alone or with a few trusted confidants. Other than a few outbursts in private to God, I internalized my anger. As mentioned in chapter 3, I tried to cage it. Well, I learned the hard way that the anger beast doesn't stay caged, so processing anger and getting through this stage is vital in the long run.

Anger usually occurs when we feel helpless or powerless.

Our anger may be directed toward our ex-spouse, inanimate objects, complete strangers, friends, family, or even the mirror. Our anger may even be directed at God. Remember, grieving is a personal process that has no time limit; nor is there only one way to walk through it.

Part of my anger was fueled by the fact that our marriage shattered at Christmastime. Christmas has always been my favorite time of year, but now it felt tainted and less joyful. That year, I did not even unpack the usual Christmas decorations. I made one trip to the store and bought a fake tabletop tree, a fireplace wreath, and a candle with greenery for the table by my living room chair. Christmas cheer was absent, and it was the first time that I actively wished away the Christmas season.

Eventually, my anger was too exhausting to maintain. After months of struggling, prayer, and counseling, I surrendered my anger to God, which kick-started the next grief stage: bargaining.

Grief Stage Three: Bargaining

In the bargaining stage, we desire to counteract our feelings of helplessness and vulnerability by regaining control (either real or imagined) of our situation. Bargaining often goes hand in hand with denial as we look for any possible way to make the relationship work through negotiation, threats, or promises of change.

When you start making "If . . . then" statements, you have reached the bargaining stage: "If my spouse would ____, then _____." Part of this process may include bargaining with God. "If You restore my marriage, then _____." This stage is marked by persistent thoughts about what could have been done to prevent the relationship's failure. Mine looked like this:

- If only we had sought marital counseling after his first affair six years ago, then . . .

- If I had only paid closer attention to how he spent his time, then . . .

- If I would have been a nymphomaniac, then . . .

- If I would have been a perfect Martha Stewart homemaker, then . . .

If not properly resolved, these feelings of remorse, guilt, and not facing vital facts can interfere with the healing process.

GRIEF STAGE FOUR: DEPRESSION

This stage of grief occurs when we realize the true extent of our loss. It surfaces in many different forms, such as feeling tired all the time, withdrawing from the outside world to simply lie around the house, feeling disconnected from people even when you're with them, and bursting into tears at the slightest provocation.

During this stage, I experienced two types of mild depression that may resonate with you. The first type was my initial reaction to the loss of my marriage, which showed itself in sadness and worry. I worried about how I would make it on my own again and what that would feel like. For this type of depression, I simply needed clarification and reassurance along with practical guidance.

The second type of depression was more subtle and infinitely more private. It was my quiet preparation—spiritually, emotionally—to bid my marriage farewell. Some days I needed to spend hours in Scripture to remind myself how much God loves me and that He is my refuge and strength. Other days I really just needed a big hug.

Signs that you have reached this stage of grief include trouble sleeping, loss of appetite, lack of energy and concentration, and crying spells. This stage hit me hard, and I lost thirty pounds over a four-month period simply because my appetite was gone and I hardly slept. Feelings of loneliness, emptiness, and isolation are normal and can trigger depression if not dealt with in short order.

This grief stage is particularly hard because you may need to combat depression with medication. There is no shame whatsoever in admitting it. Consult with a mental health professional for assessment if you experience severe depression consistently for several weeks. Although medication was not part of my story, it has been part of many. Don't be afraid to seek the appropriate help you need.

GRIEF STAGE FIVE: ACCEPTANCE

This final stage of grief is one not reached by everyone. If your divorce was sudden or unexpected, you may struggle to move beyond anger or denial. This is the stage in which we are able to make peace with the loss, God, our ex-spouse, and ourselves. Normally, acceptance happens gradually, interspersed with some of the other stages. Acceptance doesn't always involve harmony and flowers; there is usually lingering sadness marked by calm and withdrawal. Acceptance lets go of the relationship and allows you to slowly move forward into a new phase of life.

Once I accepted that my marriage was over, I felt calm and at peace. Still, I needed to withdraw and process that acceptance. For me, this stage often looked like long, uninterrupted walks alone while listening to worship music. It felt like the more I walked, the more God was healing my heart and soul. I needed time to shift to life on my own again and make peace with myself.

After acceptance, I began to earnestly seek the Lord's guidance about my new life and future through prayer and His Word. Acceptance can be misconstrued as depression, but it must be properly distinguished. Acceptance is not necessarily a period of happiness, but a rather somber assessment of your new life and embracing what lies ahead.

Coping with the loss of your marriage is a deeply personal and singular experience; only you can fully understand all the emotions you experience. However, others can be there for you and help comfort and guide you through the process. Grieving is like digestion: there is nothing you can do to hurry it along. It takes time.

The best thing you can do is allow yourself to feel the grief as it comes over you. Mine was an intensely private process. I realized very quickly that I could not feel and respond freely to my stages of grief if I was concerned about how others would react to my grief. The more I processed grief—alone or with my counselor—the more easily God navigated me through the natural healing process.

Meet Cheryl

She never imagined that her marriage would abruptly end almost nineteen years after marrying her best friend. Cheryl and her ex-husband had both been raised Missouri Synod Lutherans; they attended church together and experienced many years of making good memories. In fact, when her ex-husband suddenly announced that he no longer loved her and wanted a divorce, it completely surprised Cheryl and their two teenage children.

The month before he announced that he wanted a divorce, her ex-husband had lost his job and dealt with resulting legal issues. He had also been seeing a VA counselor to treat post-traumatic stress disorder (PTSD). After his bombshell divorce announcement, Cheryl asked that they see a counselor together:

> I asked for us to see a counselor, but he said it didn't matter—his mind was made up. I continued [for two months] to argue with him to fight for our marriage, but he wouldn't have it. He searched online for filing for divorce without lawyers. He found the paperwork and emailed it to me. We went to the courthouse and filed the divorce paperwork.

A year before announcing his decision to divorce, Cheryl's ex-husband had suggested they move from Minnesota to California so that they could be closer to Cheryl's mom. Little did she know at the time that the move was part of her ex-husband's plan to move Cheryl and their kids in with her mom before he filed for divorce. Then, one month before the divorce was final, he drove Cheryl, their two teenage children, three cats, and a few belongings from Minnesota to California and deposited them at her mom's house. Cheryl remembers:

> I told him that since the court date was in Minnesota, he would need to get permission from the judge for me to appear via telephone. I was NOT going to pay to go back there for something I didn't want. He got permission from the judge. I dialed in, and within less than twenty minutes my whole adult life was changed. I met my ex when I was nineteen and now, at the age of forty, I was another statistic: a divorced mom of two.

Perhaps you can relate to Cheryl's story. She discovered that there were many things she found difficult to handle following the divorce, including accepting the fact that she was no longer married. Cheryl and her children struggled to understand how their life as a whole family had ended so suddenly. During the divorce, Cheryl experienced many grief stages, including denial, anger, bargaining, and acceptance:

> Acceptance came because I was pretty much forced to accept. He left, he hurt me, and then he got married. . . . It was hard to maintain my self-worth and not get depressed—struggling through feelings of anger, betrayal, loneliness, feeling unlovable, and more. . . . I know I have not handled this well. But I also know that I have been doing the best I can with what I have.

As she prayed and journaled, the faith that God gave Cheryl saw her through. Although her future is unclear, she says, *"I don't know what's in store for me, but I'm looking forward to it."* The verse that God gave her as a child helped to see her through the divorce: *"I will never leave you nor forsake you"* (Hebrews 13:5).

Even after such heartbreak and life change, Cheryl offers us this wisdom, in the form of some of the words her mom would often say to her during that first year:

> Don't lose sight of yourself. You are important; you are valued. Your worth is not with that other person. You are strong and you are loved. God WILL NOT leave you. He has your best interests in mind. You may not see it right now, but He's got plans for you, and you will be fine.

Don't lose sight of yourself. You are important; you are valued.

God's love never fails us. Walk faithfully through your grief stages, trusting that God carries you each step of the way.

Meet Emily

Emily and her husband (an associate minister) enjoyed a good life together. They met at church and their dads (both ministers) were friends. They married at twenty-two and welcomed three children in their first eleven years of marriage. He worked and finished college while Emily worked from home and cared for their three children.

When their youngest child turned six, Emily went back to college to get her nursing degree. Her husband did not support her decision, and her life soon took a turn she never expected.

Emily and her husband knew each other's email passwords their entire marriage. One day she needed to retrieve a recipe that she had emailed him a few weeks before but had accidentally deleted from her own account:

> His email password didn't work, so I answered the security questions, found the recipe, and forwarded it to my email. Then I found pages and pages of emails from all hours of the day and night to a name I didn't recognize going back several months. I opened them and discovered he was having an affair. Explicit emails of their secret meetings, details of them having sex at work, and how he was going to lie to me and sneak away to be with her for a few hours here and there. I thought I was going to be sick. He had just preached a sermon the previous Sunday. Nothing had changed in our marriage, in our bedroom, in his parenting—how could I not know?

Emily forwarded all of the emails to her account, printed them out, and asked a neighbor to pick up the kids. She confronted her husband when he arrived home from work. He admitted that he was having a midlife crisis and confessed that he made a mistake, and he promised to end it. He cried, begged for forgiveness, and begged Emily not to tell anyone. She needed time to process what had transpired, so she retired for the evening. But the situation didn't improve after she went to school the next morning:

> I logged on to his cell phone account and discovered he had texted her over a hundred times that morning and they'd talked several times. I called my friend to

drive by my house, and sure enough, a strange car was in my driveway. Not only was he seeing her—she was at my house.

When Emily arrived home and asked her husband what he had done that day, he said he had slept most of the day and picked up the kids from school. She told him what she had discovered. He accused her of being a psycho stalker and stormed out of their home. The nightmare continued:

> He returned home later and smelled like alcohol. What? He preached that drinking was a sin. In all the years I'd been with him, I never saw him drink a drop. I told him I wanted to talk to the girl who was sleeping with my husband. He hit me across the face while my three kids watched; he had never laid a hand on me before. He then took my phone and locked me in our bedroom so I couldn't call for help. He tried to convince me all night that I'd had a nervous breakdown and that he'd never hit me.

When her husband went to work the next day, she changed the house locks, changed the garage code, transferred half of their money to a new bank account, packed his things, and put them out on the porch. When he couldn't get into their home, he started banging on the door. Later, Emily threatened to call the police, and he eventually left.

Within weeks, her husband moved in with his girlfriend, and Emily learned that his girlfriend was pregnant. Even though her husband denied it and called Emily delusional, the truth was confirmed by the appearance of a baby girl several months later.

The whole ordeal was tremendously difficult for Emily and their three children. Her husband became physically abusive toward their children, and on a few occasions Emily was forced to involve the police and Child Protective Services. After an eighteen-month legal separation, Emily filed for divorce. When I asked Emily which part of the divorce process itself was hardest, she responded:

The hardest part for me was losing my church family. He was one of the associate ministers. The church officials told me that I needed to prove that he was in a sexual relationship with the girl or I had no right to divorce him. The wives of the church officials asked me if I had "withheld" myself from him, "causing" him to be unfaithful. We had been a part of this church for fifteen years—all of my friendships were there, and I became a pariah. I left there within a couple of months of being separated.

Needless to say, the grieving process has been a long, painful one for Emily, and she admits that she has not yet forgiven her ex-husband even though the divorce was final almost five years ago. She has struggled in her faith as well:

I prayed and looked for answers and comfort, but I was so hurt by what the church officials were saying to me that I left there. I took the kids to the church we attend now, but it was for them, not me. I quit praying. I felt abandoned by God too. After all, He had allowed all this to happen when I had served Him since I was fifteen and taught my children like I was supposed to. I had a real crisis of faith and went down a bad road for a time, but I never kept my kids from church. I eventually asked God for forgiveness and turned my life back over to Him.

Perhaps you find yourself somewhere in Emily's story. What breaks my heart about her story is that her husband was a member of the clergy. That element causes significant damage because clergy are tasked with being our earthly shepherds—our protectors and guardians who should be known for impeccable reputations, truth-filled words, and Christlike behavior. But the bottom line is that clergy are sinners just like you and me. They succumb to temptation and need God's forgiveness and grace as much as we do.

A church position does not make someone more like Christ.

Only diligent prayer, study of God's Word, genuine love for Jesus, and humble service keep us mindful of what God has called us to do—especially clergy and church workers who have devoted their full-time vocation to serving Jesus.

Over time, Emily experienced all five stages of grief. At first, she battled denial that her marriage was really over and kept hoping that her husband would come to his senses. She also isolated herself on social media and told only her family and the church officials what was happening. She remembers:

> I was trying to save his reputation. Funny how I was still putting him before myself or my kids those first weeks.

Emily moved into the anger stage next and admits that it still rears its ugly head from time to time. She candidly relates that her anger is not really about the adultery anymore, but "because I chose to have kids with him and he's abandoned them."

Then the bargaining stage hit: Emily offered to go through marriage counseling and go away with her husband to reconnect as a couple. She even offered to quit school and stay home as she had before—all to no avail.

The depression stage of the grief process hit Emily hard. When her husband's girlfriend turned out to be pregnant, Emily realized that she couldn't fix her marriage. She felt like a failure, and she lost fifty pounds in four months. Looking back, she confesses:

> It's embarrassing to admit, but for a short time, I went out and drank and slept with men in their twenties—anything to try to feel better, to feel wanted, but I always felt worse. I'm glad I had a mother who came to me and told me that I would never find my self-esteem that way.

I am so thankful that Emily's mother loved her courageously enough to tell her a hard truth. We all need family and/or friends who are willing to speak honestly in love when the going gets tough. But those trusted loved ones can help us only as much as we give them access to our situation and honest feelings. If you are traveling down a harmful road, stop right now and ask God to bring someone into your life who will speak His truth to you in love. Then ask God to give you the grace and strength to follow His guidance back toward faith.

Emily is still working on the acceptance stage of grieving:

> I'm successful as a nurse and am almost a nurse practitioner; I'm a great mom, daughter, sister, and friend. I realize his cheating wasn't my fault. I hope I will get the chance to be a good wife in the future.

There is so much positive self-talk and hope in Emily's words. The Scripture passage that helped her most was Proverbs 3:5–7:

> Trust in the LORD with all your heart, and do not lean on your own understanding. In all your ways acknowledge Him, and He will make straight your paths. Be not wise in your own eyes.

As Emily moves forward to embrace the new future that God has given her, she offers this advice from hard-earned experience:

> Take it just one day at a time—or just get to noon and then get to the end of the workday and then through dinner. It is all overwhelming at first, so set small goals. Don't try to look at the whole picture just yet.

God specializes in one moment, one day at a time. Trust Him and He will light your path.

PRACTICAL STEPS

As our stories reveal, several factors may hinder grief and healing: becoming a workaholic; abusing drugs, alcohol, food, or other substances; avoiding emotions; and minimizing feelings. Many strategies can help you move through and resolve grief:

1. Express thoughts and feelings openly or capture them in a journal.

2. Allow yourself to grieve.

3. Confide in a trusted person.

4. Seek professional help and spiritual guidance.

5. Most important, rely on God and His promises of hope and healing.

Divorce is a loss; it is similar to death, except people don't send flowers and sympathy cards. The pain you have experienced is beyond the comprehension of those who have not gone through divorce. There were some days when I did not believe I would survive the pain. Others cannot fathom the depth of pain and the mental, physical, emotional, and spiritual toll of divorce.

One of the first security blankets that divorce rips off is our peace. Suddenly, our carefully planned future lies in shards and tomorrow is uncertain. But there is a place where we can find peace in the storm—at the foot of the cross.

Perhaps the pain has caused your heart to harden toward God; yet He understands how you feel (Isaiah 63:9). He endured excruciating pain on the cross, so He understands best how to comfort you in your suffering. Most people naturally look for a painless way out of the terrible storm, but there is no way around it. However, God will get you through it. *Lean in and let Him.* Over time, you will see that healing is possible because with God *all things* are possible.

CONCLUSION

Even though we grieve, the apostle Paul reminds us that we do not grieve as those who have no hope (1 Thessalonians 4:13). With the same power that God used in raising Christ from the dead, He reaches down to rescue you when the storm threatens to sweep you away. Like baby Moses plucked from the water, God will not abandon you to drown.

Divorce means that your surroundings and life look vastly different. As you grieve,

Divorce is a loss; it is similar to death, except people don't send flowers and sympathy cards.

allow trusted loved ones to come alongside you in prayer. Let them show their love for you because you need that vital reminder after such a hurtful trauma. When friends asked what they could do for me, I requested Scripture written on index cards. Before long, letters full of Scripture passages arrived, and I hung them on my refrigerator, bathroom mirror, and on the dashboard in my car; I tucked them into my Bible and my journal. I put them anywhere that I spent significant time. Those passages reminded me that Jesus understands suffering:

> He has sent Me to bind up the brokenhearted, to proclaim liberty to the captives . . . to comfort all who mourn; . . . to give them a beautiful headdress instead of ashes, the oil of gladness instead of mourning, the garment of praise instead of a faint spirit. (Isaiah 61:1–3)

All you may see right now are the ashes, mourning, and faint spirit. But when you look with the eyes of faith, you will see a beautiful headdress, the oil of gladness, and a garment of praise. God provides exactly what we need precisely when we need it:

> And God is able to make all grace abound to you, so that having all sufficiency in all things at all times, you may abound in every good work. (2 Corinthians 9:8)

Like baby Moses plucked from the water, God will not abandon you to drown.

As you travel through the stages of grief, allow God's life-restoring comfort to pour like oil over your head. He opens wide the floodgates of compassion and enfolds you with His love. You can surrender your grief to Him because He cares for you (1 Peter 5:7).

Loss and heartache are unfortunate parts of our human experience. But you and I have the hope of Christ, and we know that His strength carries our burdens (Matthew 11:30).

Pastoral Wisdom

You've probably heard it said that "everyone grieves differently." That is true. And part of the truth of that statement is that everyone grieves. It is part of our existence in this fallen, sinful world.

In this chapter, Donna referred to 1 Thessalonians 4:13, which says NOT **to grieve "as others do who have no hope."** The context of this passage refers to those who have died, but the principle is the same in any grieving process. As a follower of Jesus Christ, you will grieve, but you do so with the confident hope that God is in control of all things, and that includes your current situation. Your hope comes from knowing that Jesus is your Savior, that He has paid the penalty for all transgressions, and that He did that for you. He also conquered death for you when He rose to give you the certainty of eternal life with Him in the joy of heaven. Your faith in the living Lord changes your overall perspective. Yes, you will grieve, but do not grieve as those who have no hope!

Something else I try to share with those who are grieving is that Jesus understands. That is not just another pious platitude. He understands because He became one of us and went through what we go through, including grief. The prophet foretold this:

> He was despised and rejected by men; a man of sorrows,
> and acquainted with grief. (Isaiah 53:3)

When Jesus was in the Garden of Gethsemane, some translations say, His soul was grieved to the point of death. He understood sorrow and grieving because He lived as a man and felt the impact sin had on this world. He understands what it is to grieve.

As you grieve, I hope you will remember this promise:

> And we know that for those who love God all things work together for good, for those who are called according to His purpose. (Romans 8:28)

Again, this has to do with your perspective. Please understand that this does not say that all things are good, but that even awful, horrible, painful, terrible things can be and are used by God to bring about good in the lives of His dearly loved children. It may take awhile before you see and experience that, but you have God's promise that it *will* happen.

COUNSELOR'S CORNER

Wow, Donna just took us on an emotional roller coaster with her own story and the stories of both Emily and Cheryl. But you are riding your own roller coaster, aren't you? Do you need to pause for a moment and acknowledge that truth?

Emotions are hard, aren't they? There is a wide range of emotions that can change so quickly—especially in times of crisis. It's easy to stay focused on the surface emotions: I'm mad. I'm sad. I'm glad. Part of the healing process involves digging below the surface emotions to deeper emotions.

Delving into the muck of deeper emotions can create movement between the phases of grief toward lasting healing. What deeper emotions hide behind those on the surface? What thoughts are driving those emotions?

I will explain in greater detail how our thoughts fuel our feelings (which directly impacts our behaviors) in chapter 7, on counseling. But understand right now that processing thoughts and emotions is not clear-cut, smooth, or quick.

Donna described the stages of grief beautifully. Each stage differs greatly and looks vastly different from individual to individual. It seems an easy task to decide—for others or for ourselves—what grief is supposed to look like. We can exert pressure and judgment on ourselves and others by predetermining how grief should look.

We also place expectations on ourselves and others to "handle it well." We need to allow room for emotional reactions. Sometimes they are ugly and raw. However, allowing such room does not excuse inappropriate reactions that can cause harm. Remember: hurting people hurt those around them, and forgiveness and grace are required in great measure.

My clients often misunderstand grief. They find it difficult to name the stages, and they believe that they will move through the stages one at a time. They have an enormously difficult time understanding that people don't always—even usually—move through the stages in order. They often return to stages multiple times. People want to believe that it's a straight shot through steps 1–5, but grief is much more like a knotted, tangled mess of Christmas tree lights.

Patience is a great friend to you and others during the grieving process. Everyone needs to remember that individuals grieve differently, in different times, at different rates, through the different phases.

In your journaling, talk to God about patience during your grieving process. Ask Him to help you not expect yourself (or others) to "get over it" or "move on" quickly. Continually pray for God-size patience.

Donna would be the first to admit that she really struggled with patience. She would often get frustrated and ask me when this would just be done so she could move on. I had to consistently encourage her not to hurry through stages or be frustrated when she returned to a stage, because things would be missed and eventual blessings could be skipped.

I know you are probably asking, "Great, how do I be patient? How do I deal with my anger? How do I let go of my depression and get to acceptance?" I'm sorry to say that there is no easy answer. But here are a few things that can assist you:

1. Journal your heart out! It really does make a difference, and it serves as a safe place to unload. Later, when you feel as if you are not getting anywhere, it will show your progress.

Grief is much more like a knotted, tangled mess of Christmas tree lights.

2. Write a letter to your ex-spouse. NO, you will not give it to him or her, even if you REALLY want to! But it is very cathartic to physically write down your thoughts and emotions in black and white to vent and release your anger and pain. When we trap anger inside without releasing it, it can easily turn into depression and, later, into bitterness. God does not want that for us! We need to get it out.

Working on your thoughts and feelings and facing the death of your marriage (or any trauma) can be overwhelming at times. In your pain and/or depression, if you ever experience thoughts of self-harm or wanting to kill yourself, seek professional help immediately! It's one thing to have thoughts about disappearing or "If I weren't here, this wouldn't hurt so bad," but thoughts of harming yourself are your soul's way of crying out for help and support. *Get it!*

You will make it through the stages of grief in time. It might take significant time if you are willing to sit in each grief stage and return at times to redo them.

It's challenging to look at the hard truth, but you will be blessed and become a stronger person by doing so. You cannot do it alone, so stop trying now! God will provide tangible, Jesus-with-skin-on people to walk this journey with you—but remember: He is also walking right next to you the whole time!

How do I be patient? How do I deal with anger? How do I let go of my depression and get to acceptance?

5: Pausing to Breathe, Pray, and Reflect

Everyone grieves in different ways at different paces. Simply because someone in your circle of friends who has gone through a recent divorce seems to be bouncing back beautifully does not mean that he or she does not struggle when they lie in bed at night. Comparison is lethal, and it interferes with your grieving process.

Walking through the battleground of grief following divorce can feel like tiptoeing through a minefield surrounded by snipers. But you do not fight this battle alone or unprotected. God never fails to wrap you with His armor and see you to the other side to victory.

Through the following exercises, cling with confidence to this hope-filled truth: though your feelings come and go, God's love for you does not. Take your time walking through the following Bible passages, questions, prayer time, and journaling time before you move on to the next chapter.

Scripture to Read, Meditate on, and Memorize

Blessed are those who mourn, for they shall be comforted. *(Matthew 5:4)*

God is our refuge and strength, a very present help in trouble. Therefore we will not fear though the earth gives way, though the mountains be moved into the heart of the sea. (Psalm 46:1–2)

My flesh and my heart may fail, but God is the strength of my heart and my portion forever. (Psalm 73:26)

115

For I am sure that neither death nor life, nor angels nor rulers, nor things present nor things to come, nor powers, nor height nor depth, nor anything else in all creation, will be able to separate us from the love of God in Christ Jesus our Lord. (Romans 8:38–39)

Questions for Reflection

As you walk through the grieving process, several questions can, with God's guidance, help you navigate the journey. Take a minute to answer these questions honestly. No one is looking over your shoulder. It's just you and God. So get real and raw so that God can continue the healing process in your heart.

1. What stage of grief are you currently experiencing?

2. What tools and Scripture passages has God given you to use in this stage? How have they helped?

3. The grieving process can take a toll if we don't actively seek uplifting activities. Do you like gardening? Plant something new and nurture its growth. Do you like photography? Grab your camera and tennis shoes and head to the nearest park. Walking, enjoying fresh air, and focusing your lens on God's beautiful creation will do wonders for the soul. What do you love to do? Do it!

Pause for Prayer

Take this time to pour out your feelings to God. His big shoulders can take it. Little by little, piece by piece, He will restore you. Let's pray:

A—Acknowledge God's sovereignty: Sometimes the heaviness and depth of our grieving makes it hard to see that God is still in control of everything, even your situation. Read 1 Peter 1:3–9 aloud with confidence.

C—Confession: Walking through the stages of grief and emerging healed by God on the other side takes time and diligence. Take this time to confess to God any actions or thoughts that have not honored Him in the way in which He calls His children to behave. Narrow it down and get specific. He already knows each circumstance, but verbally expressing those feelings ejects them from your heart, mind, and soul so that He can begin the healing process. Please pray aloud to God now.

T—Thanksgiving: It is hard to express thanks when you are drowning in pain. Yet even in the midst of your circumstances, God has blessed you with people and/or things for which you owe Him thanks. During my grieving process, I thanked Him for the gift of tears that released toxic feelings and allowed His healing to take place in my heart and mind. List three things you are thankful for right now, and thank God for them.

1.

2.

3.

S—Supplication (requests): God promises that when we pray, He faithfully hears us. The grieving process can be a long road. Identify what you need from Him right now, and ask Him in faith to provide it.

EXHALING ON THE PAGE

If you have not started the journaling process, begin TODAY. God will use your journaling as another way to release grief and pour His love into you.

Here are some suggested questions to answer as you journal:

1. What happened today?

2. How do you feel?

3. What made you angry or made you grateful?

4. How did someone encourage you today or show kindness?

5. Where did you see God at work in your circumstances today?

You did it! Take a deep breath and exhale slowly. God is with you, dear one. He will NEVER leave you or forsake you. He will see you through each day and every circumstance.

6

Using Kid Gloves to Walk Children through Divorce

Children seldom misquote. In fact, they usually repeat word for word what you shouldn't have said.

—Author Unknown

Children are the innocent casualties of divorce. The majority of children believe that somehow their actions or words contributed to or caused their parents' divorce. Regardless of how old children are when divorce happens, the split affects them deeply.

Some parents are so intent on hurting their ex-spouse that they use their children as pawns, failing to realize the extent of the emotional and spiritual damage that their actions cause in their children.

Although I did not have children, I have been exposed to both scenarios through family and friends. This chapter relies heavily on the wisdom of our expert consultants and interviews with divorced parents who successfully navigated their children through divorce. They provide sound, biblical guidance to minimize the disruption and damage of divorce on these innocent bystanders.

Meet Loren

Of all the challenges that children face in this world, divorce was the last thing Loren thought he would have to walk his two young sons through. Loren and his wife had been married almost seven years before the bottom dropped out one heartbreaking day:

> I came home from a business trip the day before Valentine's Day and had an amazing day planned for my spouse the next day. The day was a lot of me showering her with love and gifts. That night, I could tell something was wrong and [my feelings were] not reciprocated, so I asked a few questions. That is when she started sharing her lack of love for me, her love for other men, and her previous actions.

Loren immediately shut almost everyone out of his life, withdrew from social media, and trusted only a few confidants. Although he knew that his ex-wife had been physically and verbally abused in her previous marriage, she never disclosed to Loren until after they were already married that she had been sexually abused as a child. At last, he finally understood the night terrors that she frequently experienced.

Over the next two years, there were numerous attempts at reconciliation, counseling, dealing with his ex-wife's numerous affairs, separation, and broken promises. The final straw came when Loren was struck with Bell's palsy:

> During this time, I was bedridden for a few weeks and I really came to forgive her and understand I could move forward with the divorce. It was in this time of prayer and healing that I knew I could stop fighting divorce.

> [It was difficult] understanding God's plan for my vows

in a broken world. When was "for better or worse" not valid anymore? After my marathon of a divorce (almost a two-year process) was final, it was a bit stunning. In the first ten minutes, it was like the pain and sorrow of two years rushed upon me. There was the relief of closure, then the stark realization of finality. I remember after praying for God's wisdom and forgiveness, asking Him to mold me into the father, son, brother, man, and leader that He could use to point people to Him.

Loren loves his two sons more than anything on earth and couldn't imagine not having them part of his daily life, so he was determined to ask the court for custody. Although friends advised him that his chances were slim since mothers were usually granted custody, Loren trusted God and pressed on, never giving up or losing hope. The court eventually awarded Loren 85 percent custody of his sons, giving his ex-wife two weekends and one night each month.

There was the relief of closure, then the stark realization of finality.

As a devoted Christian, Loren considered custody important because he wanted to be sure that he could pass his Missouri Synod Lutheran heritage and faith along to his sons. He and his ex-wife still attend the same church. Although they don't sit together, Loren and his ex-wife go to the same service when he has the children, and he attends a different service when he doesn't. Though awkward for some church members, he reminds them that it isn't about them or him, and he believes it will get easier over time.

Loren's parents, family, friends, and co-workers worried about him, but he found it difficult to share his deep feelings or accept their offers to help. Though he was (and sometimes still is) quiet, he truly appreciated their support and prayers.

It has been a difficult road to determine the best ways to walk his boys through divorce. His younger son was five years old when Loren and his ex-wife finally divorced:

I saw [the struggle] in his behavior, through anxiety and longing for the other parent. He didn't verbalize it much, was pretty resilient, and also seemed to accept it pretty easily. When I told the boys what was happening, I could tell he didn't understand but knew it was important for him to hear what divorce meant and what was happening to Mommy and Daddy.

Loren's older son, eight years old at the time, was devastated when he learned about his parents' divorce. He was more verbally and socially understanding of the significance of divorce:

He asked me many questions and constantly was seeking a foundation. He began always asking about the future—where would I be when he went to bed, how long would we be at places, random need for hugs and affirmation. It was harder on him. He has adjusted fairly well, but he references a lot of memories of when we were married and he was younger.

Loren diligently walked with his sons through the emotional aftermath. He discovered the things that helped most were prayer, honesty, consistency, individual dad/son time, verbal support of their mother, verbal and physical time together, signs of affection, and engaging them away from electronics and digital media:

I have been overly dedicated to making sure time with both sides of the family increased—even on my ex's side. I think creating a lot of routine at these ages helped, [along with] open conversation and a dedication to never placing blame or discussing negatives. They clung to what was familiar and embraced it. I tried to keep as many things the same as I could.

Interestingly, it doesn't bother Loren to see his ex-wife with her new boyfriend. However, it was extraordinarily difficult the first time he saw her boyfriend with his sons. Loren worries how his ex-wife's boyfriend will influence his children.

Loren's family was very hurt and struggled with his divorce. Though they supported him and the boys, some have still not accepted it. As for how Loren's divorce affected him personally, he says:

> I have ALWAYS been a positive person. I still am—and very confident—but at the same time, I have caught myself doubting for a moment myself and a positive outcome. Although it passes quickly, it never used to be there.

Above all, Loren's faith and his relationship with his Savior saw him through, and this continues to be the filter for every aspect of his life. He teaches his sons likewise. He summarized it beautifully: "There is my plan and there is God's plan. Trust in God's."

Meet Nancy

Despite the still, small voice discouraging Nancy from getting married, she took the plunge. Their marriage went off without a hitch, and they welcomed their first child nine months later. She and her ex-husband both drank excessively and smoked marijuana at the time and, looking back, Nancy is grateful that their children were born healthy.

There is my plan and there is God's plan. Trust in God's.

By their second year of marriage, Nancy's husband had had the first of many affairs that he would have during the course of their fourteen-year marriage. Even though they attended church regularly and Nancy helped teach Sunday School, her ex-husband never attended Bible study for himself, although he made sure that their boys did.

Over time, Nancy discovered her ex-husband was not a good father or helpful husband. Since her job required a lot of overtime, many times Nancy came home past the kids' bedtime. Frequently, she would find them still playing while their dad slept in his chair; they had not done homework, had baths, or eaten dinner. She recalls:

Because I had to work so much, my paychecks were abundant. My ex took it as a challenge to see if he could spend it all.

His repeated infidelity and irresponsible living took a toll on Nancy. She began praying and asking God for guidance regarding her marriage, but she stayed committed despite years of enduring her ex-husband's behavior. Then one evening, everything changed:

> The final straw came when we were waiting for [my ex] to come home from work so that I could go to work. My oldest came and sat on my lap and started to cry. I asked him why he was crying, and he told me that his dad said I worked all of that overtime because I didn't want to be at home with them. My heart melted and my blood pressure soared! That could not have been further from the truth. My younger son looked at [his brother] and said that I worked so they could have a better life. . . . I knew then that it was time to make a change. I filed for divorce.

Nancy and her ex-husband sought Christian counseling. After hearing all of the issues, the counselor concluded that divorce was the best solution. Counseling revealed to Nancy how incompatible she and her ex-husband were, and she learned tools for moving forward as a single mom. Nancy and her ex-husband were given joint custody, but their boys struggled:

> The hardest part was seeing the toll it took on my boys. They were so torn because they loved both of us. They would come home after being with their dad, and it was like they had to go through withdrawals. . . . At his house, they did whatever they pleased. The school-teachers could even tell when they were with him and would call me to let me know they needed my guidance.

Her boys are now young men. It was not an easy road, but she faithfully worked with them:

They did not understand why my ex and I could not stay together . . . and had a hard time understanding what was true and what was not. I took them to counseling and that helped them a great deal. We also spent a good amount of time discussing their concerns. My mother was great with my boys. She would share wonderful wisdom and worked alongside them on projects that she would line up for them to do. My boys and I grew throughout experiences working together—the time helped us grow as a single-parent family.

Through her grief stages of denial, anger, mild depression, and guilt, Nancy's strong faith was her lifeline. She faithfully attended church and immersed herself in Bible study. She leaned on a strong support network from her family and her co-workers, who were like family.

Nancy has been divorced for sixteen years now. Looking back on that time, she says:

> I have learned that staying in the Word, worshiping, praying, and listening for that still, small voice will get me through any circumstance I may encounter, no matter how tough it seems. God led me through divorce, and I have learned to follow His leading no matter how much of a leap of faith it seems to be.

What Children Need

Most of the people I interviewed for this book have children and had to learn to walk their children through that very difficult time of divorce. Here is valuable insight about what children need most from those who have learned it firsthand:

I have learned to follow His leading no matter how much of a leap of faith it seems to be.

- Don't put your children in the middle:

I am eleven years down the road from divorce now, and my kids are grown. They tell me often that the fact I never put them in the middle between me and their dad was a huge blessing. Parents need to be accountable to keep their speech edifying, no matter what. Basically, you have to love your children more than you hate what your ex is doing. —Kathleen

- Create a familiar environment and nurturing routine:

My ex-husband wanted nothing of the kids' things—no toys, games, pictures, movies, books, clothes, bedding, nothing that belonged to them. It was as though he wanted nothing to do with them. I focused on showing the kids how much they had, how they could always take things to their dad's house and always use their imagination to get by. My older two kids bonded a lot more as an alliance of sorts with a mission to survive the time at their dad's house together. We started doing evening devotions more frequently together. We prayed together in the evening, started going back to church, and started spending more time together as a family of God. —Tiffany

- Let your children know that it's okay to freely love and grieve:

Make it okay for them to love both of you. Your divorce impacts everyone around you; allow them to grieve. —Linda A.

- Maintain a healthy relationship with your ex:

Keep on good terms with your ex because you will be connected with him/her for as long as your children are alive. That means graduations, weddings, babies, etc. You will have to get good at sharing the children without being jealous of the time they spend with your ex. —Catherine

- Children are not pawns:

  The children are off limits. The divorce was your decision
  and they have no say in it, but they have to live with it.
  To them, you are both still their parents. Children are not
  pawns, bargaining chips, a way to get back at each other, or
  tools to get what you want. —Tony

Insights from Children of Divorce

Parents going through divorce are constantly looking for helpful advice on how to raise grounded, resilient children despite the emotional whirlwind. Through my interviews, I discovered that some of the best answers came from the children of divorce themselves. Now adults, they graciously agreed to share their hard-earned insights.

Meet Samantha

Samantha's parents divorced when she was very young, so she does not remember her parents being together. Her parents had joint custody for a while, but she found it difficult going back and forth and living by different rules on different days.

Her mother is an alcoholic, which was very difficult to handle alone as a young child. She eventually went to live with her dad and never talked to or heard from her mother again. Both of her parents have remarried, but the cycle of toxic relationships continues.

Samantha's older sister is now divorced, which actually improved their relationship. Where her sister used to isolate herself from the family during her marriage, Samantha now sees her a lot more. Though sad for her sister's heartache, she is happy to see her sister slowly find her way back to her happier old self.

Now in her early twenties and not yet married, Samantha's experiences through both her parents' and sister's divorces have helped her figure out what type of relationship she wants for herself:

  Watching them all over the years has taught me a lot.
  Through my parents' and step-parents' negatives, I have
  created a positive for me. My sister's divorce made me

take marriage more seriously. It also made me realize it is okay to admit defeat. Divorce isn't a lonely death sentence; it can be a new beginning, if you let it.

Meet Matthew

Like many children, Matthew thought his parents' relationship was normal. However, as a young adult, Matthew became curious about his parents' lack of physical affection and emotional connection. Consequently, it was not a complete surprise when his parents divorced when Matthew was in his thirties.

Even though he wasn't shocked, Matthew was still devastated by his parents' split. His family had always been a fixed point on the horizon from where he could discern his own location (kind of like nautical "triangulation"). After his parents divorced, Matthew felt adrift and found it difficult to navigate life for a while—even as a thirty-something.

Matthew and his brother were faced with reconciling their dad's faults and frailties—integrity gaps, an affair, and unwillingness to repair the marriage. Matthew's dad eventually remarried and tried to start over several times, but he eventually took his own life.

Matthew gave his life to Christ in the midst of his parents' divorce. He learned how to reconcile the positive things that his dad provided for their family, while at the same time acknowledging that his actions ultimately destroyed it.

Because of his experience with his parents' divorce, Matthew works hard at maintaining a good marriage for himself, his wife, and their young children:

> I became pretty hard on men who are failing in marriages, and perhaps I still am. But I'm learning more grace now that I'm married and understand how much work that marriage is. More grace seems to come with age, more so than being affected by divorce.

Meet Lily

Lily cannot remember a time during her youth when her parents were happy together. Despite being regularly churchgoing Christians, her parents constantly argued. Her mom regularly belittled her dad in front of Lily and her sister, and though her mom never committed a full-fledged affair, she tended to lean too heavily on the emotional support of other men. Eventually, her dad told Lily and her sister that he was filing for divorce because their mother had committed emotional adultery.

Lily's parents were too busy being wrapped up in their own anger to help her and her sister cope with their mourning process. Even at such a young age, Lily leaned heavily on God through prayer. At sixteen years old, Lily remembers praying night and day for God to fix her parents' marriage. When He didn't, she became angry. She tried clinging to God but felt betrayed, empty, and numb. She survived by putting her emotions on hold.

The tradition of faith that her parents instilled in her saw her through. When she began dating, the emotional backlash of her parents' divorce resurfaced with a vengeance, but she faithfully sought God to heal her.

Today, as a more spiritually mature thirty-three-year-old, when anger or bitterness triggered by that old pain surfaces, Lily handles the situation differently:

> The huge difference now is simply God's grace—for me and others. How can I withhold it from anyone, my parents included, when He doesn't?

ADDITIONAL EXPERIENTIAL WISDOM

I took to social media and asked other adults to share wisdom they gleaned from growing up with divorced parents:

- Don't expect your children to walk through their pain alone:

  Speaking as one whose parents were divorced, take time to walk kids through their pain and grief, minimizing their losses as much as possible. As a pastor, I've seen kids get lost in the shuffle. They lost a parent and now they often lose their home, friends, school, and security. These losses add up, and the soul always grieves its losses. Kids are not equipped to cope, so they act out while their parents are focused elsewhere. I'm very proud when parents can manage to put their kids first during the very elongated trauma of divorce. —Bill

• Emphasize their identity in Christ:

As a child of divorce, it's important to learn very quickly that your identity is not in the family but in Christ. If your identity is in the family, which is very reasonable as a child, the breaking up of that leaves a long scar that only Christ can heal. —Tina G.

• Adjust your schedule to be home when your children are:

I experienced divorce in high school when my mother and step-father got divorced. I felt so lost, alone, and mostly abandoned. My step-dad moved out and really had nothing to do with me after raising me for ten years. Then my mother started working night shifts, so I started hanging out with the wrong crowd. I soon moved out of state and lived with my cousin, who helped put me through school. —Shelby

INSIGHTS FROM PARENTS OF DIVORCED ADULT CHILDREN

One of the most difficult scenarios outside of experiencing divorce yourself is watching your grown children go through divorce. You agonize over how to best counsel and support your grown children while not overstepping important boundaries. The situation becomes infinitely more painful when you see the negative effects on your grandchildren.

How you react to your child's announcement of divorce will pave the way for your future relationship with your child, your grandchildren, and soon-to-be-ex in-law. You are still an important figure in all of their lives, so here are steps to help your journey:

- **Show loyalty:** Nothing changes the fact that your child is your child. Show loyalty by being in his or her corner, though that does not mean you have to agree with what they've done.

- **Lend them your strength:** Through the painful emotions of divorce, your adult child still needs to know that he or she is loved. Let your child know that you realize they are hurting, and ask what you can do to help. You can't take away their pain, but you can lend them your strength.

- **Offer help before they have to ask:** Divorcing children may need to move back in with their parents or borrow money until they get on their feet again. Pride can often get in the way of adult children asking for help, so offer first before their situation deteriorates too far.

- **Avoid alienating your child's ex-spouse:** You may think you're showing support if you trash your child's ex, but your child doesn't want to hear that they were a bad judge of character. Focus on the positive, because access to your grandchildren may be at stake.

- **Create a stable environment for your grandchildren:** With their whole world turning upside down, your grandchildren need to know that their whole family isn't disappearing. They worry about where they will live and go to school and who will take care of them. Create a routine when they visit that creates a sense of belonging, comfort, and consistency. Stock their favorite treat, provide their very own teddy bear to cuddle with if they sleep over, and eat sit-down meals at home. Stability is key when their young lives are so transient.

CONCLUSION

One of the most frequently quoted verses in Scripture about children comes from Proverbs: *"Train up a child in the way he should go; even when he is old he will not depart from it"* (Proverbs 22:6). Despite divorce, it means that parents patiently discipline, prune, and shape each individual child in the way that *he or she* should go.

In other words, no two children are alike. Although your family has experienced divorce, each child will process it differently according to how God created him or her. Parents need to be careful to understand their children well enough to guide them effectively rather than taking a one-size-fits-all approach.

Children are blessings from God; they are His unique and precious creations. Despite your feelings about your ex-spouse, God gave YOU those children. He chose YOU as that child's parent. Regardless of past or future relationships in your life, your children are always your children. There's no such thing as ex-children, only ex-spouses.

You are not the only casualty on the battlefield of divorce. I have seen children who survived and thrived following their parents' divorce, and others who endured significant emotional damage that has dramatically affected the rest of their lives. The main difference came down to the parents.

When the waves of divorce crash, be sure that your children know beyond the shadow of a doubt that God is their refuge and safe place. Tell them how much Jesus loves them. Often. Then demonstrate that truth to them in real time by cherishing your time with them—regardless of how often that may be.

You are not an ex-parent. There is no statute of limitations on Proverbs 22:6. Your children still need you to train them in the ways of the Lord, and they always will—no matter how old they are.

PASTORAL WISDOM

Children, obey your parents in the Lord, for this is right. "Honor your father and mother" (this is the first commandment with a promise), "that it may go well with you and that you may live long in the land." Fathers, do not provoke your children to anger, but bring them up in the discipline and instruction of the Lord. (Ephesians 6:1–4)

You are not the only casualty on the battlefield of divorce.

Although the temptation will be strong to speak ill of your ex to your children, you will be better off in the long run to heed Martin Luther's explanation of the Eighth Commandment, "explain everything in the kindest way" (or, as earlier editions of his Small Catechism have it, "put the best construction on everything").

Children are perceptive. They often understand a lot more than you think they do. If you are the wronged party, they will ultimately understand what that means. If they see you retaliate in unkind and unloving ways, you will teach them that that is appropriate behavior. If you speak ill of your ex to your children, you encourage them to think or speak ill of their other parent, which is leading them to sinful behavior. And Jesus warned against that:

> "Whoever causes one of these little ones who believe in Me to sin, it would be better for him to have a great millstone fastened around his neck and to be drowned in the depth of the sea." (Matthew 18:6)

Leading children to sin goes against the calling you have received as a Christian parent. Mom does not stop being Mom after the divorce. Dad does not stop being Dad after the divorce. Sometimes in their pain, anguish, and anger, they are not very good at being Mom and Dad, but they still occupy those roles. Those children were entrusted to you by God.

Children love their parents and look up to them:

> The glory of children is their fathers. (Proverbs 17:6)

And there will be plenty of teachable moments. They will know (or learn) that you are far from perfect, but they still love you and need you to be their parents. Don't neglect the training and instruction of your children in the Lord. Pray WITH them. Read Scripture WITH them. Admit you don't know all the answers, but encourage them to trust God, who is always in control. Believe His promises, which are often shared in terms of a loving parent:

> As one whom his mother comforts, so will I comfort you. (Isaiah 66:13)

> As a father shows compassion to his children, so the LORD shows compassion to those who fear Him. (Psalm 103:13)

Perhaps the greatest opportunity you have will be to teach your children about sin and forgiveness. If they see that you refuse to forgive your ex, they may wonder if you will stop loving them when they do something wrong. But if they see you forgive your former spouse, they will understand that forgiveness is available no matter how great the offense may be.

This is not something that will happen overnight, but it is part of the process you will undergo.

Perhaps the greatest opportunity you have will be to teach your children about sin and forgiveness.

COUNSELOR'S CORNER

Divorce is painful for everyone involved, and I know you are feeling and seeing that right now. Honestly, as painful as divorce is for you right now, it's even more painful for your kid(s). Now please know I'm not saying that to rub even more coarse salt into your already hemorrhaging wounds or to heap on another extra-thick layer of guilt; it's just truth, and truth is painful, as you well know.

I point that out simply because I have never met anyone who didn't realize on some level that there were dynamics in their marriage. Although there are varying levels of marriage dynamics, you are aware of potential train wrecks. However, kids don't know this information. They are oblivious to the extent and roots of the dynamics that they see played out at home between Mom and Dad. All they see is that Mom and Dad fight a lot or that one is gone all the time. They don't know the details behind their observations. This often leads to self-blame on their part. They struggle with feeling like they contributed in some way to their family falling apart. You need to be aware of this and continually refute this irrational thought each and every time it arises. And it will arise a lot!

One of my most important pieces of advice is do not expect your kids to understand or think logically about the divorce. The younger they are, the less they understand. Developmentally, they are not equipped. Teenagers also struggle, so don't expect them to understand either. I know you are experiencing an emotional roller coaster, but so are they—and they didn't ask for admission to the ride! Extraordinary patience is required. When your children are being irrational and emotional, simply love them through it. Love reinforces that you are still safe and able to be their stability, even when you feel the opposite!

The statistics focusing on divorced kids are heartbreaking and seem overwhelmingly grim, but you can change some of that with the nuggets of wisdom in this chapter. You were given great pointers from parents and the now-adult kids who have survived and learned from their experiences. Do not ignore their advice!

Hinged on that, I can say from professional experience, DO NOT use your children as weapons! NOTHING good comes from such destructive motivation—it only reaps destruction FOR EVERYONE! At all times, no matter how angry, hurt, or anxious you are, do not speak against your ex to your child whom you love dearly. It places them in the middle emotionally, and no child should EVER have to choose which parent they love more—NEVER! They will never fully recover from such emotional damage.

If you are tempted to say something negative about your ex, give yourself a time-out. Explain to your child that you are upset in that moment and need time out to calm down. They will understand and respect you for your self-control. Then go into another room and call a trusted, godly friend to vent to, journal, scream into a pillow, punch a pillow, take a hot shower, or cry your eyes out, but do it out of the sight of your child to preserve the God-ordained love they have for their other parent. When a child of any age feels trapped between two parents, it only breeds depression, insecurity, anxiety, and low self-esteem, to name only a few.

When it comes to adult children, they usually want to know more details. They want to know more of the nitty-gritty dysfunction that caused the divorce. I caution you as to how much you tell them— even though they are adults. You are still talking about their other parent, whom they still love at some level.

No matter how old a child may be, it will always be devastating to deal with the death of his or her parents' marriage and the family as he or she knew it. If you do decide to talk to your adult child, remember that he or she is not your friend or counselor but your child. Do not put your child in the position of counseling you through your divorce and healing. Children have their own healing they need to journey through. Instead, lean on a godly friend or a godly therapist. It will help all of you.

I love the fact that Donna brought up walking through the divorce of your own adult children. It's easy to think of divorce just from the framework of your own divorce and its effects on younger kids. The death of your adult child's marriage is a death for you as well. Offer them support as needed; but again, watch your own emotions and actions. Do not get drawn into speaking ill of your child's ex-spouse in order to justify or support your child. This can be very difficult because you love your child. However, it doesn't help them heal by bashing the person they once loved. It only lengthens the distance of the journey toward healing.

Instead, ask your adult child what he or she needs from you for support—and ask regularly. Does it mean helping with laundry? bringing a meal once a week? short-term financial help? living with you? picking kids up from school or events or taking the kids for the weekend? a text of encouragement? Above all, you can always support them by praying!

In regard to grandkids, make extra time for them—and A LOT of it. Their world is falling apart, and you very well could be the only stability in their lives right now. Make room for a lot of emotion. In fact, when they understand that you are safe and stable, you could see more emotion or acting out when they are with you because they feel safe enough to express it the only way they may know how.

Do not put your child in the position of counseling you through your divorce.

Within loving boundaries, love them through it and remind them that you are there for them no matter what. Make your house the "boring" house of comfortable traditions—it will give them the stability they need when their young life is anything but stable.

Seek counseling for your kids and/or grandkids. They need it even if you or they think they are doing fine. They aren't. They need a place to talk with someone who isn't involved. A safe place where they can express their honest thoughts and feelings. A place where they can learn different ways to deal with their stress and emotions in a healthy way. In chapter 7, Donna describes DivorceCare® and DivorceCare for Kids™. Look in to them. I have known many individuals who say that the group was a vital part of surviving and healing.

6: Pausing to Breathe, Pray, and Reflect

As innocent bystanders of divorce, your children need diligent care to process the emotional, physical, and spiritual impact on their world.

Take your time walking through the following Bible passages, questions, prayer time, and journaling time before moving to the next chapter.

SCRIPTURE TO READ, MEDITATE ON, AND MEMORIZE

"And these words that I command you today shall be on your heart. You shall teach them diligently to your children, and shall talk of them when you sit in your house, and when you walk by the way, and when you lie down, and when you rise."
(Deuteronomy 6:6–7)

Behold, children are a heritage from the LORD, the fruit of the womb a reward. (Psalm 127:3)

All your children shall be taught by the LORD, and great shall be the peace of your children. (Isaiah 54:13)

QUESTIONS FOR REFLECTION

Walking children through divorce takes kid gloves filled with love, patience, and gentleness. Spending some time pondering and answering these questions may lend valuable insight:

1. When was the last time you sat down with you children and asked how they feel?

2. How does your children's outward behavior reflect how they are dealing inwardly with the divorce? Are they acting out, needing more hugs, asking more questions, or stuffing down emotions?

3. If you are dating or remarried, how does your significant other treat your children?

Pause for Prayer

Each child processes divorce in his or her own way and in his or her own time. Even though you as a parent are struggling with your own issues, remembering to pray for and encourage your children is vital. Be still before the Lord, and pray:

A—Acknowledge God's sovereignty: Even though you probably wish you could instantly take away your children's pain, God is still in control of everything. He knows your children better than you do. Read Luke 10:21 aloud with confidence.

C—Confession: Even though you may be doing everything you can to shield your children, you may still feel guilty for their pain. God never asked for your perfection; He asked that you seek Him in all things and follow Him. Confess those feelings to God so that He can eject them from your heart, mind, and soul and so begin the healing process. Please pray aloud to God now.

T—Thanksgiving: God always provides exactly what we (and our children) need when we need it—no matter how great or small. List three things you are thankful for right now and thank God for them.

1.

2.

3.

S—Supplication (requests): God promises that when we pray, He faithfully hears us. Identify what you need from Him right now and ask Him in faith to provide it.

Exhaling on the Page

As you know by now, God uses journaling as another way to release pent-up feelings and allow Him to fill you with His peace that passes all understanding. You may not see the benefits of journaling today, but you will one day. Trust Him.

Here are some suggested questions to answer as you journal:

1. What happened today?

2. How do you feel?

3. What made you angry or made you grateful?

4. How did someone encourage you today or show kindness?

5. Where did you see God at work in your circumstances today?

You did it! Take a deep breath and sit back. God is with you, dear one. He will NEVER leave you or forsake you. He will see you through each day and every circumstance.

7

The Vital Roles of Counseling and Immersion in Scripture

For the Word of God is living and active, sharper than any two-edged sword, piercing to the division of soul and spirit, of joints and marrow, and discerning the thoughts and intentions of the heart.

—Hebrews 4:12

There is no way on planet earth that I would have survived the trauma of divorce without pastoral and professional counseling and immersing myself in Scripture. Divorce affects every aspect of our life, and we do not have the time or bandwidth (or on some days, the inclination) to look at our situation objectively, tie thought patterns together, or discern motives behind our reactions to work toward emotional and spiritual healing.

This chapter provides a clear, firsthand look at the experience and benefits of professional counseling, along with wisdom from pastors and trained professionals. I will share Scripture passages that God used powerfully in my life and the lives of dozens of other Christians to restore hope and a solid foundation on Christ alone.

I believe that this chapter is one of the most vital chapters in the whole book.

My Counseling Experience

My hands shook uncontrollably the first time I stepped into the counselor's office. Even though Kristin is a friend and the wife of one of my pastors, walking into her office felt like defeat. That may sound odd, but taking that step meant admitting that it was beyond my capacity to recover from the trauma I had endured without professional help. But stepping into her office also felt hopeful because I was embracing constructive steps toward my new phase of life, relying wholly on God.

At forty-two years old, I had never sought professional counseling. That fact is neither good nor bad, just my reality. God has blessed me with three incredible sisters and other close friends over the years with whom I could talk through issues and benefit from their honest, loving counsel—even if the truth hurt. After I became a Christian at twenty-three, those friendships included much-needed godly counsel.

However, the vast majority of those cherished people had never experienced the heartache of divorce. The layers of grief and wide swath of destruction caused by divorce made counseling a necessity.

I remember feeling bone-numbing exhaustion as I walked into my first counseling session. Only a week had passed since the F5 tornado hit my marriage, and I didn't want to talk about it. Any of it. It just hurt too much. I am not much of a bawler, but I felt like just bawling. I wanted to disappear to another country and start over so that I wouldn't have to discuss or face what had happened.

COUNSELING 101

Since Kristin was the first person I reached out to after discovering my ex-husband's betrayal, she knew the basics before I arrived. The fact that we were already friends helped. To her enormous credit, she asked before we began our first session if I would feel uncomfortable letting her counsel me because of our friendship. I assured her that it was exactly what I needed. We didn't have to spend valuable time going over my life story—we could get started at a more meaningful level.

Kristin instantly put me at ease by starting our session with prayer. Then she began by asking me to fill in what had happened since that first day. Although she asked a few questions during my monologue, she listened without interruption.

When I was finished talking (which took most of our first session), she asked how I felt, whether I was eating properly, sleeping regularly, and handling other basic necessities. Beyond needing to know the facts, her questions let me know that I was still important—that I mattered. I didn't fully realize until that moment, when I heard her genuine concern and words of affirmation, how fragile and discarded I felt. Her questions helped to momentarily remove my external focus and place it back on my basic survival and well-being. It touched me deeply.

I often found it difficult to pinpoint exactly how I felt.

To my surprise, I often found it difficult to pinpoint exactly how I felt because all of the life changes were so dramatically overwhelming. When Kristin pulled out a chart containing little emoji faces, I smiled. I confess that I found the chart very cute because below each little emoji face was a label identifying a feeling. The downcast emoji had "Sad" below it, the red-faced emoji had "Mad" below it, and so on.

Even though I smiled at such a basic tool, it proved to be invaluable for sifting past surface emotions and identifying how I truly felt in that moment. Once my emotions were properly identified, she could walk me through each of them appropriately.

Feel It, Then Let God Heal It

As a hopeless optimist, all of my negative, sad emotions affected me deeply. I just wanted to cast off the hurt and unearth joy again. The divorce process had barely begun, but I already wanted to be done with it and find joy. Kristin had her work cut out for her.

The truth about hurt and dark valleys is that you have to walk through them before you reach the light of healing at the end. Simply put, you have to feel it before God can heal it. I have known many Christians who pray away their valleys rather than diligently seeking the Lord for lessons learned in them.

Kristin helped me discover small steps that brought joy during the difficult healing process. For example, since I love nature and music, she suggested that I take long, uninterrupted walks while listening to my favorite music. The combination worked beautifully. I often took along my journal on those walks in the park. Fresh air, soothing music, and special time with the Lord helped to slowly begin peeling back the layers of sadness.

I taped a copy of Kristin's emoji faces chart inside my journal to help identify my feelings. That may sound strange, and it certainly felt that way at first. I mean, who can't identify their emotions, right? Well, when so many were bombarding me at once, the chart helped me unearth the prevailing emotion so that I could pray more effectively. In subsequent counseling sessions, we sometimes discussed what my journal revealed, and we would process it together.

The truth about hurt and dark valleys is that you have to walk through them before you reach the light of healing at the end.

When Do I Get Back to Normal?

As a results-oriented Type A personality, I asked Kristin more than once how many sessions were required before I was "all better." To her credit, she didn't laugh at my absurd question. She patiently explained that healing from such trauma takes significant time. Although I balked at first, I trusted her. So I embraced the process and asked God to guide me through.

I initially sought to avoid any more pain. Unfortunately, there are many layers when it comes to divorce. Pain arrived with unwanted friends: sadness, frustration, loneliness, and hurt, among others. We have little choice but to deal with them in order to heal properly.

God faithfully walked me through every step, maturing my faith along the way. I am thankful beyond measure for each session. Some were infinitely harder than others, but they were all necessary tools to bring about God's healing in my heart.

I will confess that my one year of counseling felt like five, but that's my impatience talking. I would not change a thing.

Meet Marguerite

After thirty-five years of marriage, Marguerite never expected her life or marriage to take such a drastic turn. Both she and her husband were very involved in church activities. He was a director of Christian education at their church as well as the principal of their parochial school. They always planned and took special five-year anniversary trips, and they enjoyed a loving, close-knit family with their two children.

Marguerite noticed behavioral changes in her husband around the time of their son's wedding. A shower for their son was held at their congregation, and the shower's primary host was a woman involved in the child development center of the school. Although Marguerite mentally questioned the woman's involvement, she swallowed her thoughts and pressed on. But that was not an isolated incident. At their son's wedding reception, she recalls:

> I went to the ladies' room and when I came out, I saw my husband dancing with that same woman. My husband and I did not dance with other partners, so for this to happen was crushing.

Marguerite's husband began working later at school and spent more time away, working on the business they jointly owned. Then one Saturday, he announced that he was going to visit their pastor. A few hours later, her husband returned home, sat down with Marguerite, and confessed that he'd had an affair:

I was shocked, completely devastated, and crushed, and I began crying. We talked about counseling. He said he would start counseling and then I could be included later, when he worked through his issues. We began spending more time together.

Six months later, when she was returning from out-of-town church-related meetings, Marguerite's husband picked her up at the airport and told her that he had moved out while she had been away. However, Marguerite remained hopeful because they talked every night on the phone, even having devotions and prayers together. But the situation continued to deteriorate.

For both Thanksgiving and Christmas that year, Marguerite's husband refused to visit out-of-state family with her as was their usual custom. She ended up having Thanksgiving dinner alone at Denny's, but she decided to travel alone to see their children at Christmas. It was the first time their children had a clue that something was amiss in their parents' long-standing marriage. She had never told anyone about their marital difficulties, but later she realized that keeping silent covered his actions so that he would not be held accountable.

Marguerite faithfully asked her husband when she would be able to attend counseling with him and when he would be moving back home. He promised he was working on both, which she later discovered to be untrue.

Although her husband had filed for divorce before Thanksgiving, he told Marguerite to disregard the legal papers because he had decided to work on their marriage. She put the papers in a drawer and never read them. But the day after Valentine's Day the following year, her husband sat Marguerite down once more and told her that the judge had granted their divorce because she had never contested it.

She hired a lawyer to contest the divorce, but after more lies and questionable financial dealings by her husband, Marguerite finally realized that he would not stop seeking a divorce. Eventually they reached a mutual agreement regarding their business and finances, and the judge signed their agreement for divorce in September. Six months later, her ex-husband remarried. As she adjusted to her new life alone, Marguerite remembers:

> I found myself to be downtrodden, broken, weak. I kept quiet. I didn't feel strong enough to speak in a public setting, in Bible class, in a voters meeting, etc.

Eventually, Marguerite reached a place where she began to pray that God would enable her to forgive her ex-husband. God graciously granted her prayers. A few years after their divorce, Marguerite discovered that her ex-husband had suddenly died of a heart attack. Although she was shocked, she was thankful that God had allowed her to forgive her ex-husband before he died.

Marguerite's story is a beautiful picture of diligence and commitment to marriage. But you cannot hold on to someone who willfully chooses a different path. Marguerite sought counseling from a professional Christian counselor who helped her process the whole ordeal.

When asked how the divorce experience affected her, Marguerite said:

> It strengthened my faith. I completely relied on God. He is the only thing that got me through. I don't know how people survive if they don't have a loving relationship with God. Romans 8:28 was a constant Scripture passage that I said many times throughout the day. God can work good out of anything for those who love Him.

Meet Nicole

Nicole met her ex-husband in their church's youth group when she was fourteen and he was eighteen. Since she had a difficult relationship with her dad after discovering that her dad was having an affair, her ex-husband became her confidant with whom she shared everything. She didn't realize that he would later misuse her trust for personal gain:

> The summer before my sophomore year of high school (I was fifteen), he was a camp counselor at a youth

camp. After a "True Love Waits" message, we took a walk and he told me that if I had sex with him, he would never break my heart or do to me what my dad did to my mom. But if we didn't, we couldn't stay together. I lost my virginity that night. Over the course of the next couple of years, he introduced me to porn, sex toys, and alcohol. Whatever he said, I did. My parents were clueless. He played the part (as I did) of the perfect Christian.

Their relationship continued until Nicole left to attend college. She broke up with him and became interested in someone new a few months later. She never expected their first date to end in violence:

I thought I had met someone. He was nice and not pushy. That night we went on a little date. As it came to a close, he tried making a move. I tried to politely say no. He did not accept my no and pushed me to the ground, where he raped me. I was devastated.

Three months later, Nicole was back with her now-ex-husband. At college, she repeatedly heard that men wanted women who were pure. Since she wasn't, she felt that her only God-honoring path would be to marry her first boyfriend. They married when Nicole was twenty, though she knew it was a mistake the day she married him.

Compared to her parents' marriage, she felt that hers was satisfactory, but she felt empty. They attended church, had what they needed, and didn't fight:

By twenty-two, I had my first child and my world changed dramatically. Life was filled with so much joy. For the first time for what felt like my entire life, I was happy. I had purpose. And so it began. Every thirteen months, I got pregnant. My babies were my everything. They kept me going and kept me with my ex-husband.

Her ex-husband was a traveling salesman who was only home on weekends. Although she felt like a single mom, she was fine with it until his job moved them three hours away from family. Being alone with him and without family and friends took a toll on their marriage. Soon things began to fall apart. Her ex-husband was emotionally and verbally abusive, so she told him that she was done. He begged to go to counseling and Nicole agreed:

> Our counseling consisted of meeting with an associate pastor at the church we had attended for eight years. I was told I needed to pray for him, submit more, and pray that God would reveal the sin in my life that was causing his behavior. I was at a loss but did what I was told. This went on for several months. Our marriage quickly deteriorated. We were sleeping in separate bedrooms, barely communicating. I detested the sight of him.

Her ex-husband threatened to take away their children, and Nicole battled with depression. He moved out, and Nicole began to notice that people were treating her differently. She discovered that her ex-husband had spread rumors that she was having an affair. Then, sadly:

> I received a letter from my church placing me on church discipline for having a reckless spirit. I was no longer attending that church, as I had begun visiting another, so this letter came out of the blue. Every friend I had from church was told by the pastors they were no longer to speak with me, as I was walking in sin. Pretty much everyone in my life abandoned me.

Over the months that followed, her ex-husband had an affair and hired a private detective to track Nicole's every move. He finally served Nicole with separation papers. Despite the horrible counseling advice Nicole had received before, she and her ex-husband began going to counseling again. Finally, after listening to both sides of their stories, the new counselor called out her ex-husband:

> The counselor looked at my ex and said, "You have completely broken her spirit. You are a man who will take down anyone he has to in order to accomplish

his agenda." He asked [my ex] to leave the room and spent time talking and praying with me. On the car ride home, my ex spent the entire ride on the phone making business calls as if nothing had happened. It was in that moment that I knew I no longer wanted to be married to this man. I did not want God to fix it. I was done.

Many things happened over the course of the next few years that culminated in Nicole obtaining a restraining order against her ex-husband for physical abuse before they finally divorced.

It took several years for Nicole to recover from her traumatic experiences. Looking back, Nicole reflects on how God strengthened her faith:

The experience grew my faith in tremendous ways. I had no one and became so desperate for Jesus. He was all I had. I learned to rest in Him, to trust Him and walk with Him. I know Him now in a way that I never knew Him before.

As you can see from Nicole's story, choosing the right counselor is crucial. If you believe that your current counselor (whether pastor or otherwise) is not providing sound biblical advice, do not hesitate to end sessions and search for a new counselor.

There is too much at stake.

We Need Wisdom

We need wisdom to recover from divorce. Wisdom comes from God and is available to all: *"If any of you lacks wisdom, let him ask God, who gives generously to all without reproach"* (James 1:5). Those last four words are particularly important since divorce often revolves around the issue of fault. God promises wisdom to ALL who ask Him for it. He does not discriminate. All means all.

God often uses others to impart wisdom we need during divorce and the aftermath, so choosing the right professional is crucial. Specifically, we need to seek structured wisdom from professionals, licensed counselors, and pastors who have been trained to provide wisdom in navigating our journey. Yes, we have God's Word and the

Holy Spirit to guide us, but going through divorce distracts our focus toward simply surviving. We desperately need an outside, objective assessment.

God promises wisdom to ALL who ask Him for it. He does not discriminate.

CHOOSING THE RIGHT PROFESSIONAL

1. Counselors

First, as a believer, you need to seek out a licensed Christian counselor. Secular counselors possess the appropriate list of steps to walk people through drastic life changes, but they do not address the spiritual aspect that is at the very core of our created beings.

If you are a woman, I highly recommend that you seek a female Christian counselor, if at all possible. The trauma of divorce makes us vulnerable. The last thing you need is an inappropriate emotional or physical connection with a male counselor to interfere with your healing process.

2. Pastors

Although a few trusted pastor friends offered to counsel me following my divorce, I declined for three reasons: (1) I felt fragile and vulnerable, so (as stated above) I did not want opposite-sex factors to hinder the journey; (2) I wanted to protect these honorable men and their marriages for the same reason (regardless of vocation, men can be tempted just like women); and (3) I did not trust men. Since the one man I was supposed to be able to trust above all had betrayed me, I was unable to see past gender in order to fully share my deepest feelings.

Although I seriously doubt that those first two reasons ever would have come into play, I took special, proactive care to guard my mind and heart against the possibilities. Our goal is healing, so we need to remove any barriers that might inhibit the process.

3. Trained Professionals

Many people whom I interviewed found other faith-based options. For example, many churches (mine included) offer the popular, Christ-centered DivorceCare® and DivorceCare for Kids™ groups. One of the women I interviewed for this book, Linda Paden, now serving as a DivorceCare® facilitator following her divorce, says:

> After months of getting some nonbiblical counseling . . . I joined the DivorceCare® program at my church home. DivorceCare® was the best thing I could have done. I was far younger than anyone else in the room, but we felt the same hurt, rejection, and pain. It was a room where I wasn't alone. Where being sad and broken was okay. DivorceCare® recognized how big of a loss a marriage was, and I appreciated how much they taught reconciliation.

Search online for professionals in your area or other helpful resources, including Christian recovery groups that meet at churches, seminars, books (this book is a great example), videos, workshops, and even retreats. Some churches offer the faith-based GriefShare® program. The most important aspect is to ensure that the help you seek bases their advice on the foundation of God and His Word.

Leave Your Baggage at the Cross

The bottom line is that divorce is far beyond our own capabilities to walk through alone without godly wisdom from an outside source. We are too emotionally invested and mentally shaken to think clearly.

For example, two of my sisters are nurses. My older sister is an emergency room trauma nurse, and my youngest sister is a post-anesthetic-care nurse. Both of them are highly skilled and save lives on a regular basis. However, if one of their children were to be admitted in distress, their ability to assess the medical situation from a completely analytical vantage point would be compromised. They would be too emotionally invested and mentally

The bottom line is that divorce is far beyond our own capabilities to walk through alone.

shaken to focus properly. The same is true for divorce and the kind of professional care we need to seek.

Emotional baggage weighs us down and holds us back. Piece by piece, we need to address and then surrender our bags of anger, unforgiveness, hurt, grief, and loneliness and put in the hard work of addressing them head-on to usher in God's ultimate healing.

God's divorce recovery plan is best—leave your baggage with Him: *"Come to Me, all who labor and are heavy laden, and I will give you rest"* (Matthew 11:28).

Going through divorce most assuredly qualifies you as "heavy laden." But thanks to God, He does not want us to remain that way.

THE BENEFITS OF COUNSELING

I chose one-on-one counseling with a licensed Christian counselor because I wanted the benefit of personalized, individual time to focus on the tools, tips, and exercises that I needed to receive God's ultimate healing. There are many specific benefits that come from such counseling.

An Outside Perspective

I was an emotional wreck when everything first happened. I could barely get past feelings of surreal disbelief. Attempting to discern what to do next seemed like a Herculean task.

Counselors are trained to look at our situations objectively and identify important facts that perhaps hurt has blinded us against. For instance, I am a compassionate person by nature. I kept trying to figure out how my ex-husband could be helped. Even that first night after I confronted him, I was concerned about where he would spend the night in the pouring-down rain. I called a mutual friend and arranged for him to stay the night.

Although such compassion was helpful in the beginning, in order to heal, I needed to learn how to focus on my well-being first. Such focus is not selfish; it is necessary. Kristin gracefully taught me the balance of setting healthy emotional boundaries that, at the time, felt like survival skills. She taught me what I needed to pack

153

in my spiritual and emotional backpack to survive the hard journey through divorce.

Kristin also pointed out thought patterns and behaviors that I needed to change in order to heal and change for the better. Those were tough but necessary sessions.

If you are extremely dependent on your ex-spouse, counseling can help you work through those issues to prevent dependency that keeps you entangled with your ex-spouse in unhealthy ways.

Biblically Based Counsel

Christian counselors use Scripture as the foundation for any advice they impart. Since God created us and wrote our instruction manual, relying on His Word is crucial. You need a counselor who knows the Bible and how to apply it properly.

Accountability

Kristin kept me accountable—not only to the process but also to God. Even though I was fully committed to giving it my all in our sessions, some weeks were hard to survive.

She exhibited much grace in her questioning, but she did not let me slide by with sloppy homework, so to speak. She gently but firmly kept me accountable regarding the various tasks I needed to complete or work through.

You and I ultimately determine how well we will get through counseling and take their professional advice and spiritual guidance to heart. God put them in your path for a reason.

The Importance of Immersing Yourself in Scripture

Even though Christians are encouraged to spend daily time in God's Word, it becomes vital when we face the heartbreaking situation of divorce.

Since you may feel discarded, unloved, and devalued, spending time in Scripture reminds you how much He loves you. Satan will do everything in his power to kick you while you're down. I highly recommend reading Ephesians 6:10–18. Those crucial passages reveal the armor that God has given you to not only survive but thrive. You are HIS soldier, wearing HIS armor—you are never at the mercy of Satan or his legions.

We need to be reassured that God will never leave us or forsake us. For example, when you pray, take a leaf from King David's example: *"Cast me not away from Your presence, and take not Your Holy Spirit from me"* (Psalm 51:11). David knew what mattered most: God's presence.

Satan will do everything in his power to kick you while you're down.

God's Word heals, but it also convicts us regarding our thoughts and intentions. My thoughts and intentions were certainly not God-honoring toward my ex-husband during the divorce. Only spending time in the light of His Word dispelled the darkness I kept hidden in my heart.

God's Word reminds us who is in charge. It also reminds us that nothing can separate us from His everlasting love. And when we are nursing a broken heart, that truth provides a healing salve to our soul.

Lessons from the Valley

Like you, I wanted to experience the mountaintop joys, not the low valleys. But I have discovered an important truth: water runs in valleys, not on mountaintops.

There are no streams above a mountain's tree line. It's bare and exposed. Greenery and growth take place because of water, not due to high altitude and cold temperatures. Valleys—especially in deserts—are places where greenery flourishes. Life is found in the water.

Spiritually speaking, our eternal life is found in God's living water:

> Jesus said to her, "Everyone who drinks of this water will be thirsty again, but whoever drinks of the water that I will give him will never be thirsty again. The water that I will give him will become in him a spring of water welling up to eternal life." (John 4:13–14)

As we walk through the valley while listening to God, trusted professionals, and pastors, we grow and learn vital life lessons that we can learn only there.

One day, mountaintop experiences will happen to you again.

But right now, faithfully walk through the valley, remembering that His living water still flows in you.

PASTORAL WISDOM

"For I did not shrink from declaring to you the whole counsel of God." (Acts 20:27)

A big part of being a pastor is sharing the counsel of God. All of it. Law and Gospel. We point out what Scripture says is sin, but we also share the forgiveness Jesus accomplished for all sin. So pastors are in a very real sense "counselors."

People will come to their pastors for advice on a wide variety of topics. The wise pastor will spend a lot of time listening. He will also recognize his limitations. Pastors are trained to share God's Word, to be spiritual counselors. Paul gave this advice to the young pastor Timothy:

Do your best to present yourself to God as one approved, a worker who has no need to be ashamed, rightly handling the word of truth. (2 Timothy 2:15)

That is what we have to share with people. People who are hurting need to be directed to God and His love and His promises. You find those in the pages passed down to us, God's written Word. And a person who is hurting and angry and grieving and confused needs to be pointed to the certainty of God's forgiveness and acceptance. Pastors give spiritual counsel. That is foundational:

Let the word of Christ dwell in you richly, teaching and admonishing one another in all wisdom, singing psalms and hymns and spiritual songs, with thankfulness in your hearts to God. (Colossians 3:16)

If God's Word is filling you, that will be what comes out of you as well. The important thing is to keep your focus on the one who loves you and wants to help you:

> I lift up my eyes to the hills. From where does my help come? My help comes from the LORD, who made heaven and earth. (Psalm 121:1–2)

It is vital that you have that understanding and confidence. However, in most cases more is needed. While God's grace is sufficient, people often need practical suggestions for coping and moving on, and that comes from a different kind of counselor. In my experience, most pastors have little or no practical counseling training. Many do it, and some do it well, but some are not very good at it. That is why professional Christian counselors are blessings to the Body of Christ.

The role of the pastor is primarily confessor and comforter. He provides spiritual counsel, listens to confessions, assures individuals of God's forgiveness for Jesus' sake, provides emotional and spiritual support, and points people to Jesus, the rock on which our lives are to be built:

While God's grace is sufficient, people often need practical suggestions for coping and moving on.

> According to the grace God has given me, like a skilled master builder I laid a foundation, and now someone else is building upon it. Let each one take care how he builds upon it. (1 Corinthians 3:10)

In the construction business, you want to have a solid foundation. It is essential for a sound structure. But the person who lays the foundation is seldom the same one who frames the building, puts on the roof, or does the finish work inside the building. Different skill sets are needed for different jobs. But it is all sitting on the firm foundation.

Donna uses the analogy of a tornado. I've seen firsthand the devastation they do to homes. Sometimes you clean everything away except the foundation of the building. And that may be where you are: rebuilding your life after a divorce. You still have the foundation of Jesus and His love. Just be careful in selecting the "builders." If you are building on the foundation of God's Word and promises, you will want to select a trained Christian counselor as you rebuild. Let each one take care how he builds upon it.

COUNSELOR'S CORNER

I am starting this section with a straightforward statement: you get out of therapy what you put into it. That might be a tough way to start, but it's true. If you view counseling only as an avenue to prove your ex's faults and assign blame to him or her (even if it's true), you will miss a God-given opportunity to grow, heal, and flourish. Bravely taking steps to look at all angles of a fallen relationship is vital. Yes, that includes you. If you are willing to look at yourself, you will gain wonderful insights into your thoughts, feelings, and choices and why you do the things you do. You will also learn how to evaluate and improve those skills to create healthy coping skills.

You get out of therapy what you put into it.

Divorce creates a multitude of emotions. Many emotions are very painful, so our human psyche wants to protect us. In that protection, we can "numb out" so that the emotions are not as intense or not there at all. We can live for weeks, months, years, even decades numb and out of touch with emotions. Until we are willing to face those emotions and FEEL them—yes, I said FEEL them—we can't completely heal.

I LOVE Donna's words "You have to feel it before God can heal it." AMEN! I know you just said, "But, Kristin, if I feel them, they will consume me and _____ will happen." You fill in the blank. So, what will happen if you feel them? What do you FEAR will happen? Congratulations—you just *felt!*

If you have been protecting yourself through the emotion of FEAR, here are some practical questions and exercises to help:

- How connected are you to your emotions?

- Are you in touch with them or have you become numb?

- Are you only in touch with a couple of emotions and life is mostly sadness or anger?

- Over the next week, notice what emotions you feel, and list them. If you realize that you aren't sure what you feel or you only identify a few main feelings, then search "feeling lists" online. Print a couple of copies—my personal favorite is one with funny faces to match the emotions! Put the list in front of you because you will need it below.

As much as I believe and encourage you to identify your emotions and sit with them, don't just stay in the pit. The pit will keep filling with emotions, and before you know it, you will drown in them. One of the many lifelines out of the emotional pit is to look at our thoughts and gain the skill of recognizing when they are rational or irrational.

I often use a counseling theory called Cognitive Behavioral Therapy (CBT) because it is based on looking at the relationship between thoughts, feelings, and behaviors. The premise of CBT is this: *If you change the way you think (thoughts), you can change the way you feel (feelings), which can change the way you respond (behaviors).* That being said, you are NOT going to go from livid to happy or devastated to appreciative in a single bound! By changing your thoughts, you can change the *intensity* of your emotions, which gives you a chance to make wiser, less emotionally charged choices in your responses.

So it sounds great, but how? Follow this:

- Search "thought distortion lists" online. Identify one that contains ten to fifteen types, and print it out.

- Ask God to open your heart and mind to reveal to you which thought distortions are your go-to favorites. We ALL do them. We all have our go-tos.

- Mark your go-to favorites on the list. When do you use each one? Certain situations, people you hang around, or seasons of life can bring out certain distortion types.

So, now you have a list. Now what? Keep this list handy. When you notice your emotions are changing, grab some paper and a pen:

- List your emotions (use the list, if needed).

- Write down the thought that is going through your head.

- What evidence do you have that the thought is *factually* true?

- Does one of the distortions fit the thought?

- "Rewrite" the thought based on fact, not distortion, and pray over it.

- Did the intensity of the emotion lessen? If not, do the same with other thoughts.

7: Pausing to Breathe, Pray, and Reflect

Immersing yourself in Scripture and Christian counseling offers the best combination of tools to enable you to survive your divorce and thrive afterward. God will use them to heal your heart and open doors in your future.

As I and many others have discovered, God will use you one day to speak hope and encouragement to others struggling with divorce. But you can only do it effectively through a heart healed by God.

Through the following exercises, cling with confidence to this hope-filled truth: though your feelings come and go, God's love for you does not. Take your time walking through the following Bible passages, questions, prayer time, and journaling time before moving to the next chapter.

SCRIPTURE TO READ, MEDITATE ON, AND MEMORIZE

My sheep hear My voice, and I know them, and they follow Me. I give them eternal life, and they will never perish, and no one will snatch them out of My hand. (John 10:27–28)

Make me to know Your ways, O Lord; teach me Your paths. Lead me in Your truth and teach me, for You are the God of my salvation; for You I wait all the day long. (Psalm 25:4–5)

Listen to advice and accept instruction, that you may gain wisdom in the future. (Proverbs 19:20)

QUESTIONS FOR REFLECTION

Devote a block of time to answer these questions from the gut. No one is looking over your shoulder. It's just you and God. So get real and raw so that God can continue the healing process in your heart.

1. What part of the divorce process or its aftermath are you struggling most with right now? Narrow it down and get specific.

2. Have you sought outside help or wisdom from a pastor, counselor, other trained professional, or support group? If so, how has it benefited your journey? If not, why not?

3. Do you set aside time each day to read and meditate on Scripture? If so, how has it helped you? If not, have you considered starting?

PAUSE FOR PRAYER

Take this time to talk to God. He is waiting for this time with you.

A—Acknowledge God's sovereignty: Sometimes we dwell on our situation, forgetting amidst the pain and emotion that God is still in control of everything. Even your situation. Read Hebrews 4:12 aloud with confidence.

C—Confession: Working through emotions and emerging healed by God on the other side takes time and diligence. Take this time to confess what you are feeling to God—narrow it down and get specific. He already knows each circumstance, but verbally expressing those feelings ejects them from your heart, mind, and soul so that He can begin the healing process. Please pray aloud to God now.

T—Thanksgiving: It is hard to express thanks when traveling down a painful road. But each day, God blesses us with what we need. Perhaps someone encouraged you today. Maybe God provided beautiful weather. List three things you are thankful for right now, and thank God for them.

1.

2.

3.

S—Supplication (requests): God promises that when we pray, He faithfully hears us. Identify what you need from Him right now, and ask Him in faith to provide it.

EXHALING ON THE PAGE

If you have not started our journaling process, begin TODAY. You don't need a fancy journal. Pick up the nearest yellow pad or some loose-leaf paper and start writing. God will use your journaling as another way to release toxic feelings and show how He is pouring His love into you. You may not see the benefit of journaling today, but you will one day. Trust Him.

Here are some suggested questions to answer as you journal:

1. What happened today?

2. How do you feel?

3. What made you angry or made you grateful?

4. How did someone encourage you today or show kindness?

5. Where did you see God at work in your circumstances today?

ADDITIONAL EXERCISE: SCRIPTURE IMMERSION

Spending time in Scripture studying verses specific to your struggle reaps incredible benefits. For example, during my divorce there were days when I needed to be reminded of how much God loves me. I used an Internet Bible website (such as BibleGateway.com or BlueLetterBible.org) to search every instance in God's Word where the word *love* appeared. The resulting list turned out to be several pages long. I printed the list out and spent hours, sometimes large blocks of time on the weekends, reading those passages about God's love. I rewrote on index cards the verses that I wanted to commit to memory and then carried those cards in my purse. I cannot tell you how often I needed to pull them out and read them aloud.

I highly recommend that you try this, at least for a time. Identify your biggest struggle right now—whether it's anger, loneliness, etc.— and perform your own Scripture word search. Spend time reading and praying through the passages and then rewrite on index cards or sticky notes the ones that you feel led to commit to memory.

God's Word never returns void: *"You will seek Me and find Me, when you seek Me with all your heart"* (Jeremiah 29:13).

You did it! Take a deep breath and exhale slowly. God is with you, dear one. He will NEVER leave you or forsake you. He will see you through each day and every circumstance.

8

The Important Role of Your Church and Faith Family

Bear one another's burdens,
and so fulfill the law of Christ.
—Galatians 6:3

Going through divorce instantly creates feelings of isolation. You have been deeply wounded and are amazed that you aren't bleeding out of your skin. Most people cannot understand the depth of pain.

That's where our church and faith families play a vital role, because they point you to God's hope and healing. Unchurched friends may point you to self-help books, twelve-step programs, or the most ruthless attorney to go after your ex-spouse, but that's not what you need most. You need Jesus. You need to link arms with other believers in fellowship and in corporate worship because during those fleeting minutes, Christ takes your mind off the brokenness and puts it back on Himself.

THE KIND OF FRIENDS WE TRULY NEED

What comes to mind when you think of your closest friends? I'm not talking about acquaintances who barely know you. I mean those inner-circle friends who have walked beside you through life's stinky trenches and still stuck around. They've shared your joys, heart-breaks, long-running jokes, arm-in-arm victories, bold prayers of faith, laughter, failures, and mountaintop experiences.

One of life's greatest blessings and sweetest rewards is the bond of intimacy and joy experienced through one-of-a-kind friendships knitted together by Christ—iron-sharpening-iron kinds of friends centered in God, who have His calling in their hearts and His words on their lips. They aren't afraid to challenge you, protect you, hold you accountable, and provide a safe place for transparency and honest communication.

And for those tough days when we can't stand on our own, we need friends who pray us through the gap. During the chaos and sadness of my divorce, my three closest friends did just that. They called to check on me, they got me out of the house when I just want-ed to shut out the world, they texted Scripture passages and encour-agement to me, and they simply loved me unconditionally.

My closest friends serve side by side with me at my home church. Whenever I spend time with these women, I gain a greater appreci-ation for who God made them as friends, moms, wives, and Christ followers. They provide regular glimpses of Jesus' unconditional love.

They reflect the kind of friend I want to be.

To get a friend like that, we have to be one like that. Cultivating and maintaining such friendships takes commitment. But the result is priceless. Those kinds of friends walk beside us through the fires of life without flinching.

They turn our gray days into vivid tapestries of JOY.

CHOOSE WISELY

One of the very first people I sought out during my divorce was my best friend. Luanne has an amazing faith in the Lord, and I knew beyond the shadow of a doubt that God would use her powerfully to walk beside me through the terrible storm ahead. I mention that for one reason: *who you choose as travel companions during this time is crucial.* Be sure you choose wisely. Surround yourself with people who genuinely love you and will support you, encourage you, help you, and pray for you. God works powerfully in our lives through other people. Solomon said:

> Two are better than one. . . . If they fall, one will lift up his fellow. But woe to him who is alone when he falls and has not another to lift him up! (Ecclesiastes 4:9–10)

Keep in mind, it may be a new person God has recently sent into your life. It doesn't have to be a friend from grade school.

Surround yourself with people who genuinely love you.

I thought long and prayed hard about who I wanted to walk alongside me through the storm of divorce. I sifted friends through a quality-check system, if you will. That may sound scientific, and you're right. You may automatically gravitate to your BFF, but he or she may not possess the specific qualities you need at this crucial juncture. Here are the qualities I sought in friends when selecting my "divorce posse":

Godly wisdom. To honor God as you walk the tough road of divorce, seek out friends who love the Lord, know Scripture, and are prayer warriors. You need friends who will speak godly wisdom into your situation, not personal preference or platitudes.

Love. Your love tank is pretty low during divorce, so you need a reservoir of people who love you deeply just as you are, especially on those days you don't feel very lovable.

Support. You will encounter risk, fear, anger, sadness, and a myriad of other emotions. For those tasks that seem too daunting to face, your support team will build your courage and lend their strength.

For example, the day I had to go to court and sign my divorce papers, I wanted to go alone. I didn't want to talk to anyone on the phone afterward, either. However, I needed their prayers desperately. I texted my posse when I left my house married, then texted them when I left the courthouse divorced a few hours later. They texted prayers, encouragement, and love—and honored my wishes not to call. You need friends who understand the importance of what you truly need, so be sure to articulate and communicate your needs well.

Morals. Your morals will guide you as you walk toward the new future God has planned for you. Your morals and values guide how you make decisions, so you need others who have the same high standards. You do not need to surround yourself with those who believe lying and cheating are the means to a worthwhile end.

Accountability. When your judgment is clouded by hurt, you may be tempted to make less-than-honorable decisions. You need trustworthy friends who are not afraid to keep you accountable if you begin traveling down the road of recklessness or revenge. Trust me, you will be tempted to travel both at some point.

Experience. Seek out those who have experienced divorce and emerged strong in their faith and their new life. They understand what you are experiencing like no one else can. They understand what you need, even when you don't.

Worldly wisdom. You need friends who are wise regarding finances, legal matters, and household organization. They can help you set a solid budget, navigate court issues, and teach you how to effectively manage your home and schedule alone.

You need trustworthy friends who are not afraid to keep you accountable.

Church Family

I stayed away from my church the first two weekends after everything first happened. I didn't want to have to answer questions as to where my husband was, and I wanted to give my pastors a chance to field uncomfortable questions if word had gotten out.

I didn't realize how much staying away affected me until I went back on that third weekend. The beautiful simplicity of singing beloved songs and hymns, receiving Communion, and opening God's Word in the pew among my fellow believers during the sermon filled my heart and soul with indescribable joy. I was HOME, and it felt so good.

My posse sat with me in a heartwarming show of loving unity in the Lord. It was hard to attend church without my ex-husband and even harder to sing songs we had often led together. But more important than memories, I experienced the presence of God in that place.

Thank You, Lord.

One Day, Return the Favor

Have you ever received a gift so lavish that words failed you? one that touched your soul so profoundly that your heart experienced tangible waves of God's relentless love?

My lavish gift arrived on a chilly March evening exactly one month following my divorce as I stood on the cold concrete floor in the middle of my bare living room. I was in the rebuilding process—spiritually, physically, and emotionally. I was doing some remodeling to replace my carpet with wood floors, so the emptiness echoed loudly.

Into that emptiness, the phone rang. It was one of my pastors, and he asked if I was sitting down. Looking around at the bare concrete floors, I laughed and said, "Not quite."

He told me that an anonymous benefactor had just paid for my passage on a nine-day cruise with the seniors group from my church to sail up the New England coast into Canada to see the fall foliage in October. All I had to do was say yes.

I stood, opening and closing my mouth like a fish out of water, as the tears flowed. That person (or persons) from the church simply wanted to provide an avenue for me to get away with God to nurture my healing process.

The spiritual and emotional benefits of that amazing, soul-refreshing time still ripple in my heart today. Not only was the cruise beautiful and relaxing, but the group of seniors I traveled with took me under their wing and loved on me.

I still don't know whose anonymous hand extended that amazing gift to me. *But I know whose hand was behind it.* Their generosity far exceeded monetary value. Those nine precious days away allowed me to breathe again, slow life to a stroll, refocus direction, listen to God's guidance, and allow Him to resurface my heart.

I know without a trace of doubt that one day, I'll pass such a blessing forward to someone in the future. I don't know what that will look like or who will receive it, but God will let me know.

As you walk through divorce, there will be people who bless and love on you in unique and incredible ways. One day in the future, after God has healed your heart and set your feet on a new path, consider passing along blessings to others facing the road that you've traveled. God will use those blessings to bless them just as they did you.

GIVE TO OTHERS

Have you noticed that when we focus on helping others, God lifts our eyes and hearts off of our problems and onto His mission?

As you walk through divorce, there will be people who bless and love on you in unique and incredible ways.

Last October, my church tried something called Impact Sunday. The goal was simple: instead of gathering in the pews, we spread out in our community. I volunteered to spearhead the music/singing for a Houston inner-city organization called Church in the Driveway.

My team and I arrived to discover it was *literally* a church in the driveway. Tents had been erected over a few dozen folding chairs along two connecting driveways occupied by men and a few women from area community housing. The ten-minute sermon was to the point, the singing was done a cappella, and the day was rainy, but it was God who reigned there that morning. That experience impacted me greatly, and I have continued volunteering there on the fourth Sunday of the month ever since.

There's just something about sacrificial serving that lifts sadness, about generous giving that ends grumbling, and about leaping faith that ushers love. As Jesus followers, we are here to be His hands and feet despite our circumstances. So the next time your situation pulls you low, instead of venting to a friend, volunteer for an organization. It does wonders for your soul, your community, and God's witness.

CONCLUSION

The bottom line is that we need one another. Scripture often challenges us to do something to, with, or for "one another." The family of God is about true community in which His people enjoy the blessings of fellowship with those who share one big thing in common—a love for Jesus Christ and His inerrant, infallible Word.

True fellowship happens when believers spend time praying together, bearing one another's burdens, encouraging one another to do good works, encouraging one another from the Bible, and keeping one another focused on what truly counts. When trouble comes and you need someone you can trust with the core issues of your heart, no one can compare with another believer who can pray with you and help you carry the cross.

Without a doubt, there are times when we fail and let one another down—that's part of living in a fallen, imperfect world. But Jesus will never disappoint you. Each day, you are called to walk with Him, take part in His suffering, experience His lavish love, and be free from sin. Jesus said:

> No longer do I call you servants, for the servant does not know what his master is doing; but I have called you friends. (John 15:15)

Welcome to the joy of not having to go it alone—welcome to the community of fellowship with one another and with Jesus.

171

PASTORAL WISDOM

A pastor went to visit a member who had stopped coming to church. It was cold out, and when the member opened the door, the pastor walked into the house. Neither of them said a word as they sat down in front of the roaring fire. The pastor quietly used the tongs to pull an ember out of the fire and set it on the hearth. They both watched as it glowed for a while but then started to go out. Before long, it was cold and dead. The pastor got up to leave, but as he did so, he picked up the dead ember and threw it back into the fire. Almost immediately, it began to glow from the light and warmth of all the other coals around it. He had preached a convincing sermon without saying a word.

It is important for us to be a part of a fellowship of faith. We are all in this together. Paul describes believers as the "body of Christ" in 1 Corinthians 12:12–31. God has put us into this Body; it is where He wants us to be, and we are to be concerned about one another. This is especially true when someone is going through a difficult time.

> If one member suffers, all suffer together; if one member is honored, all rejoice together. (1 Corinthians 12:26)

You may feel like isolation is the way to cope with your sorrow and grief and bitterness. But remember that God has placed you in the Body of Christ. When you shut out other parts of the Body, you deprive them of the opportunity to help you, and you deprive yourself of the help Jesus wants to give you through His Body.

> Let us . . . not [neglect] to meet together, as is the habit of some, but [encourage] one another. (Hebrews 10:24–25)

It is more than commiseration. It is encouragement with the message of love and reconciliation and forgiveness that is yours because of what Jesus has done for you. You need to be built up in that Good News when you are feeling despair and failure because your marriage is over. That building up takes place in the fellowship of faith.

Be aware that other believers may not always say and do the right thing. They are sinners too. But we all have the same Head: Christ (Ephesians 4:15). And we want to do the best we can to care for other parts of His Body, especially when they are hurting.

> So then, as we have opportunity, let us do good to everyone, and especially to those who are of the household of faith. (Galatians 6:10)

Ideally, other members of the Body of Christ will reach out to you. Sometimes they will not because they are unsure of what to say or how to help. But your brothers and sisters in Christ do want to help you. They know you are part of the same Body. If they don't take the first step, don't let that keep you away from the communion of saints.

Sharing your concerns with others allows them to pray for you.

In worship and small-group settings, you can confess your sins and be assured of the forgiveness that Jesus earned for you. Sharing your concerns with others allows them to pray for you. That is all part of the healing process.

> Therefore, confess your sins to one another and pray for one another, that you may be healed. (James 5:16)

8: Pausing to Breathe, Pray, and Reflect

Remaining active in church and among the fellowship of believers is crucial to our spiritual and emotional healing after the significant hurt of divorce. Take your time walking through the following Bible passages, questions, prayer time, and journaling time before moving to the next chapter.

SCRIPTURE TO READ, MEDITATE ON, AND MEMORIZE

That which we have seen and heard we proclaim also to you, so that you too may have fellowship with us; and indeed our fellowship is with the Father and with His Son Jesus Christ. (1 John 1:3)

Jesus answered him, "If anyone loves Me, he will keep My word, and My Father will love him, and We will come to him and make Our home with him." (John 14:23)

And they devoted themselves to the apostles' teaching and the fellowship, to the breaking of bread and the prayers. . . . And all who believed were together and had all things in common. . . . And day by day, attending the temple together and breaking bread in their homes, they received their food with glad and generous hearts. (Acts 2:42, 44, 46)

QUESTIONS FOR REFLECTION

If you are having difficulty remaining connected to and enjoying the fellowship of believers, perhaps considering these questions will help:

1. When you spend time with believers, is it about having fun or is there a deeper purpose?

2. Do you have a Christian friend whom you are comfortable asking to be your accountability partner?

3. Are you an active member in your church (whether in Bible study, worship, and/or missions)? If not, why?

PAUSE FOR PRAYER

Despite our circumstances or how we feel, time with the Lord in prayer is essential. Exhale now and be still before the Lord. Let's pray:

A—Acknowledge God's sovereignty: With all the changes in your life right now, it helps to acknowledge that God is still in control of everything. Even your situation. Read Matthew 19:26 aloud with confidence.

C—Confession: Working through divorce and emerging healed by God on the other side takes time and diligence. Take this time to confess to God what you are struggling with most—narrow it down and get specific. He already knows each circumstance, but verbally expressing those feelings ejects them from your heart, mind, and soul so that He can begin the healing process. Please pray aloud to God now.

T—Thanksgiving: It is hard to express thanks when the future is uncertain. Yet even in the midst of your circumstances, God has blessed you with people and things for which you owe Him thanks. List three things you are thankful for right now, and thank God for them.

1.

2.

3.

S—Supplication (requests): God promises that when we pray, He faithfully hears us. Identify what you need from Him right now, and ask Him in faith to provide it.

EXHALING ON THE PAGE

As you know by now, God uses journaling as another way to release pent-up feelings and allow God to fill you with His peace that passes all understanding. You may not see the benefits of journaling today, but you will one day. Trust Him.

Here are some suggested questions to answer as you journal:

1. What happened today?

2. How do you feel?

3. What made you angry or made you grateful?

4. How did someone encourage you today or show kindness?

5. Where did you see God at work in your circumstances today?

You did it! Take a deep breath and sit back. God is with you, dear one. He will NEVER leave you or forsake you. He will see you through each day and every circumstance.

9

Repeat after Me: "I Cannot Change My Ex" (Communication 101)

You are not only responsible for what you say,
but also for what you do not say.

—Martin Luther

When someone hurts you deeply, the last thing you desire to be is civil to them—especially if you were blindsided. Your natural self-defense mechanisms kick in, and you want to lash out and hurt them as much as they hurt you.

Although spewing ugly words may feel good for an instant, it proves extremely harmful in the long run. There are two things we can never recover: wasted time and hurtful words.

Even though you may think that your ex-spouse's behavior hasn't earned your civility, there's much more at stake—especially if children are involved.

There are two things we can never recover: wasted time and hurtful words.

TAKING THE HIGH ROAD

Each conversation you have with your ex-spouse can go one of two ways: productive or destructive. I had to remember that each and every time my ex-husband and I exchanged an email or text. The only reason I mention that is because my ex-husband and I handled our entire divorce through written communication; I haven't seen him since the day he left our home.

If you and your ex-spouse have children, such distance may seem completely foreign. Even though I could barely function through the hurt on some days, I continually asked God to give me words of grace whenever I communicated with my ex-husband. There were some days when I wanted to use poisonous words, but God faithfully reminded me that I wouldn't be able to unsay them. Sometimes when I could find no graceful or kind way to respond, I simply wouldn't respond myself and I would let the attorney handle the communications.

By God's grace alone, I never called my ex-husband any of the ugly names that sometimes popped into my head. Ugly names and curses spewed without restraint when I first confronted him. Later, I repented to God and received His forgiveness, remembering how awful it felt knowing that I could not take back my words. I resolved to never again repeat that mistake with my ex-husband. The self-loathing that I felt afterward was too high a price to pay.

Perhaps it would have felt better momentarily to rant and call him names, but how many of those names would have been true of me in different circumstances? Although I never committed marital adultery or put another man above my husband, I couldn't say the same about my relationship with God. Over the years, I have cheated on God by putting myself, my ex-husband, others, and even my career above Him. God could have shouted "Adulterer!" at me and been justified. Instead, He showed grace. You and I are no different.

JESUS COMMUNICATED GRACE

As His followers, we are bound to show grace. Even when it hurts most. When Jesus hung on the cross as the innocent sacrifice for our sins, He did not curse the ones who hung Him there. He said, *"Father, forgive them, for they know not what they do."* I do not know what drove my ex-husband's actions, but I cannot believe that he intended to end up where he did.

I used Jesus' prayer for my ex-husband: *"Father, forgive him, for he knows not what he does."* In those early divorce days, I prayed it through gritted teeth. But I learned firsthand that you cannot pray for someone without God changing your heart. Eventually, I prayed it through tears of genuine care and concern. God's pretty amazing like that.

Taking the high road in communicating with your ex-spouse may result in biting your tongue until it's bloody. I can certainly empathize. But when all was said and done, I could look at myself in the mirror without regretting ugly words said during the divorce process.

Yes, it can be exhausting always climbing to the higher road, but it's an exercise toward freedom. The rewards of self-respect and the ability to sleep peacefully at night, knowing that you honored God with your words and actions, are priceless.

Meet Janetta

Following a whirlwind three-month engagement, Janetta married her first husband. The problem was that he could not seem to tell the truth about lots of things. In one of his biggest lies, she discovered that the wedding ring set he'd given to her had originally been bought for a previous girlfriend. When their relationship didn't work out, he gave the ring to Janetta. She remembers:

> Let's just say it looked great flying through the air (when I threw it at him), and we made a trip to the jewelry store for a simple band to replace it.

Over their nearly three-year marriage, they separated countless times. Janetta finally went to visit family, advising her husband to think about how they could get back together and make their marriage work:

> I got back a few days later and asked if he wanted our marriage to work. His reply: "Yes, but I'd like to date other people." End of our relationship.

Her ex-husband even lied about actually starting the divorce proceedings. When Janetta called the court to find out why it was taking so long, she discovered they had never heard of her ex-husband. She called him to meet her, and they went to the courthouse together to file for divorce.

Janetta has long since forgiven her ex-husband since they have been divorced for years. And when it came to post-divorce communication, she discovered a surprise:

> Actually, we've remained friends. I know that's strange since we didn't have kids, but I'm one that moves on. We make much better friends than husband and wife.

Following her experience all those years ago, Janetta has been remarried for more than three decades now and has a strong relationship with the Lord today. I have seen it firsthand because she is a fellow writer and talented editor, and we have been friends for several years now. When I asked her to share the most important lesson she learned from her divorce, she said:

The Lord is there to help you through whatever you're going through.

> If you're not in church, go back. This was home when I wasn't sure what was going to happen next. The Lord

is there to help you through whatever you're going through. Also, if family and friends had not prayed fervently when my second marriage hit a serious spot for a number of years, we'd be divorced today. Pray! God can and will work miracles.

What sweet hope God brings out of our ashes.

Meet Tim

When Tim married his first wife, he worked as a prison guard. He was rough, crude, and mean; he used foul language and was unchurched. His wife loved all of that. However, five years into their eleven-and-a-half-year marriage, Tim became a Christian. She despised the new man he had become. He recalls:

> Our relationship went downhill from there and never recovered. I became way too weak, which allowed her to become way too strong. She wanted to fight, and I refused to fight. She verbally and physically abused me in front of our two children constantly for many years. She hit us all a lot. My refusal to fight back would only make her even more furious and abusive. When we separated for the fourth time, I filed for divorce.

Needless to say, communication was a challenge. His ex-wife was granted custody of their children, and he had visitation rights. Tim focused on his relationship with his children:

> I visited them regularly and attended their school events. Their relationship with me grew stronger while their relationship with their mother grew weaker and more strained. I was at a loss as to how to best help them. Only by the grace of God did they turn out okay. I have forgiven her, but I do not like to talk to her or spend time around her.

Tim touches on an important point. When your ex-spouse is determined to be contentious, the best alternative is to limit your exposure to him or her. Taking the high road in such a situation can certainly go a long way toward maintaining civil communication.

Three years after his divorce, Tim married a wonderful Christian lady, and they have been married for twenty-four years now. During that time, God called Tim to serve in full-time ministry. Today, he is a blessing to many at my home church, where he serves as pastor of life care.

God has placed Tim in a unique position to counsel others, not only from a biblical standpoint but also from an experiential one as well. He vividly remembers his personal struggles following his divorce:

> Because I was a Christian, the most difficult thing was the feeling of a tarnished witness. I knew God hated divorce, but I did it anyway. I felt like a second-class Christian. It was tough handling the limited time I had with my children. Everything in my life I saw through the distracting lens of personal failure.

Tim's divorce experience strengthened his faith and changed his future outlook. He explains:

> It humbled me, which is what I needed a lot. It also completely changed the direction of my faith toward grace—not law and self-righteousness. My divorce eventually helped the way I saw my future. I felt relief more than grief. I felt optimism about what God might do with my life instead of defeat over the embarrassingly fragmented pieces of my past. I have a lot more grace and patience with people now.

As a sheep under this shepherd of God's flock, I can tell you from firsthand observation that God is using Tim in mighty ways to spread His grace and love.

His incredible book, *The Executioner's Redemption*, outlines his years as a prison guard and member of the Texas death squad. His journey of faith from God's hand of judgment to His gentle servant is a beautiful display of God's transformative grace. The ways that God used Tim to communicate the hope of eternity to the condemned death-row inmates, their families, and the families of their victims is a riveting must-read.

TIPS FOR EFFECTIVE COMMUNICATION

Communication between ex-spouses can either improve over time or become a constant source of hurt. I am not sure where you fall along that spectrum, but having effective communication tips at your disposal doesn't hurt.

In any divorce, things get heated occasionally (or more often). It is a difficult, stressful experience, and we sometimes react emotionally as a result of the hurt we feel. Here are some helpful tips that I learned through trial and error to help maintain constructive communication:

1. Don't email or text in anger. I cannot count the number of angry texts or emails that I drafted to my ex-husband before I deleted them. I quickly learned that the email drafts folder was my best communication-saving friend. I would draft an email, let it sit overnight in the drafts folder, then open and read it again the next morning. Eighty-five percent of the time, I ended up changing language and toning down the anger or sarcasm before hitting Send. You may be angry and hurt, but a mean, ugly email or text will cause damage to a relationship that you need to maintain—at least for a while.

2. Don't dwell on blame or fault. I realize that is much easier said than done, but it can be done with the help of God. Blame or fault looks back. In Christ, we look forward in hope, not backward in hurt. Arguing fault and assigning blame is divisive and hinders reaching important agreements.

3. Don't communicate verbally when angry. See number 1 above. Voicemails can cause significant legal problems as well as unnecessary hurt. Pray for God's guidance, strength, and peace *before* you call.

4. Don't negotiate directly with your spouse—you need an attorney. Even in the most straightforward divorce proceedings, arguments can occur, especially when it comes to children and finances. Even though my ex-husband admitted his adultery and indicated in a moment of sorrow that I could have the house, when push came to shove, he decided that he wanted half after all.

Since I kept the house, I was required to obtain a professional appraisal and arrange for mortgage refinancing so he could receive half of the value of the house when our divorce was final. Although this was difficult to swallow at first, it turned out to be a wonderful blessing.

I added additional money to my new mortgage amount to finance some modest remodeling. Wood floors replaced the carpet, and a warm cappuccino color softened the white walls. My home is now my oasis, far removed from a chaotic world.

My attorney was instrumental in navigating me through that whole financial process. She discovered a savings account that my ex-husband had failed to disclose, which helped reduce the amount that I owed him for the house. I never fought with my ex-husband over material items, but I still needed an attorney with my best interests at heart to perform the due diligence to ensure that it was a fair, legal, and smooth process.

5. Focus on the bigger goal. Any time you focus on the small details, it becomes much easier to get into arguments. Ask God to help you see the bigger issues and how to achieve your higher goals. Since I've worked in the legal field for more than twenty-five years, I have witnessed family relationships destroyed by fighting over kitchen china. Even if the legal issue is resolved in court, the emotional damage and hurtful words take years to heal, if ever. That creates entirely too much emotional and spiritual baggage.

My ultimate goal was to start over with a clear conscious, clean slate, no baggage from the past, and forgiveness leading the way. That goal and my peace of mind were worth more than all the money and possessions in the world.

A word to the wise: beware of the devil's attacks to drag you back down and entice you to fight over material things. Case in point: A few years after the divorce, my ex-husband emailed me out of the blue and asked me to sign over a joint stock-trading account that he had opened while we were married. This account was never disclosed during the divorce.

However, rather than fight, I simply signed it over. Although the account held a five-digit sum, my higher goal was to live in peaceful freedom, not waste energy fighting over something as dirty and transient as money.

Beware of the devil's attacks to drag you back down.

Focus on Christ and the bigger goal at all times. You will sleep better and live more joyfully.

THE LIE YOU CAN'T BELIEVE

When we struggle through divorce, there is one particular Christianese phrase that you have probably heard: "God will never give you more than you can handle."

Many Christians hold that statement as absolute truth. Actually, it's an absolute lie. God never said it. Jesus never taught it. Don't fall for it.

I mean, just think about it. If God will never give us more than we can handle, then what do we need Him for? When I was going through my divorce, I heard that phrase often. You probably have as well. Honestly, it made me want to kick the person who said it. Hard. (Just keeping it real.)

All of us face seasons when we are overwhelmed. Sometimes it's a product of our own doing, sometimes not. But ALL of the time, it feels like spinning out of control—like you've lost grip on the pieces of your life as they are sucked away in that F5 tornado. Then, in the midst of your storm, some well-meaning person comes along, grabs your arm to ensure that he or she has your full attention, and lays that line on you. *Sheesh.*

Those words are not welcoming or comforting. In fact, they often create discouragement that suggests the hurting person can't seem to control his or her life.

The quote implies that you can handle every situation on your own. It's the old pull-yourself-up-by-your-bootstraps mentality—and it's dangerous sinking sand. It provides a false sense of control, only to be wept over later when the enemy attacks once again.

May I suggest a new phrase as you walk toward hope and healing following divorce? <u>God never gives you more than *HE* can handle.</u> He alone provides living water as we stumble through the desert of divorce. When our soul thirsts after God, He meets us in the midst of our pain, mess, and suffering. He demonstrated His willingness to be our ultimate comforter by coming down to earth in the person of Jesus Christ.

Jesus knew that our sin was not something that we could handle—even on our best days. Even when we're playing our A game, we have no way to get ourselves out of our sin situation. We cannot handle it, but He can. And He did.

When we are suffering and remember His promises, we will find Jesus right there in our time of need. In divorce court. In the unemployment office. In the counselor's office. Jesus never leaves you or forsakes you. <u>And He *never* asks us to handle any situation outside of His guidance, strength, and love.</u>

So the next time someone tells you "God will never give you more than you can handle," switch it up for the truth: God will never give you more than *HE* can handle.

Now *that* is effective communication.

Pastoral Wisdom

God is big on communication. He also understands it is not always easy. He is probably more often misunderstood than understood correctly. But God wants us to know who He is.

In order for us to be able to relate to Him in terms we can understand, He became one of us. He came down here—was born to live among us, interact with us, have face-to-face contact—not only to pay for our sins but also to make Himself known. He wanted to make sure we can understand Him and relate to Him. God understands the importance of good communication.

God will never give you more than HE *can handle.*

Our loving God also knows how important it is for us to have good communication with one another. He encourages it in His Word:

> He who loves purity of heart, and whose speech is gracious, will have the king as his friend. (Proverbs 22:11)

When I came across that passage recently, I thought "What a friend we have in Jesus," who is the King of kings. It is because of our friendship with Him that we want to have pure conversations and effective communication with others.

Because the Lord knows how difficult this is in our lives, Scripture has many warnings against harmful and hurtful speaking. James 3:1–12 speaks of the difficult yet necessary task of taming the tongue:

> With [the tongue] we bless our Lord and Father, and with it we curse people who are made in the likeness of God. From the same mouth come blessing and cursing. My brothers, these things ought not to be so. (James 3:9–10)

Peter also reminds us of the importance of good communication this way:

> Whoever desires to love life and see good days, let him keep his tongue from evil and his lips from speaking deceit. (1 Peter 3:10)

Life will go better for us if we speak the truth in love (Ephesians 4:15). When we do things God's way, it always goes better for us.

When I think of the importance of good communication, especially when dealing with someone who has wronged you or with whom you have a conflict, I am reminded of some wisdom that was shared with me early in my ministry: "You will never regret taking the high road. You will never regret doing the right thing." If you have not done anything wrong, Satan will not be able to pile on the guilt! Doing the right things, speaking in a kind way, is in your own best interest.

Scripture has many warnings against harmful and hurtful speaking.

187

When considering how to have God-pleasing communication with your ex, don't forget the importance of your communication with God. The One who went to such lengths to make Himself known to you wants you to be in dialogue with Him:

Call upon Me in the day of trouble; I will deliver you, and you shall glorify Me. (Psalm 50:15)

COUNSELOR'S CORNER

Ah, communication. It's so easy, isn't it? Communication was so easy when you were dating, engaged, and then married, right? It's been so easy with friends and family over the years, hasn't it? If you answered yes, then good for you—you can write the next best-selling communication book.

But if you are honest, communication is never easy, is it? Healthy communication takes a LOT of work, even between emotionally healthy people! There are a few tips to keep in mind about communication in general, but also when communicating with your ex, which can be difficult.

Healthy communication takes a LOT of work.

I once took a Bible class at my church, and the wise woman who was leading it talked about an "emotional elevator." Now, I have been a professional counselor for almost two decades, and I had never heard it presented this way. It was wonderful, logical, and helpful in its direct impact on communication, so I stole it (but give her credit).

Think of an elevator. An elevator can travel many floors up or down. The upper floors represent positive emotions. The higher the floor, the more intense the emotion. For example, the upper floors feel like elation, joy, gratitude, cheerfulness, gladness, pleasantness, and mellow, and they lessen in intensity as the elevator travels down.

The floors below ground represent negative emotions, increasing in intensity the farther down you go. The below-ground floors feel like dissatisfaction, irritation, anxiousness, unhappiness, anger, panic, outrage, and depression, to name only a few. Please don't get trapped in how many floors or which floor is which; simply recognize that positive emotions elevate while negative emotions push down.

It is very important to know where your emotional elevator sits when you are communicating. Studies show that when your mood elevator is down, your ability to think clearly is GREATLY diminished. Thus, it greatly affects your ability to have effective, healthy communication and the ultimate results.

You need to become a superstar pro at knowing where you are emotionally in the moment. Ask yourself whether communicating right then is the healthiest time for all involved. It is totally acceptable to give yourself an adult time-out. Again, pray, take a walk, or read Scripture. Give your elevator a chance to come up before attempting to communicate.

When you finally decide to communicate, be a hawk! Watch several key things:

- Watch the language you use. Are you using calming or inflammatory words?

- What is your tone?

- What is your body language saying?

Our nonverbal communication speaks much more loudly than our actual words. In fact, words (what people hear) make up only 7 percent of communication. Our tone makes up 38 percent, and our body language is a staggering 55 percent of what is communicated and heard! Look at how much power is simply in nonverbals—93 percent! Use that 93 percent to the best of your ability to bring about positive communication and results.

Be aware of using "I" versus "You" when communicating. "I" statements stick to you as an individual and have the least amount of negative impact. "You" language can feel hostile and attacking, thus invoking defensive feelings where everything deteriorates rapidly.

Also, analyze your motivation for the communication. If it is in any way based in negative emotions and thoughts, then your reaction (the need to say something immediately) will also be negative, and nothing good will result from it.

Healthy listening skills are imperative! They can be compromised when stress and emotions run high. The other skills discussed in this chapter are critical in placing boundaries around yourself so that you possess the best listening skills possible for the healthiest communication possible.

There are several types of listening skills, which vary from theory to theory, but typically they range from poor to best:

- Nonlistening: totally tuned out

- Limited listening: distracted but understanding bits and pieces

- Moderate listening: interrupting to give your thoughts on what you have heard before you receive all information

- Active listening: listening for understanding; clearing your mind to truly hear what is being communicated verbally and nonverbally by the other person

Each listening skill works in various times and places, but higher-level listening is critical when dealing with stressful situations. Push yourself to higher listening skills when communicating with your ex.

Don't get stuck in the little things and the emotions. Put those aside and try to hear what your ex is *really* trying to communicate. Then you will be able to prayerfully respond in a healthier way, and you will be able to determine if he or she actually made a point that you could have easily dismissed, thus costing you both a chance at a healthy outcome.

9: Pausing to Breathe, Pray, and Reflect

Effective communication can be difficult even in the best of circumstances. But when you add trauma and heartache to the mix, it may seem impossible. Few of us escape the journey through divorce innocent of slinging hurtful words at our ex-spouse.

Through the following exercises, cling with confidence to this hope-filled truth: although your feelings come and go, God's love for you does not. Take your time walking through the following Bible passages, questions, prayer time, and journaling time before moving to the next chapter.

SCRIPTURE TO READ, MEDITATE ON, AND MEMORIZE

Let the words of my mouth and the meditation of my heart be acceptable in Your sight, O LORD, my rock and my redeemer. (Psalm 19:14)

A word fitly spoken is like apples of gold in a setting of silver. (Proverbs 25:11)

For by your words you will be justified, and by your words you will be condemned. (Matthew 12:37)

QUESTIONS FOR REFLECTION

When you are not in a highly charged emotional state, there are several questions that, with God's guidance, can help you assess your communication skills. Be sure to answer these questions from the gut so God can continue to impart wisdom in your mind and heart.

1. What do you find most challenging about communicating with your ex-spouse? Go deeper than the divorce process in general; narrow it down and get specific.

2. Are you aware of any "hot buttons" that your ex-spouse may be pushing in your mind and heart that thwart efforts toward effective communication?

3. When you think of your higher goals and taking the high road in communication, do you believe that is possible for you? Why or why not?

PAUSE FOR PRAYER

God promises that when we submit all things to Him, He will bring beauty out of ashes. Take this time to pour out to God any anxiety, frustration, or difficulty about communication that you may be feeling. Let's pray:

A—Acknowledge God's sovereignty: Sometimes we dwell on our situation, forgetting amidst the pain and emotion that God is still in control of everything. Even your situation. Read Psalm 50:15 aloud with confidence.

C—Confession: Relying on God for His strength and graceful words when your ex-spouse may be quite a challenge takes time and diligence. Take this time to confess what you struggle with. Narrow it down and get specific. He already knows each circumstance, but verbally expressing those feelings helps to usher in God's healing process. Please pray aloud to God now.

T—Thanksgiving: It is hard to express thanks when effective communication collapses. Yet even in the midst of your circumstances, God has blessed you with people and/or things for which you owe Him thanks. List three things you are thankful for right now, and thank God for them.

1.

2.

3.

S—Supplication (requests): God promises that when we pray, He faithfully hears us. Identify what you need from Him right now, and ask Him in faith to provide it.

EXHALING ON THE PAGE

When communication is difficult, journaling may be hard. God can use your journaling in powerful ways. You may not see the benefit today, but you will one day.

Here are some suggested questions to answer as you journal:

1. What happened today?

2. How do you feel?

3. What made you angry or made you grateful?

4. How did someone encourage you today or show kindness?

5. Where did you see God at work in your circumstances today?

You did it! Take a deep breath and exhale slowly. God is with you, dear one. He will NEVER leave you or forsake you. He will see you through each day and every circumstance.

10

How to Handle Family, Friends, and Nosy Neighbors

The things most people want to know about are usually none of their business.

—Lewis Carroll

We all have acquaintances in our lives who simply want to know what's happening to populate the gossip chain. I hope that you also have family and friends in your life who truly love you and hold your best interests at heart. Trust me, you will know the difference when divorce hits.

Divorce involves enough confusion and hurt, so the last thing you need is to confide in the wrong person. And although family members may mean well, sometimes their help crosses over the line to meddlesome or even downright interference.

That being said, how do we handle family, friends, and nosy neighbors in a kind yet firm way that conveys our appreciation for their concern while setting healthy boundaries? Before we answer that question, let's establish what we need most as we walk through divorce.

What Hurting People Need from Friends and Family

You have a family member or friend who is going through a divorce. What in the world do you say? How are you supposed to act? How can you determine what they need most?

Unless they have experienced divorce, most people feel unequipped to relate to a divorce crisis. The situation is even more complicated if they were mutual friends of your ex-spouse. Many people simply react with silence for fear that they will say or do the wrong thing.

Most people feel unequipped to relate to a divorce crisis.

As I walked through my divorce, I discovered firsthand some practical ways you—our family and friends—can best demonstrate love and support.

Remain Engaged

Please break the silence. One of the most meaningful conversations I had was with a friend who stopped me in the church parking lot almost six months after my divorce was final. He worked with the youth of our church and had been good friends with my ex-husband. He confessed, "I have been silent because I didn't know what to say. I was working through my own hurt and avoided talking to you. I am sorry. Will you forgive me?" Of course, I forgave him, and that one exchange cleared the air.

It served as a valuable reminder to me that people around the hurting are hurting as well. Be patient and remain engaged.

Don't Leave Us

At first, some people simply wanted to hear the juicy details of what happened. Well, I had already decided not to share the vast majority of what had happened since it felt like casting stones. After the initial flurry of curiosity, many people were nowhere to be found. They didn't know who or what to believe, so they simply vanished from my life.

Make a note on your calendar to check in with us every month or so. Keep letting us know that you love us and you're praying for us. When Satan whispers in the dead of night "You're all alone" and "No one cares," your ongoing presence will remind us otherwise.

Offer Grace

We have endured something traumatic that has affected every area of our life and altered our view of life. Everything becomes magnified: details, emotions, needs, and reactions. New triggers may cause us to overreact on seemingly small issues. We need time to recalibrate and settle down, so please extend grace when our passionate responses seem disproportionate to the circumstance.

It also takes us twice as long to get things done. When we were married, there was a built-in divide-and-conquer mechanism for chores, errands, and commitments. Now it's just us. Please be patient if it takes us a little longer than normal to respond to you or complete a task. Our to-do lists just doubled.

Avoid Indifference

When you don't know what to say, please resist the urge to make dismissive comments like "People go through divorce every day, so you'll be fine." No two losses are the same. When it comes to divorce, the tearing apart of one into two again is dramatic and hurts. A lot.

Rather than brushing our pain aside, find ways to encourage. Point us to Scripture. Pray for us right there on the spot. Give us a hug. Such meaningful responses can change our outlook for the day.

It's okay to celebrate our good memories with us.

Reminisce with Us

Even with divorce, such loss needs to remember and celebrate the good. I have so many more good memories than bad from my thirteen-year marriage. It actually feels good to share cherished moments, because it helps reinforce the fact that our married years were not wasted.

Even today, when I share a tender or good moment from my marriage, it tends to make people uncomfortable. It's okay to celebrate our good memories with us. It helps alleviate the pain of the bad ones that followed.

Ask What We Need

We tend to give love in a way that we like to receive it. For instance, I like receiving gifts, so I give gifts to show love or appreciation. However, gifts may not be what that person needs. It's tempting to think we know what a hurting person needs without ever asking. Instead of filling a person's life and home with trinkets, ask what the person needs.

When friends asked what I needed both during and after my divorce, I said, "Send me Scripture passages of comfort, love, and peace." I have an entire shoebox filled with those wonderful passages that met my needs far better than a lasagna in the freezer.

Get Silly with Us

In the middle of a crisis, our focus naturally lasers in on meeting basic needs. But we also need to get out and play to be reminded that life can still be good and there's a great big world out there waiting for us to reengage.

Take us to the park, the movies, a live sports event, or a concert. We may not realize it at the time, but we need people who are willing to do something ridiculous and fun. It reminds us that we are still loved and included by you.

The Worst Advice I Ever Received

Whether founded on common sense or not, people love to offer unsolicited advice. The key word is "unsolicited"—you know, people you hardly know who believe they have the perfect solution on how to get through a divorce.

Just for grins, here are a few of the worst pieces of advice that I received before my divorce was even finalized:

- Throw a divorce shower to recoup what was lost in the split.

- "Reinvent yourself!" (What does that even mean?)

- Clean out the bank accounts and take him to the cleaners.

- Here, I have the phone number of a great guy I know. You've got to get back out there!

Enough said.

What Helps Most

I asked each person I interviewed for this book what helped them most during the time of their divorce. Some ideas are simple, and others are not, but all are insightful as to how we can best help those around us who are experiencing divorce:

- The cards and support from friends. —Carolyn

- My faith, talking to friends, time, counseling, music, prayer, support from family, exercise, new focus on the roles and opportunities God had placed in my life, and the talents He has given me. —Loren

- The greatest help to me during that time was my Christian network of friends along with deepened Bible study and prayer. Without those, I can't say how I would have made it through that tough time. —Nancy

- My pentecostal style of Christianity dealt mostly with Law, not grace, so that heaped a ton of guilt, shame, and condemnation on me. I became a Lutheran, which introduced me to grace. I learned that, yes, God hated divorce, but He did not hate divorced people. —Tim

- In my first divorce, it was people, family, and friends. My pastor was not one I connected with on any level. I kinda vacated religion for a while. No one from church even tried to talk to me or help me in any way. My pastor never once offered to speak to me. In my second divorce, DivorceCare® existed, and I attended a thirteen-week session. I had regained my faith by that time. The Bible and prayer. —Jeanette

- I was not a believer at the time. The faith in which I was raised as a child was not any sort of belief I had ownership in. I never really knew God then. My family became the lifeline and support I needed to get through the heart-wrenching pain of divorce. They were committed to helping me physically and emotionally. Without them, I would have fallen apart. —Linda K.

- Going back to church and realizing how much I had missed it. —Janetta

- What helped me most through both of my divorces was my faith. I was raised by a single mother, and her faith was everything to her. I knew that turning my focus to Christ was the only thing that could pull me out of my despair. I poured myself into Bible studies, church, good Christian people, and jamming out in my car to Mercy Me and Third Day! I was parentless during my second divorce, so I relied heavily on my extended family and friends. —Heather

- My relationship with God, my church, and my friends. Due to the suicide of my brother at the time, our family was split up. I had no support from my mom, only my brother I was living with at the time. —Lisa S.

- My friends, my counselor, and my church. All of them pointed me to the ultimate help—my God. —Kathleen

- The support of so many, including my family, friends, and church small group. My job also helped. I think that as a man, much of our identity is related to our work, and I love what I do. —Kole

- Reading Scripture, active worship attendance, keeping busy with various activities, being involved in LWML work, friends, sister, family support, and counseling. —Marguerite

- Scripture that I would put on my mirror. It was my daily bread. There were Scriptures for different times. —Linda P.

If you have a family member or friend going through divorce, I pray that these insights provide a helpful glimpse into how you can best offer help. Your prayers, love, and patience are always needed.

Allow People to Demonstrate Love

One aspect of the divorce process that I struggled with most was accepting help from others. Whether it was a neighbor offering to mow my lawn, a friend offering to treat me for dinner, or a family member offering to help reorganize my home, I often declined. I felt the need to prove that I was not defeated and could stand on my own two feet without help, thank you very much.

You may have a different personality, but I viewed it as a weakness to admit that I needed help. I learned quickly that my mind-set stemmed 100 percent from pride. Pride is a nasty tool in the enemy's arsenal, because even though it seemed I was standing on my own two feet, the truth was that I needed to be reminded of how much I was loved by God through other people's acts of kindness.

After I started to turn down a dear friend's invitation to dinner for the third time, she interrupted me and said, "I wish you'd let me show how much I care about you and how awful I feel for what you've been through. It's just dinner. I'm not trying to rob you of any newfound independence." Her words stung, but they represented a vital truth that I needed to hear and understand. The wall I had erected around my heart against any further hurt was keeping love out as well.

One day at a time, I had to learn how to let people love me again. Not only did it make them feel useful and helpful, but it softened my heart to realize that kindness and love still existed. If you are experiencing the same struggle, I encourage you to let people demonstrate love to you.

It does wonders for your soul.

10: Pausing to Breathe, Pray, and Reflect

The people who love us most seek to offer the best advice they know in order to help us navigate through divorce. However, nothing trumps discerning and following God's wisdom for our journey.

Through the following exercises, cling with confidence to this hope-filled truth: though your feelings come and go, God's love for you does not. Take your time walking through the following Bible passages, questions, prayer time, and journaling time before moving to the next chapter.

SCRIPTURE TO READ, MEDITATE ON, AND MEMORIZE

Whoever is wise, let him attend to these things; let them consider the steadfast love of the Lord. (Psalm 107:43)

Look carefully then how you walk, not as unwise but as wise, making the best use of the time, because the days are evil. Therefore do not be foolish, but understand what the will of the Lord is. (Ephesians 5:15–17)

But the wisdom from above is first pure, then peaceable, gentle, open to reason, full of mercy and good fruits, impartial and sincere. (James 3:17)

Questions for Reflection

When I need advice, I seek out people who are able to speak wisely, either based on their experience or their profession. You need sound, biblical advice on how to walk through divorce. But the truth is that sometimes people you don't know well give advice out like candy, whether you ask for it or not. Take some time to ponder and answer these questions:

1. How do you usually respond to unsolicited, unhelpful advice?

2. Who in your circle of influence do you trust to offer sound, biblical, wise advice?

3. When family and friends ask what you need, do you tell them or brush them away?

4. If you find it hard to accept help from others, why is that?

Pause for Prayer

Regardless of advice you receive from people, you need the Lord's wisdom in order to make progress through this valley. Ask Him to still your heart and give you His insight as you pray.

A—Acknowledge God's sovereignty: Sometimes we follow the advice of others without involving God. God is still in control of everything, and He has your best interests at heart. Read Deuteronomy 10:14 aloud with confidence.

C—Confession: It is tempting to follow our own self-absorbed agenda as we work through divorce. And it's also easy to belittle someone's offer to help. Whatever you are struggling with today, confess it to God so that He can begin the healing process. Please pray aloud to God now.

T—Thanksgiving: It is hard to express thanks when each day is a struggle to survive. However, God still provides what we need, whether it's a loving family, supportive friends, or caring neighbors.

List three things you are thankful for, and thank God for them.

1.

2.

3.

S—**Supplication (requests):** God promises that when we pray, He faithfully hears us. Identify what you need from Him right now and ask Him in faith to provide it.

Exhaling on the Page

If you have not started our journaling process, begin TODAY. God will use your journaling as another way to work through your feelings and as a reminder of how much He loves you. You may not see the benefit today, but you will one day. Trust Him.

Here are some suggested questions to answer as you journal:

1. What happened today?

2. How do you feel?

3. What made you angry or made you grateful?

4. How did someone encourage you today or show kindness?

5. Where did you see God at work in your circumstances today?

You did it! Take a deep breath and exhale slowly. God is with you, dear one. He will NEVER leave you or forsake you. He will see you through each day and every circumstance.

11

Sleeping Single in a Double Bed: Managing Loneliness and Midnight Madness

Fear not, for I have redeemed you;
I have called you by name, you are Mine.
—Isaiah 43:1b

One of the most difficult aspects of divorce is the intense loneliness you experience—especially in the first year or so. As a bona fide snuggler, it was particularly difficult for me. In the beginning stages, loneliness may turn into anger and bitterness toward your ex-spouse and God. This stage is where you're most likely to throw the best pity parties. However, staying in this stage too long morphs into unhealthy behavior patterns, depression, and perhaps even emotional or sexual promiscuity. It's time to hit loneliness between its beady eyes.

Understanding Loneliness

Ironically, loneliness does not mean being alone. Loneliness may impact us most deeply when we are in a crowd of people. That's because loneliness is a heart issue.

God created us to know Him and be fully known by Him on an intimate basis. Crowds are superficial, not intimate. Even those who know us best still do not know or understand the deepest and most desperate desires of our heart.

This may sound strange, but I never felt lonely while I sat in court waiting to sign my divorce papers. Even though everyone in that room (aside from my attorney) was a complete stranger, they understood the heart issue. They, like no one else, understood through hard-earned, heartbreaking experience the mess that divorce creates in every area of your life.

Over time, I realized that most of the people in my life were uncomfortable with the reality of my situation—especially if they had been friends of both me and my ex-husband. Some would say, "So, I heard you and your husband are having difficulties." No, we are DIVORCING. That goes way beyond mere difficulties. It's a ripping and tearing, and no one understands who hasn't experienced the categorical damage. I had very short responses to those people because they did not connect with the heart issue.

My close friends helped me get past loneliness. They let me talk about the small, ordinary things from my married life—how I would smile when hearing my ex-husband singing in the shower, how he wore a hand towel on his head when he mowed the lawn, how he loved being a teacher, or how he snored so loudly that he could pull the paint off of any wall.

When I was around people I didn't know well, they couldn't ease the hurt of loneliness because they didn't want to talk about such simple but real things. And they certainly didn't want to hear such tender moments "after what he did." So, I felt lonely a lot of the time.

I also found it hard to enter into people's conversations about everyday things when my heart bled with rejection and hurt. Discussing the latest Crock-Pot recipe or new social media trend sometimes left me feeling like an alien from Mars. It felt wholly unrelatable. I wanted to talk about real issues, but let's face it, they're a party killer.

JESUS UNDERSTANDS LONELINESS

Although Jesus was God in the flesh, He experienced acute loneliness. In the hour of His greatest need, as He hung on the cross of our making, the disciples abandoned Him. Even God the Father turned His back on His only Son so that God's full wrath could be poured out on Jesus to be judged once and for all.

Jesus even taught His disciples about loneliness by talking about events that had not yet occurred:

> Behold, the hour is coming, indeed it has come, when you will be scattered, each to his own home, and will leave Me alone. Yet I am not alone, for the Father is with Me. I have said these things to you, that in Me you may have peace. In the world you will have tribulation. But take heart; I have overcome the world. (John 16:32–33)

Jesus' words provide the antidote to loneliness: His presence. Jesus is the friend who lays down His life for His friends (John 15:13–15), sticks closer than a brother (Proverbs 18:24), and who has promised never to leave us or forsake us but to be with us until the end of the age (Matthew 28:20).

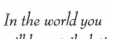

In the world you will have tribulation. But take heart; I have overcome the world.

We—all believers—have the presence of God in us through the power of the Holy Spirit. He lives *in* us and is our interpreter with God. In Christ, even though we may feel lonely, we are never alone.

LONELINESS IS NOT DEPRESSION

When people asked me how I felt during my time of divorce, I found it difficult to discern between loneliness and depression. After looking up definitions and reading a few helpful articles, they were easier to identify.

Loneliness doesn't feel good, but we are still able to function and carry on the tasks of everyday life. On the other hand, depression inhibits our ability to function. In other words, loneliness says, "I don't want to get up and go to work," while depression says, "I can't get up and go to work." Loneliness is more a state of mind, whereas depression translates physically. My lack of appetite for a period of time was due to mild depression, not loneliness.

Loneliness can certainly lead to depression if it continues unchecked over long periods of time. That's why those friends who stop by and insist on getting you out of the house even when you don't feel like it are truly lifesavers.

TWO DANGERS OF LONELINESS

Two common phrases come to mind when we feel the effects of loneliness: (1) *"I need to keep busy to keep my mind off of it,"* and (2) *"I need to find someone so I don't feel so lonely."* The first is common, the second is dangerous, and neither is the long-term solution.

1. Busyness

Divorce, by nature, makes you busy. You are busy reorganizing your home, your finances, your priorities, and your relationships. But at some point, the busyness will subside, and then what? Although nonstop activity can ease your stress and temporarily distract you from feeling overwhelmed, eventually you need to slow down and let the Lord heal your heart. Otherwise, you will career into the nearest wall at 200 miles per hour in full-blown burnout.

Loneliness is more a state of mind, whereas depression translates physically.

2. Replacement Love

It's normal to find yourself longing for someone to replace the love you lost. However, it's dangerous when you are hurting from divorce. Although I didn't long for someone to move right in, I certainly missed the touch, smell, and feel of a man. There are certainly days when that is still true.

Instead of giving in and letting neediness make me vulnerable, I shifted my focus. I pursued interests that I had put aside when I got married, such as my love for travel. I rekindled that interest with enthusiasm and have since traveled to many states and other countries. I also spent significant time investing in my relationship with the Lord through increased personal Bible study, worship, attending conferences and retreats, and listening to sermon/Bible study podcasts.

Once you center your life in Christ and gain confidence without relying on a spouse, you will be in a much better place spiritually and emotionally to embrace a new, healthy relationship when the Lord opens that door.

DECLARE WAR ON LONELINESS

You don't have to live with loneliness. Period. Although it will inevitably happen, you don't have to resign yourself to feeling like that until the Lord calls you home. We find the antidote in Scripture:

> The secret of the LORD is with those who fear Him, and
> He will show them His covenant. (Psalm 25:14; NKJV)

The "secret of the Lord" is what God calls His people. They are those Jesus-loving special friends that we discussed in chapter 8. The word *secret* doesn't mean a hush-hush utterance—it references our close, intimate friends who fear the Lord and with whom we share our joys, sadness, weaknesses, and strengths. They are the friends you let into your messy home while you're wearing sweats and no makeup. They are the precious few in whom we can confide real issues in real time.

We need those "secrets of the Lord" in our life to declare war on loneliness. Their love may look like chatting over a cup of coffee, but in the spiritual realm it's like an impenetrable shield of love surrounding you in faith against the enemy's darts of loneliness.

May we be that in their lives as well.

"MIDNIGHT MADNESS"

During my divorce, and even for months afterward, I had trouble keeping a normal sleeping schedule. It's not that I didn't want to sleep; there were just nights when I could not sleep due to the weight of sadness or anxiety sitting on my chest.

I cleaned house at all hours. Wrote and studied the Word at all hours. Made lists of all that needed to be done. Methodically went through every room, purging the unnecessary and organizing what remained. My home was extraordinarily organized, but it left me weary to the bone.

I realized that everything takes much longer to get done because there is no longer a divide-and-conquer mechanism for sharing household duties and errands. Loneliness affected me even when I was busy around the house because it was there that my ex-husband and I had jointly worked.

CONCLUSION

Loneliness and "midnight madness" can erect significant barriers that can prevent God's access to heal our heart and empower us to live life to the full.

The answer is short and simple: instead of giving in to midnight madness, lay claim to the nearness of God. *"I will never leave you nor forsake you"* (Hebrews 13:5).

PASTORAL WISDOM

The LORD God said, "It is not good that the man should be alone; I will make him a helper fit for him." (Genesis 2:18)

You thought you had found the one. Now that person is gone. There is a void in your life that you never thought you would have to fill. The intimacy, the special things only you knew about each other, the trust of that relationship—those are no longer things in your possession. How do you cope?

One night not too long ago, my wife and I were both arriving home late from our jobs. Without her knowledge, I ordered and picked up her favorite pizza, bought her some flowers, and made my way home. She was already there when I walked in. I was feeling rather proud of myself as I carried in her gifts, placed them on the counter in front of her, and asked, "Who's your hero?" Without missing a beat, she said, "Jesus!" While that deflated me for a moment, I realized the beauty of her answer. The reason I am so blessed by her is that she puts Him first. She knows that the value of her relationship with Him is the most important thing in her life.

I share this because when I am gone, she will still have that certainty. That will not preclude loneliness, but it will be the way she will cope with it. She has confidence in the promises of her Lord. You need to remember that Jesus is your hero too, and listen to His assurances:

And behold, I am with you always, to the end of the age. (Matthew 28:20)

I will not leave you as orphans; I will come to you. (John 14:18)

Be strong and courageous. Do not be frightened, and do not be dismayed, for the LORD your God is with you wherever you go. (Joshua 1:9)

This does not remove the loneliness, but it is how you cope and take the next steps in your life. When I counsel those dealing with loneliness after a death or a divorce, one of the steps I encourage them to take is to look for ways to serve others. Scripture encourages followers of Jesus to do that:

Have this mind among yourselves, which is yours in Christ Jesus, who, though He was in the form of God, did not count equality with God a thing to be grasped, but emptied Himself, by taking the form of a servant. (Philippians 2:5–7)

Look for ways to serve others.

For you were called to freedom, brothers. Only do not use your freedom as an opportunity for the flesh, but through love serve one another. *(Galatians 5:13)*

The King will answer them, "Truly, I say to you, as you did it to one of the least of these My brothers, you did it to Me." *(Matthew 25:40; NIV)*

Service to others helps fill the void. There is joy in service. That joy will not eliminate loneliness, but it can certainly temper it. And I know of more than one instance when someone offered himself or herself in service and ended up finding someone with whom they could share their life! That was not their goal or purpose in serving, but it was a happy consequence!

While doing acts of mercy and service may not provide you with that special someone, God can and will bless you in your service to others. And as you live for others, you are reminded that you are a part of something greater than yourself. You are part of the Holy Christian Church, the communion of saints:

You are a part of something greater than yourself.

For none of us lives to himself, and none of us dies to himself. For if we live, we live to the Lord, and if we die, we die to the Lord. So then, whether we live or die, we are the Lord's. *(Romans 14:7–8)*

Remember that Jesus is your hero. You belong to Him.

Counselor's Corner

Loneliness is inevitable. I'm sorry, but it's true. Go ahead and throw the pillow across the room. Loneliness is another part of healing that requires a lot of time and patience on your part. Remember, you are going to have to feel it before God can heal it.

God has created us as relational humans. He designed us that way because He wants to be in a relationship with us. Thus, it's normal to want earthly relationships as well. When earthly relationships break down and are lost, we grieve them at some level. Maybe you experienced relief in the beginning, but just know that at some point, loneliness will rear its head. You are better off working through it instead of ignoring it or substituting for it.

I have seen too many people rush out and start dating quickly after separation or before finalizing their divorce. That is playing with fire. Again, if you find yourself in that situation, ask yourself, "What is my motivation?" Make that question a life mantra, even long after healing from divorce! If your motivation is to escape _____ (fill in the blank) or "I'll show him" or "I'll make her feel the same," then you have a serious red flag.

To help ward off loneliness, take a look at the support system around you. Do you have one? Who is in it? Are they healthy, encouraging people? Or are they people who like to gossip, bash, and criticize? Do they push you to do the right, healthy thing? to be a better person? You may need to take an inventory of who's in your life and whether they are helping or hindering your healing in a godly way.

Support comes in many different forms. Sometimes we see it, and sometimes we don't. Sometimes we want it and sometimes we don't. Remember that in a crisis, we often can't objectively see what we need. We have to trust godly people to speak to us and encourage us toward what we need.

You may realize that you don't have a support system or that it's not a healthy one. Adjustments need to be made. When we battle loneliness, we eventually seek supportive relationships. When our emotions are at the helm, it's easy to look in the wrong places. That's when we can get into a new relationship prematurely (not recognizing warning signs of unhealthiness) or look for companionship in the wrong places (like the Internet), both of which are extremely dangerous.

Be careful and look for relationships and support people in healthy places like a church group, small group, healthy family members, or old friends of the same sex with whom you can reconnect. Healthy support groups like DivorceCare® can be helpful, but remember that your class is filled with people who are also healing, so make sure the relationships stay positive and God-focused instead of negative or a "quick romance"-focused.

The initial difficulty of being home alone and midnight madness are common. Give yourself a break and acknowledge that your world is topsy-turvy right now. It will settle down, but it may take a while. Make your alone time restorative, as Donna did; she rediscovered old hobbies and interests and pursued them. She rediscovered parts of herself that she had shelved. What about you? What things did you love and put aside for whatever reason? What interests has God given you that you never really pursued? Now is the time to discover those together with Him.

Give yourself a break and acknowledge that your world is topsy-turvy right now.

As Donna admitted, sleep can be difficult at first. This is a time to use the deep breathing and progressive muscle relaxation techniques we discussed in chapter 3. You can also journal before bed to get your thoughts and emotions out before you try to fall asleep. Keep your journal on your bedside stand so if you wake with your mind going, you can jot it down and roll over, knowing you gave it attention. Play soft music or a noise machine if you need some noise to distract your brain.

When you are relaxing for sleep, do NOT use electronics as a means to distract yourself. Here's why:

1. It's easy to get distracted and then stay awake longer than you intended.

2. It opens the doorway for Satan to tempt you into unhealthy places because you are tired and alone and your guard is down. Remember, Satan does his best work in the dark—literally!

3. Studies show that the backlight of electronics interrupts brain patterns and waves and actually harms your ability to rest and fall asleep.

If you are struggling to sleep over a longer period of time, you can try one of the natural sleep aid products on the market, or you can talk to your doctor about a temporary sleep aid to help for the short term.

Finally, watch your thoughts. When you are tired, alone, and lonely, it's easy for your thoughts to turn irrational, which only exacerbates your emotions. Revisit my discussion in chapter 7 about Cognitive Behavioral Therapy. Make sure your thoughts are rational, healthy, and based on truth. It will help you feel better and, I hope, help you sleep better too.

11: Pausing to Breathe, Pray, and Reflect

Loneliness and midnight madness can be a struggle, but no struggle is beyond God's strength to defeat victoriously. Take your time walking through the following Bible passages, questions, prayer time, and journaling time before moving to the next chapter.

Scripture to Read, Meditate on, and Memorize

The Lord your God is with you, the Mighty Warrior who saves. He will take great delight in you; in His love He will no longer rebuke you, but will rejoice over you with singing. (Zephaniah 3:17; NIV)

Fear not, for I am with you; be not dismayed, for I am your God; I will strengthen you, I will help you, I will uphold you with My righteous right hand. (Isaiah 41:10)

He heals the brokenhearted and binds up their wounds. (Psalm 147:3)

Questions for Reflection

If you are battling loneliness or midnight madness, take a moment to consider these questions. The answers may lend valuable insight:

1. Do you have people to talk to when you are feeling lonely? If so, when was the last time you talked with them?

2. What are some of the things you do to shake off loneliness?

3. To determine what pursuits may interest you, what do you love to do most that you would still do if no one paid you to do it?

Pause for Prayer

It takes time to adjust to your new life. Many changes and unfamiliar routines can wreak havoc on our mind, body, and soul. Exhale now and be still before the Lord. Let's pray:

A—Acknowledge God's sovereignty: With all the changes in your life right now, it helps to acknowledge that God is still in control of everything. Even your situation. Read Psalm 115:3 aloud with confidence.

C—Confession: Working through periods of loneliness and midnight madness can be exhausting. Take this time to confess to God what you are struggling with most; narrow it down and get specific. He already knows each circumstance, but verbally expressing those feelings ejects them from your heart, mind, and soul so that He can begin the healing process. Please pray aloud to God now.

T—Thanksgiving: It is hard to express thanks when you feel lonely. Yet even in the midst of it, God has blessed you with people and things for which you owe Him thanks. List three things you are thankful for right now, and thank God for them.

1.

2.

3.

S—Supplication (requests): God promises that when we pray, He faithfully hears us. Identify what you need from Him right now, and ask Him in faith to provide it.

Exhaling on the Page

As you know by now, God uses journaling as another way to release pent-up feelings and allow His Holy Spirit to fill you with His peace that passes all understanding. You may not see the benefits of journaling today, but you will one day. Trust Him.

Here are some suggested questions to answer as you journal:

1. What happened today?

2. How do you feel?

3. What made you angry or made you grateful?

4. How did someone encourage you today or show kindness?

5. Where did you see God at work in your circumstances today?

You did it! Take a deep breath and sit back. God is with you, dear one. He will NEVER leave you or forsake you. He will see you through each day and every circumstance.

12

Practical Tips for Managing Your Home and Finances Alone

Pray like it all depends on God, but work like it all depends on you.

—Saint Augustine

Many women who experience divorce have not been part of the outside workforce for many years due to raising children. Not only are you faced with the pain and hurt of divorce, but you have to relearn business skills in order to survive at a time when you're not in the best state of mind to learn.

Since I never had children and have worked in corporate America since I was twenty years old, this was not a difficult transition.

I didn't get married until I was twenty-nine, so I spent many years taking care of my own home and finances. But it was still a challenge, after thirteen years of marriage, to learn how to budget and live on one salary again.

This chapter will walk you through very practical, biblical steps in managing your home and finances well, but there's one thing we have to learn first: contentment.

Let's take an outdoor stroll together.

LEARNING CONTENTMENT

There's one thing we have to learn first: contentment.

There are mushrooms in my backyard. A cluster function all their own. I didn't plant them, but I don't intend to do anything about removing them either. Next week, they'll be a distant memory anyway.

It's been more than six years, three books, countless Bible studies, and lots of travel since the day my ex-husband closed the door behind him and left this house forever. We had looked for a modest home a year after we got married. One that we could sustain on one income, should something happen economically. We chose this house in North Houston because it suited us and made for an easy commute between church and jobs. The house bustled with life as we unpacked boxes and furnished it to welcome visitors. On the first night, between the stacks of boxes, we told each other we would be here for a very, very long time. We were content. We planted roots. We invited Jesus in. We sowed seeds for our future.

Then, one rainy night, he closed the door behind him one last time and my life was uprooted; I didn't know if I would be able to keep our home. I never thought our plan of surviving on one income would become a reality. I didn't plan on putting down roots here alone, but this house wrapped its arms around me and became my safe haven from an uncertain future. There are memories in every corner of my home, many more good than bad. I remodeled the interior to reflect my personality, and the roots sank deeper. I budgeted, cut back, and pressed forward. No matter how fiercely the spiritual or emotional storms raged during that terrible season, this house was home.

Jesus has done a lot of ministry in my heart between these walls. I am content, because true contentment isn't about the place we inhabit; it's about recognizing that our Savior inhabits our days. When we grasp that truth, God turns our surviving into thriving, regardless of our circumstances.

I didn't dream for a bigger and better house. I dreamed for God to fill this one with joy, love, and laughter again. And He has.

As wonderful family gatherings, lunches with friends, ministry celebrations, and holidays filled it, I saw John 10:10 take on new meaning within the very walls of my home: *"I came that they may have life and have it abundantly."* An abundant life isn't about a bigger house. It's about our big God who turns a house into a home. So much life and love spills out of this house that the very walls have stretched to accommodate it. And with it, the roots of His grace have gone even deeper.

I look at the mushroom cluster again, get down on my knees in the flower bed, and pull weeds. It's amazing, the beauty God allows us to see when contentment reigns. The same soil produces flowers and weeds—it's what we allow to take root that makes all the difference. My unexpected life, in all its glorious disarray. Life and grace.

My home became my sanctuary. The world could storm and rage, but my home was my safe place—and God, my refuge. I know what the bottom of the barrel looks like, and I found Jesus there, waiting to lift me out.

This house holds memories old and new. A cluster function of uninvited mushrooms and a bed of beautifully planted roses. Just like life.

I stand and shake the dirt off my knees, exhale, and walk back inside—content.

MANAGING FINANCES

Being single again means that you're suddenly an expert in more things than you care to be. The burden of life's daily responsibilities falls squarely on your shoulders. Eventually, you realize that if you don't take care of details, they slip by, neglected.

You have to learn how to do taxes, car maintenance, lawn care, and basic house repairs. Some days you feel empowered, while other days you simply want to hire an Alice (like on *The Brady Bunch*) to deal with it.

It was much easier living on two incomes than one. I didn't have to watch every penny, and I knew "generally" how much should be in our joint checking account on a regular basis. However, being single again changed all that. Divorce was a rude awakening. One of the people I interviewed for this book put it like this:

> Seeing your entire married life reduced to a ledger was jarring to say the least. All the things you both put so much time and effort in to building divided down the middle, from retirement accounts to dishes. I remember telling a friend of mine that it was the best way to make you feel like the world's biggest failure. —Whitney

I have never excelled at budgeting money. What came in usually got spent. Well, I learned very fast that such a sloppy financial attitude would lead to homelessness if I wasn't careful. I needed an expert. I needed Dave Ramsey.

Now, this is not a commercial for Dave Ramsey. There are many solid, biblically based plans available for handling your finances. However, I had heard his name many times over the years and knew people who experienced financial success after going through his program, so I checked out his website. Although I could not afford the whole fancy package that contained DVDs and downloadable planners, I ordered his basic book and got to work.

There are many solid, biblically based plans available for handling your finances.

I learned how to set up an emergency fund, make a proper budget, and save for big-ticket items. Most of all, I learned to follow the biblical basis and experiential wisdom he taught. Through trial and error, here are the most helpful tips for managing your finances after divorce:

1. Give.

I felt very strongly that I needed to follow God's command and tithe my firstfruits to Him because Scripture instructs: *"Every tithe of the land, whether of the seed of the land or of the fruit of the trees, is the LORD's; it is holy to the LORD"* (Leviticus 27:30).

Consequently, the first "payment" out of each paycheck goes to God. Yes, it was tough in the beginning, but God never failed to meet my needs—often in ways I least expected. I discovered firsthand the truth of Matthew 6:21: *"For where your treasure is, there your heart will be also."*

2. Open your own checking and savings accounts.

If you had joint accounts while you were married, you need to open your own checking and savings accounts in your own name with sole access. If your paychecks are automatically deposited into your joint account, provide your employer with the new account information and transfer it as soon as possible. Be sure to close any joint bank and investment accounts.

3. Transfer utilities and services to your name.

Since I kept the house, I removed my ex-husband's name from the accounts for the phone, cable, electricity, water, gas, and so forth. A few of the entities required a credit check to reassign the account to a sole responsibility, but all were transferred without a hitch. I also contacted my car loan company to transfer my car to my name. When I paid it off, I received the title with only my name on it. When I decide to sell it, I can do so without issues.

4. Set a budget.

List all income and expenses, and then total both. If your expenses total more than your income, you will need to make some lifestyle adjustments. For example, my ex-husband and I had a housekeeper who cleaned our home every two weeks. My new budget wouldn't allow for that expense, so I had to let her go.

5. Assess your health benefits.

My ex-husband and I both had full-time jobs with benefits. However, the law firm where I work offered better benefits, so my ex-husband was on my insurance. After the divorce, his name was removed, which actually increased my paycheck due to the lower premiums. Health insurance is vital in today's expensive medical industry. Explore your options carefully.

6. Ascertain debts and assets.

My ex-husband and I both had cars that carried notes. I had to ensure that I could continue those car payments after the divorce. Fortunately, I had only one year of payments left, so I was able to eliminate that debt fairly quickly, which freed up capital to put toward my credit card debt. My car went from debt to asset.

Since I had to refinance my home after retaining it following the divorce, I will have house payments for many years to come. However, I have budgeted accordingly. I chose to pay my property taxes separately at the end of each year rather than escrow them into my home mortgage. I save and plan accordingly, and I benefit from a much lower house payment than when I was married.

7. Change your beneficiaries.

My ex-husband was listed as the beneficiary on my life insurance and health disability insurance. As soon as possible, change the beneficiary to a trusted family member or friend. Also, I asked a lawyer friend to revise my will, medical power of attorney, and durable power of attorney. I recommend that you do the same. That way, should something happen to you unexpectedly, your loved ones can take care of managing your financial and health decisions if you are unable to do so.

8. Educate yourself.

I didn't have a clear idea about what tools I would need to survive post-divorce, but I couldn't afford to make mistakes. Consequently, I sought out professionals and resources (like Dave Ramsey) in order to get it right the first time. Divorce is messy enough without having to go back and redo any changes that you may have made inaccurately. I found that people are very willing to help—especially if they know you and your circumstances.

Managing Your Home

After the divorce, I got a crash course in managing a home by myself. My husband usually did the yard work, so I needed to relearn ASAP how to mow and edge again. I had usually handled weeding, planting, and mulching the flower beds, so that part was easy. The hard part came with home maintenance.

1. Air conditioning and heating

My eldest nephew owns his own AC/heating business, and he is a whiz at it. I live in South Texas, so properly maintaining the AC is a matter of life and death. I set up regular checkups with my nephew's company to service the unit once each year. Maintenance is much less expensive than having to replace a whole unit for lack of basic care.

2. General "stuff"

For the first time in years, I actually climbed an outdoor ladder to clean out my gutters. I am terrified of heights, so I eventually hired someone to do this each spring and fall, when leaves are an issue. Clogged gutters can cause a number of water-damage issues to your home, not the least of which is the gutters detaching from your home altogether. Again, proper maintenance is key.

3. Homeowner's insurance and HOA dues

One of the first things I did after the divorce was combine my homeowner's and car insurances to benefit from the "dual account" discount. I carefully reviewed what each policy covered (and didn't) and planned accordingly. If you do not outright own your home or car, the note holders will require you to carry insurance to protect their investment.

Also, my subdivision assesses yearly homeowner's association dues. It covers general upkeep of the neighborhood. If you have an HOA, be sure to pay the dues in a timely manner, because failure to pay can result in a lien on your home or even foreclosure proceedings.

4. The car

My dad instilled good car maintenance practices in me and my sisters as soon as we were able to drive. Be sure to have your car's oil changed, fluid levels checked, and tire pressure gauged to ensure your car is running at optimum level. If your car runs out of oil and the engine throws a rod, replacing the engine will be extraordinarily expensive. Low tires can increase gas consumption and cause unnecessary tire wear at the least, and wrecks at the worst.

The bottom line is careful, diligent planning and maintenance. Helpful neighbors are also a huge benefit. Not only can they keep an eye on your house when you are away (and vice versa), but you can borrow home maintenance equipment (such as huge ladders, tree trimmers, or power washers) to save the expense of buying them yourself.

I did it. I know you can too!

12: Pausing to Breathe, Pray, and Reflect

Nothing can cause anxiety faster than feeling that your basic needs, such as a roof over your head and food to eat, are in jeopardy. But with prayer, diligence, and planning, you can succeed.

Take your time walking through the following Bible passages, questions, prayer time, and journaling time before moving to the next chapter.

SCRIPTURE TO READ, MEDITATE ON, AND MEMORIZE

Keep your life free from love of money, and be content with what you have, for [God] has said, "I will never leave you nor forsake you." (Hebrews 13:5)

Wealth gained hastily will dwindle, but whoever gathers little by little will increase it. (Proverbs 13:11)

No one can serve two masters, for either he will hate the one and love the other, or he will be devoted to the one and despise the other. You cannot serve God and money. (Matthew 6:24)

QUESTIONS FOR REFLECTION

Navigating the throes of home and financial reorganization following divorce can be a daunting yet freeing process. Take a moment to ponder and answer these questions:

1. What are you worried about? Don't focus just on the divorce process in general or your ex-spouse, but narrow it down and get specific.

2. God promises to meet your every need at the moment you need it. What comfort does this give you?

3. What intimidates you most about handling your home and finances alone?

PAUSE FOR PRAYER

Regardless of your stress or worry, God promises that when we submit all things to Him, He will provide His peace that surpasses all understanding. Take this time to pour out your heart to the Lord:

A—Acknowledge God's sovereignty: Sometimes we dwell on our situation, forgetting amidst the pain and emotion that God is still in control of everything. Even your situation. Read Malachi 3:10 aloud with confidence.

C—Confession: Working through worry and feelings of being overwhelmed and emerging healed by God on the other side takes time and diligence. Take this time to confess your struggles to God; narrow it down and get specific. He already knows each circumstance, but verbally expressing those feelings ejects them from your heart, mind, and soul so that He can begin the healing process. Please pray aloud to God now.

T—Thanksgiving: It is hard to express thanks when stress and worry take center stage. Yet even in the midst of your circumstances, God has blessed you with people and things for which you owe Him thanks. List three things you are thankful for right now and thank God for them.

1.

2.

3.

S—Supplication (requests): God promises that when we pray, He faithfully hears us. Worry saps us of vital strength that we need to survive and thrive following divorce. Identify what you need from Him right now, and ask Him in faith to provide it.

EXHALING ON THE PAGE

If you have not started the journaling process, begin TODAY. God will use your journaling as another way to release toxic feelings and show how He is pouring His love into you. You may not see the benefit today, but you will one day. Trust Him.

Here are some suggested questions to answer as you journal:

1. What happened today?

2. How do you feel?

3. What made you angry or made you grateful?

4. How did someone encourage you today or show kindness?

5. Where did you see God at work in your circumstances today?

You did it! Take a deep breath and exhale slowly. God is with you, dear one. He will NEVER leave you or forsake you. He will see you through each day and every circumstance.

13

Handling Holidays, Wedding Photos, and Your Wedding Ring

The secret of change is to focus all of your energy not on fighting the old, but on building the new.

—Socrates

Two years ago, a beautiful wedding invitation arrived in a heavy, chocolate-colored parchment envelope boasting a feather closure. It announced a special evening to rejoice with two dear friends whom God brought together. Each had lost their first spouse to illness, so they joyfully embraced this newfound love they shared, with God at the center. It was time to celebrate, complete with a special evening of glittery fun!

Excitement pounded in my chest, because somewhere deep inside, Cinderella thrives. You know, that little girl who desires to don a beautiful gown, attend the ball, and dance with a handsome prince. Walking into my closet, I made a beeline to the back where I keep my special-occasion dresses. I considered each outfit, slowly making my way down the rack, moving items aside as I explored.

That's when I saw it. *That box on the floor.* I had almost forgotten it was there. Taped shut. Dusty. I didn't want to open it. It hadn't been opened since I packed it during my divorce. But it was time. Slowly picking it up, I carried the box to the bed. Beneath the dust and duct tape rested snapshots of a life that I had thought would last until God called me home.

I took out my wedding photos and began unpacking the journey down memory lane. Seeing our youthful faces, gazing upon Dad's happy face in that time before cancer took his life, remembering the hope on that beautiful, crisp December day, knowing how it ended, I looked up and whispered, *"God, would I have still said yes?"*

After my marriage abruptly ended, a friend told me that she thought it was a complete waste of time that my ex-husband and I had gotten married—that God should have spared me the heartbreak of how it ended by never allowing it to begin. And therein lies the answer. God *did* allow it.

You see, I didn't know God before He brought my ex-husband into my life. Oh sure, I knew about God, but I didn't *know* Him. I had no clue who Jesus was and I did not understand God's amazing grace. God used my ex-husband to guide me into that saving relationship with Jesus Christ. My ex-husband introduced me to my home church, where I still love serving today. My church is one of the greatest blessings God has provided—rich in meaningful friendships, ministry, and Christ-centered purpose.

As I slowly made my way through that box, I removed the pictures from their frames and once again felt sadness over the loss of that relationship. *Yet no tears came.* Those had been shed and caught by God a long time ago. It provided a vivid reminder of His healing work in my heart, soul, and mind.

SIFTING THROUGH MEMORIES

Divorce damages many things, but one of the greatest casualties is the holidays—especially when children are involved. My marriage blew up at Christmastime, my favorite time of year. Holiday casualties are often more hurtful because they taint precious memories. All of a sudden, holidays are jarring instead of joyful.

Then there are your wedding photos. They captured a very happy time in your life, as well as images of loved ones who may not be with you any longer, such as parents or grandparents.

And what about your wedding ring? What do you do with something that symbolized a covenant now broken? In this chapter, you will learn how to create new memories and traditions, how to properly preserve old ones, and a unique suggestion for what you can do with your wedding ring.

You will learn how to create new memories and traditions.

HANDLING THE HOLIDAYS

There are no two ways around it: handling the holidays is hard—especially when children are involved. It's most difficult that first year, because those family traditions that you looked forward to will not be the same. But it comes down to determining the schedule that works for you and your ex-spouse and the kind of relationship you have.

1. Alternate the holidays.

When there are children involved, be sure to review your divorce decree to refresh your memory about what you and your ex-spouse agreed to. Some families choose an alternating holiday schedule, such as Dad has the kids for Thanksgiving this year and Christmas the next year, and then switch the following year.

The fallout of that arrangement is that you have to process your disappointment and your children's concerns about not spending every holiday together. Remember, simpler is better. The more complicated the arrangement, the more stress it creates.

2. Split the holidays.

This option means that the children get to see each parent on every holiday. However, it also creates added scheduling issues to an already-hectic day—trying to eat fast at the first parent's house before going to the second parent's house, for instance. If you and your ex-spouse still don't get along well, this option is probably not the best one.

3. Spend the holidays together.

Some parents may be at a point far enough out from their divorce that they can actually sit at the same table and have a family meal together. This option works only if the hurt feelings and negativity are checked at the door. Also, the family picture the kids create in their minds is confusing because the old family unit doesn't exist anymore.

Regardless of the option (or any variant thereof) you choose for your family, make sure you leave your boxing gloves in the closet. Holidays are no time to beat up on your ex-spouse. The post-divorce holidays are hard enough on your children without the additional sadness brought about by fighting parents.

Your Wedding Photos

While enjoying lunch with a friend at Cracker Barrel about a year after my divorce, two ladies at the table behind us were laughing so hard it seemed they could hardly breathe. Everyone around them was curious, and when the waitress went to fill their drinks, she asked what was so funny. One lady, who had apparently just gone through a bitter divorce, was talking about what to do with her wedding photos. Her friend had candidly replied, "Donate them to Cracker Barrel so they can decorate their walls with them in fifty years."

We all need friends who can make us laugh about the hard times, but the divorced lady was actually seeking advice. What *do* you do with your wedding photos?

As I looked at mine, I realized that a few friends in the photos had gone home to the Lord, including one of my bridesmaids. Also, my dad had passed away by then, and I certainly didn't want to throw away any photos that captured him. So what to do?

I saved mine in a plain envelope and tucked them away in my study. That day is part of my history, and it was one of the happiest days of my life. I don't want to tear those pictures in half or burn them. But I don't want to display them because they no longer represent my reality.

Some people burn the whole pile of them, while others cut their ex-spouse out of every one. But if you have children, they may want to see those photos someday—especially when it's time for them to marry. And your ex-spouse may want some of the photos in case they contain some of his or her loved ones who have gone home to the Lord.

Even though my ex-husband and I didn't have children, I'm keeping those photos tucked away with all of the rest of my photos. One day when my youngest niece gets married, I want her to see just how darling she was as my flower girl.

Your Wedding Ring

Following divorce, what are you supposed to do with the very thing that symbolizes a beautiful circle of married love until death do you part?

Each night during my marriage, I took off my wedding ring and put it on my nightstand so it wouldn't scratch my face as I slept. It's a habit.

When I woke up in Doug and Delo's guest room that morning after my marriage exploded, I looked over and saw my wedding ring on their nightstand.

I stared at it for a long time, remembering the first day I wore it. But somewhere deep down inside, I knew I would never wear my

What are you supposed to do with the very thing that symbolizes a beautiful circle of married love until death do you part?

wedding ring again. Before I left their home that morning, I thanked Doug and Delo for their wonderful hospitality and entrusted my wedding ring to them. I asked them to use it as a reminder to pray for me and my husband until I figured out what to do with it.

Four months later, after my divorce was final, Doug preached that life-changing sermon about forgiveness (discussed in chapter 2) that God used to help me realize that I had forgiven my ex-husband. God showed me that day what to do with my wedding ring. It became a "forgiven ring."

I retrieved it from Doug and Delo and took it to a local jeweler along with a picture of how I wanted them to redesign my ring. Here is a picture of my ring today:

Instead of discarding my wedding ring, I turned it into something that would remind me to forgive. I wear it on my right hand now. It not only represents forgiveness for my ex-husband, but it also reminds me to forgive every single person who hurts me. And it reminds me how much I have been forgiven by God. "Forgiven"

is inscribed inside the band, along with "Colossians 3:13" (not the whole verse, just the citation). In that passage, God doesn't merely suggest forgiveness, He commands it.

Over the past six years, my forgiven ring has opened doors to provide a powerful witness about God's love and forgiveness. When a store clerk or someone in the grocery line comments on how pretty my ring is, I simply say, *"Thank you. It used to be my wedding ring. After my divorce, I redesigned it into a cross to remind me to forgive others and to remember how much God has forgiven me."*

I cannot begin to tell you how many times complete strangers have poured out their own hurts afterward. Time and again, God has turned casual encounters into impromptu prayer sessions in the middle of stores, parking lots, and restaurants.

After each encounter, I thank God for faithfully bringing beauty out of ashes in a way that I never expected.

Conclusion

Knowing how it would end, I still would have said yes on my wedding day. By the grace of God, I'm a different person today. I cannot conceive of how my life would have unfolded if God had not intervened and called me toward Him in faith.

So I offer prayers of thanksgiving—not for how my marriage ended, but for the life-changing journey toward the cross that it began. Thanksgiving for the good times and the bad. For the lessons that only pain can teach. For the forgiveness that only God can work in us, then through us. And thanksgiving for the heart resurfacing and eternal life that only He can provide.

As it turns out, I *did* find my Prince. He is royalty personified, robed in splendor and majesty, and His holy, perfect love for me outshines any glittery frock in my closet.

On that day when I opened my box of wedding memories, I gathered the pictures into an envelope, tucked it away,

I still would have said yes on my wedding day.

and stacked empty frames in the empty box, ready to donate. As I steadily breathed in the soul-refreshing freedom of God's peace and healing, He reminded me of His redemptive words:

> He sent from on high, He took me; He drew me out of many waters. . . . He brought me out into a broad place; He rescued me, because He delighted in me. (Psalm 18:16, 19)

God promises to heal the brokenhearted.
When we trust Him to do it, **HE DOES.**

13: Pausing to Breathe, Pray, and Reflect

Holidays and wedding memories become tainted by divorce, but it doesn't have to stay that way. There are constructive ways to handle them in a healthy manner that help you and your children move forward.

Take your time walking through the following Bible passages, questions, prayer time, and journaling time before moving to the next chapter.

Scripture to Read, Meditate on, and Memorize

You have kept count of my tossings; put my tears in Your bottle. Are they not in Your book? (Psalm 56:8)

But the Helper, the Holy Spirit, whom the Father will send in My name, He will teach you all things and bring to your remembrance all that I have said to you. Peace I leave with you; My peace I give to you. Not as the world gives do I give to you. Let not your hearts be troubled, neither let them be afraid. (John 14:26–27)

Questions for Reflection

If you are having difficulty figuring out how to handle the holidays or your wedding memorabilia, these questions may lend valuable insight:

1. If you have children, how do you handle holiday time? How is it working?

2. What have you done with your wedding photos and wedding ring?

3. How can you best turn both of those proposed negative scenarios into positive ones?

PAUSE FOR PRAYER

It takes time to adjust to your new life. Many changes and unfamiliar routines can wreak havoc on our mind, body, and soul. Exhale now and be still before the Lord. Let's pray:

A—Acknowledge God's sovereignty: With all the changes in your life right now, it helps to acknowledge that God is still in control of everything. Even your situation. Read Isaiah 46:10 aloud with confidence.

C—Confession: Working through divorce and emerging healed by God on the other side takes time and diligence. Take this time to confess to God what you are struggling with most; narrow it down and get specific. He already knows each circumstance, but verbally expressing those feelings ejects them from your heart, mind, and soul so that He can begin the healing process. Please pray aloud to God now.

T—Thanksgiving: It is hard to express thanks when the future is uncertain. Yet even in the midst of your circumstances, God has blessed you with people and/or things for which you owe Him thanks. List three things you are thankful for right now, and thank God for them.

1.

2.

3.

S—Supplication (requests): God promises that when we pray, He faithfully hears us. Identify what you need from Him right now, and ask Him in faith to provide it.

Exhaling on the Page

As you know by now, God uses journaling as another way to release pent-up feelings and pave the way for Him to fill you with His peace that passes all understanding. You may not see the benefits of journaling today, but you will one day. Trust Him.

Here are some suggested questions to answer as you journal:

1. What happened today?

2. How do you feel?

3. What made you angry or made you grateful?

4. How did someone encourage you today or show kindness?

5. Where did you see God at work in your circumstances today?

You did it! Take a deep breath and sit back. God is with you, dear one. He will NEVER leave you or forsake you. He will see you through each day and every circumstance.

14

Save the Date: Guarding Your Heart and Sexual Integrity

I have learned in whatever situation I am to be content.
—Philippians 4:11

This issue is so critical that it could fill its own book. Today's society believes that the key to getting over a divorce is finding someone new. Friends and relatives may offer the "perfect person" and want to set you up immediately. But a new relationship is not the cure for filling the emptiness left after divorce. God must be allowed to fill that emptiness first.

Many people have not allowed God enough time to heal their heart and mind before dating again or beginning new relationships.

When young children are still at home, it adds a whole other level of care and forethought to the picture, because your home (and perhaps even your bed) could be a revolving door causing damage with each swing.

In this chapter, you will learn how to diligently invest the time and patience to allow God to heal your heart before you seek a new relationship. It also provides firsthand accounts and counsel from those who have dipped their toes into the dating water again, and advice as to how you might go about it when the time is right.

Dear Christian Single Person

During two events where I was invited to speak in 2014, I was given the opportunity to talk with young single women (late teens, early twenties) in small-group sessions about some of the challenges single Christians face as they look expectantly toward marriage.

The predominant question was how they could best live out their faith and daily lives as single Christians. Since I have lived "single again" for a good while, this topic really hit home, and I touched on several areas that I had been personally wrestling with and praying through.

I was not an active Christian the first time I was single. Let me tell you from firsthand experience: it makes ALL the difference in the world. Living a God-honoring life as a single Christian woman takes intentionality. The bottom line is that I need to act like I am already married. Let me explain.

> *Living a God-honoring life as a single Christian woman takes intentionality.*

As an unmarried woman, I am very careful not to spend significant time alone with married men. This is partly to guard against misconceptions, but it's also to guard against weaknesses. I'm not interested in opening the door for trouble. Having watched infidelity play out in my own marriage and other people's marriages, I am under no illusions that hearts are immune to physical attraction.

As an unmarried woman, I guard my speech around men. This is a hard one for me because I love to use humor to put people at ease. But teasing and sarcasm can communicate flirtation, and innuendo invites disaster. Social media and email add another layer of complexity to the problem.

As an unmarried woman, I think twice about what I wear around men. Looking nice is not a crime. Dressing to intentionally attract a man's attention to certain body parts is. I dress much more casually around my family and female friends. But when I know I will be in mixed company, I dress so that men will look me in the eye, not from neck to navel.

As an unmarried woman, I think twice about my body language toward men. This one is hard because I'm a Southern woman who loves to hug the stuffing out of people. However, I ensure there is daylight between me and a man I am sitting next to. I still hug, but never in a prolonged manner, to avoid implied intimacy. It's a "hug-and-release" policy (yes, I love to fish, so this is a fishing analogy).

As an unmarried woman, I guard my thoughts about men. If I find myself idealizing the appearance or admirable qualities of a male acquaintance (*especially* if he is married), I confess those thoughts to God and set them aside. If I find myself fantasizing about "what if" or "if only" scenarios, I ask God to shut down that dangerous thinking. I've also learned to "bounce my eyes" so that I am not disrespecting men with a neck-to-navel assessment that may invade my thoughts at night.

This list may seem fastidious, but it reflects the high regard in which I hold men, their marriages, and their personal boundaries.

My question for dating Christian singles is this: What will you give to this man or woman who is not your spouse? Don't cheapen yourself with the legalistic gymnastics like "How far is too far?" Ask instead, "What is my motive for the thoughts, words, and actions I am choosing in my interactions?"

If you can answer that question without shame, you are more likely to stay on safe ground and attract someone you want to keep.

UNLEARNING MISTRUST

Loss of trust is a casualty of war—whether through betrayal, abuse, or otherwise. However, since God can heal all wounds, there is hope! Mistrust is learned, and you can unlearn it.

DATING . . . AGAIN

When I got married, I thought my days of dating were behind me for good. Can I get an amen? Let's face it, dating at forty-eight years old looks vastly different than it does at twenty-one. Social media is the new norm, and old-fashioned courtship is so rare that it sometimes makes the evening news.

Even now, six years following my divorce, I have not stepped back into the dating world. I know, right? Sure, I could say that I've been busy. I could say that I need to focus on writing and teaching through the ministry God has given me. I could say that God has not sent the right man into my life. Even though they are true, those reasons are superficial at best.

It took many years for God to heal my heart. Am I ready to throw it out into the world again? Suffice it to say that I am a tad hesitant. Actually, most days, dating never crosses my mind as I live out my day-to-day life following God's calling.

But the truth is that I *have* started thinking about it lately. I believe it's a positive sign that perhaps I am finally ready to jump back in. But what does that even look like today? Before taking the plunge, there are a few important things to keep in mind:

1. God loves you as you are.

No one else on earth can complete us because we are complete in Christ. God never ceases to extend His love, forgiveness, and grace to all who seek Him through faith. You don't have to become someone else's idea of a perfect mate. God made you unique, so don't try to be someone you aren't.

2. Embrace the possibility.

Trust is the very fabric of human relationships. You can't enter into a new relationship if you still harbor feelings that no one is worthy of your trust. Projecting the past onto a new relationship is not fair to either of you, and it provides a recipe for certain failure.

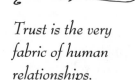

Trust is the very fabric of human relationships.

3. Be observant.

Watching how people interact with others provides excellent clues about their character. How do they treat other people? How do they talk with others? Do they gossip or share other people's secrets? Although people can put on an excellent show in public, their behavior often deteriorates in private. Do they express unkind words and actions in private before they catch themselves?

Start any relationship—romance or friendship—by sharing small things and seeing what happens. The breach of even a small confidence presents a huge red flag. Trustworthiness with little things generally means trustworthiness with big things.

OUR FOCUS POINTS

It's natural when we turn our mind toward dating to begin thinking about what we would or would not like in a person or relationship. But have we made such lists about ourselves? In other words, before beginning to date seriously, there are some key points that we need to take into consideration that have little to do with potential dating prospects:

1. Become the person that you are looking for. I have a mental list of attributes that I believe to be essential in that special someone. But do I possess those as well? Since I want him to love God, be patient and kind, and display all the other attributes listed in 1 Corinthians 13, I need to ensure that I am those things also. Time for some self-examination.

2. Say no to the physical and yes to the relationship. In his teaching series *The New Rules for Love, Sex, and Dating*, which I highly recommend watching, Andy Stanley said it perfectly: *"If you fish with your body, you're going to catch body snatchers every time."* Good point. Build a relationship first. Save the body for marriage.

3. Take notice of who God has already put in your life. I want to meet a like-minded man who loves God and embraces the same values, and whose life is moving in a similar direction as mine is. He may already be in my circle of friends. So that means that I'll continue volunteering at church, not head to the local dive. I'll continue working on my writing projects at the community library or coffee shop. I'll follow my passion for travel and continue digging in God's amazing Word with other women. I'll shop at the local farmers market, take in the theater and the arts, and embrace fun outings with friends. And I'll keep looking up to God for guidance.

Some churches offer adult singles groups, which may be an option for you. Also, online dating seems to be a popular choice nowadays. In researching for this chapter, I signed up for two online dating sites: one Christian and one secular. I truly wanted to grasp what online dating entailed so that I could offer helpful insight.

What I discovered on both sites is that online dating is 100 percent not for me. I couldn't even finish the ten-day trial period for either site due to the volume of alarming, suggestive propositions I received. However, I know friends who highly recommend online dating. The only way to discover whether or not it is a viable option for you is to try it out.

How Does It Feel to Date Again?

Since I have yet to dip my toes into the dating pool since my divorce, I asked the people I interviewed for this book (both male and female) whether dating after their divorce felt odd. Their candid answers contributed valuable insight:

- When *isn't* dating odd? Ha-ha! But yes, for someone who has been married, dating feels akin to cheating at first. That said, I believe that allowing a period of time as I did to mourn my marriage helped overcome those uncomfortable feelings. —Linda K.

- Because of my divorce, I see my future as a single woman. If God intends for me to be married again, He has not shown it to me yet. I am okay with being single, although there are times when I would love to have some companionship. —Nancy

- Ask twenty people what a date means or looks like and you will get twenty different answers with different etiquette and expectations. You have to be yourself and give the other person the same benefit of the doubt. —Anonymous

- Dating was not odd at all. It was fun and exciting to be going out and experiencing new things. I felt much wiser than I did dating in my twenties. —Kole

- If a trusted friend sets you up on a blind date, go! Your friend knows you and holds your best interests at heart. You never know what may happen. Just be sure you meet at a public place so that you feel more at ease and safe. —Anonymous

- Dating was weird—especially [for] her family, knowing she was dating a divorced man. I had an overly cautious heart, which was not healthy or respectful. —Tim

- At first it's like going back to high school. Feels kinda weird. —Jeanette

- A date should be brave. Like any adventure, a proper date takes courage and the risk of personal investment. We are to treat one another with a Christlike level of love, respect, and sacrifice. Our passion for life and honorable treatment of one another should tell the person you are spending time with that they are worthy of the risk. —Anonymous

- I wonder if I will be single forever. I think it might be best for my children right now, but I hope it might change some-day. —Tina Y.

- The few times that I have thought about [dating], it seems so foreign and odd. I am sure there are underlying trust issues,

but I usually tell myself to focus on my kids, work, and life.
—Loren

- I fluctuate between just wanting to have a good time and the feelings of inadequacy. —Cheryl

- Wait to get into a relationship too quickly after divorce. Some say you get over heartbreak by finding a new relationship, and I learned otherwise. You must heal after ripping "one" into "two." —Doris

- Few things are more intoxicating and memorable than a truly great date. Like art, a date is the pursuit of something meaningful. —Anonymous

- It is very hard to remain faithful to what we know God expects of us as a single when the world is pushing other behaviors. —Carolyn

- I had to work on being myself first. —Tiffany

- Stop evaluating whether or not the person is marriage material before the first date. If you take notice, if you are intrigued or interested, make a date! It's foolish to think that the way someone acts in a group of friends is the same way they'll act one-on-one in a friendship. Everyone is different when you get them one-on-one. —Anonymous

When I reread the journal that I kept during my divorce, I found this entry that I wrote during a trip to the Holy Land three months after my divorce was final:

> There is a large part of me that has accepted the fact that I may be single for the rest of my life. I find that I am at peace with that. God dropped my ex-husband in the middle of my life when I wasn't looking for anyone, and huge blessing came out of it by coming to know Jesus. Also indescribable hurt. I trust You, Lord, for any future relationship—it needs to be Your plan, not mine.

Interestingly enough, I find that I would change little in that entry now, six years later. In trusting God, I rest securely in His peace. I am open to whatever future He has in store for me—whether single or remarried. I trust Him completely to guide me each step of the way.

Remarriage is not how God mends our hurts. God works grace and healing in us through His Word and walking with those who love us.

CONCLUSION

Scripture describes the Church as a bride awaiting a husband-who-is-to-come. That bride is admonished to keep herself pure, to live as though she were already the wife of her bridegroom. To me, this is a powerful image of what being a Christian single woman (and man) should look like.

Whether a husband is ever in your future, a Husband is certainly in your future. Honor Him now in eager expectation of meeting Him soon.

Think like a married person whether you ever become one again or not, guarding your heart from sin, and opening it to God's incredible plans.

PASTORAL WISDOM

The sexual mores and morals of our society are more closely aligned with Sodom and Gomorrah than with God's will. It is hard enough for those who have never been married to keep themselves pure. What about those who have been in a sexual relationship within marriage but now find themselves single again? Society tells you, "Do what you want. There will be no consequences. It isn't a big deal. There is no problem."

God works grace and healing in us through His Word.

But it is a problem. Sexual immorality is condemned in Scripture dozens of times.

It has always been a problem for fallen, sinful mankind. It is still a problem for us today.

> Let marriage be held in honor among all, and let the marriage bed be undefiled, for God will judge the sexually immoral and adulterous. (Hebrews 13:4)

You shall not commit adultery. Keep yourself sexually pure. Don't have sex with anyone other than your spouse. These are not some antiquated customs, but God's will for His people, standards He established for the good of His children. Your loving Lord gave you boundaries for your own good. We call them Commandments. I like to think of them as fences: as long as we stay inside the fence, our lives go better.

But sometimes we think it wouldn't hurt anything to jump the fence and do something we were told not to do. That is where the problems and heartaches begin. In a moment of weakness, someone says, "What the heck!" or "Where's the harm?" All too soon they find themselves wracked with guilt and filled with remorse. While the death of Jesus covered that sin too, it is much better not to put yourself through it.

Let's be clear on something. Sex is not bad. The way people have abused God's gift of sex is the problem. Sex inside the loving, committed relationship of a Christian marriage is a beautiful thing. It is what God intended when He made us sexual beings. But outside of that relationship, it will not bring happiness or contentment.

Concentrate on doing things God's way. He is with you. He will help you. He wants the best for you:

> Submit yourselves therefore to God. Resist the devil, and he will flee from you. (James 4:7)

This is not simply a physical issue. It is an issue of the heart and the soul:

> For this is the will of God, your sanctification: that you abstain from sexual immorality; that each one of you know how to control his own body in holiness and honor, not in the passion of lust like

the Gentiles who do not know God. . . . For God has not called us for impurity, but in holiness. (1 Thessalonians 4:3–5, 7)

Flee from sexual immorality. Every other sin a person commits is outside the body, but the sexually immoral person sins against his own body. Or do you not know that your body is a temple of the Holy Spirit within you, whom you have from God? You are not your own, for you were bought with a price. So glorify God in your body. (1 Corinthians 6:18–20)

That is what helps me: remembering that God paid a tremendous price for me, the death of His Son, so that I could be His and live under Him in His kingdom. That is the motivation to conform yourself—your heart, your mind, and your body—to God's desire for human sexuality.

COUNSELOR'S CORNER

There is nothing like the feeling of being in love. It's amazing and intoxicating. It can bring so much joy, security, and peace when founded in God's plan. The temptation is to chase after what feels good now, in the moment, because you deserve it, right? Isn't that what the world and maybe even the people around you say? Let me warn you: if that is your focus, disaster awaits, and you can make an appointment for next week.

When we experience pain, we seek anything to stop it. We can easily become desperate for something to make the pain subside. We can be tempted to look in wrong areas for a quick anesthetic, which could be packaged as a new man or woman who might "not want anything serious, just fun." Such anesthetic could be tempting because even if you know you aren't ready for something serious, the physical can be met. You could

Concentrate on doing things God's way.

also be tempted into satisfying your sexual desires through pornography, sexting, and so forth. Be careful. That is not God's design for sexual intimacy, and you and your potential future marriage will be hurt even more in the long run!

During the time of separation and then after your divorce, focus on your healing—not just your pain, but the junk in your trunk. I know you probably want to say, "But I don't have any junk, Kristin; it was my *wife's* fault!" or "I'm fine! *He* is the one who has the issues!" I'm calling you out on that. It's not true, and the sooner you are willing to accept that we ALL have junk, the sooner you will heal.

In order to be in a healthy relationship that could lead to marriage and then the gift of sexual intimacy, you have to wrestle with your issues. No, you will never become perfect. However, you can at least gain insight into why you act, think, and say the things you do, and then you can adjust them as needed. God walks with you every step! He loves it when we gain insight into who we are—especially if we allow that insight to draw us closer to Him! Remember, if you don't feel it, God can't heal it!

When we experience pain, we seek anything to stop it.

With clients who are healing from a broken relationship, I often look at the client's priorities. We often have to take a hard, painful look at who or what occupies the top spots on our priority lists. Oftentimes it reveals that spouses reside in the top spot (honestly, a spot of idolatry), which places them even higher than God Himself. Is it the same for you? Did you at some point put your spouse out of order?

Looking at our junk is essential so we do not repeat patterns when we do get into another relationship. The foundation or starting point of that relationship cannot be physical.

After working on our junk, in order to ensure that a new relationship starts on the right foundation (other than physical gratification), I recommend making a list of the qualities you want in a partner:

- What good qualities did your ex have (yes, he or she did have a few, even if they got lost along the way) that you might want in a new spouse?

- What other qualities matter now that you have learned and matured, working on your junk and spending time wrestling with God over this?

- On your list, which are nonnegotiable?

May I STRONGLY suggest that the top quality is that they love the Lord more than you do! Keep that list close by, and when you start to get to know someone who interests you, check them against the list, ask your godly friends for their insights, and LISTEN.

If there are children involved, PLEASE read, ponder, and consider this seriously: If a physical relationship with someone happens too quickly (before marriage, which is very tempting as an adult who knows what sex feels like and the bond it creates), your ENTIRE family is at risk. Let me shine a light in a hard place. Who you bring into your home and thus your bed has access to your children! You are responsible for their safety above your physical needs. There are countless stories of children who have been abused by a parent's boyfriend (mostly) or girlfriend. They have access to your children not only physically but also emotionally in order to lay groundwork for future abuse.

When a new relationship is based on God and you wait on the physical side until marriage, it is much more likely that you will truly know the person and his or her intentions. Hopefully their true character has surfaced, and you will have noticed and/or listened to red flags voiced in your spirit, by others, and by your kids. If the physical is all they want, they will leave if they have to wait. Again, it's worth waiting—not only for you but also for your kids' protection and to support what you are teaching them.

I have a friend who, after her divorce, was talking with her college-age son about dating and a physical relationship. She told me that they made a promise together that since they were both in the dating world, she had to wait just like she had always taught him. Together they were going to wait for their future marriages. You can do it also, with God's help and foundation.

14: Pausing to Breathe, Pray, and Reflect

Entering the dating world following divorce is not a venture to be undertaken lightly. It takes courage, strength, prayer, and ensuring you enter it having allowed God to heal past hurts.

Through the following exercises, cling with confidence to this hope-filled truth: though your feelings come and go, God's love for you does not. Take your time walking through the following Bible passages, questions, prayer time, and journaling time before moving to the next chapter.

SCRIPTURE TO READ, MEDITATE ON, AND MEMORIZE

But seek first the kingdom of God and His righteousness, and all these things will be added to you. (Matthew 6:33)

*Do not be deceived: "Bad company ruins good morals."
(1 Corinthians 15:33)*

Love is patient and kind; love does not envy or boast; it is not arrogant or rude. It does not insist on its own way; it is not irritable or resentful; it does not rejoice at wrongdoing, but rejoices with the truth. Love bears all things, believes all things, hopes all things, endures all things. (1 Corinthians 13:4–7)

QUESTIONS FOR REFLECTION

Although there is probably an endless list of questions that could be asked about dating, we'll tackle only a few of the most important ones here.

1. Have you begun dating again? If so, what have you discovered about yourself? about others?

2. If you have not starting dating again, what are your reasons?

3. What do you look forward to most in dating? What do you look forward to least?

PAUSE FOR PRAYER

Following the pain and trauma of divorce, dating again can be very scary. But God walks with you and me every moment of every day, offering guidance and His loving presence. So let's pray:

A—Acknowledge God's sovereignty: God is still in control of everything—including any future relationships. Read 2 Chronicles 20:6 aloud with confidence.

C—Confession: Fear, uncertainty, and even recklessness can come into play when we think about dating following divorce. He already knows what is in your heart and mind, but verbally expressing those feelings puts them out on the table, so to speak, so that He can begin the healing process. Please pray aloud to God now.

T—Thanksgiving: God has brought you (and will bring you) through one of the hardest seasons of life anyone can face. During the process, and now afterward, He blessed you with many gifts and will continue to do so. List three things you are thankful for today, and thank God for them.

1.

2.

3.

S—Supplication (requests): God promises that when we pray, He faithfully hears us. Identify what you need from Him right now, and ask Him in faith to provide it.

EXHALING ON THE PAGE

Whether or not you discuss the topic of dating in your journal today, there are still vital questions that help us process and sift through each day's events.

Here are some suggested questions to answer as you journal:

1. What happened today?

2. How do you feel?

3. What made you angry or made you grateful?

4. How did someone encourage you today or show kindness?

5. Where did you see God at work in your circumstances today?

You did it! Take a deep breath and exhale slowly. God is with you, dear one. He will NEVER leave you or forsake you. He will see you through each day and every circumstance.

15

When the Vow Breaks: Learning to Trust Again

We're never so vulnerable than when we trust someone—but paradoxically, if we cannot trust, neither can we find love or joy.

—Walter Anderson

She looks straight at me, straight over our half-eaten lunch as my lemonade glass forms condensation circles on the table. She peers intently, as if she's trying to read straight into my soul, then straight-up asks the question so many have asked: *"So, is there someone special in your life yet?"*

My mouth goes dry and I focus on swallowing before choking. The bird in the tree becomes fascinating. *Please not now, Lord. Not today. I'm feeling fragile, and I don't know why.*

Smiling, she looks hopeful, like I'm about to launch into an epic romantic tale. My eyes latch on to the table centerpiece and I sip my lemonade, willing my voice to remain steady as I ascertain how best to answer.

She loves me and holds my best interests at heart, but how do I articulate that the heart knows no time? that the mind can play dirty tricks? that trusting someone again to that degree straight-up scares my freckles white?

It would have been different if my ex-husband and I had fought constantly. Or if I had been looking for a relationship upgrade. Or if we never had spent time together. But that's the heart of the issue: everything about my marriage had looked right.

I looked forward to our regular date nights. We shared similar life goals and dreams. We served God together in ministry. We never hit below the belt or called each other names during arguments. We loved puttering around the house together on Saturday mornings. We loved each other. It all looked right.

How do I tell her that years later, I'm still scared everything will look right on the outside again only to discover everything horribly wrong on the inside? How do I tell her that I don't think I could survive another heart-shredding betrayal?

Over the past few years, God has allowed me to discover this soul-freeing truth: there is unwavering peace today when an uncertain tomorrow is entrusted to an unchanging God.

There is unwavering peace today when an uncertain tomorrow is entrusted to an unchanging God.

God has opened doors to follow this amazing roller-coaster ministry ride, to write and teach and fully engage in what He has called me to do. I really love my life right now.

So I lay down my fork, look her straight in the eye, and say, *"I'm trusting God and His perfect timing. Yes, I get scared. Yes, I feel fragile. Some days, bravery feels alien. No, there's not anyone. Yet."*

The bottom line is that I trust God for my

daily bread, for His lamp to light my path, and for His grace to lead me home. It took divorce to fully get me to that place. I cannot imagine where I would be without God's great love demonstrated by Jesus' redemptive sacrifice.

That truth provides strength and orders the whole trust thing into proper perspective. In the dark valley of divorce, this passage became clear:

> Trust in the LORD with all your heart, and do not lean on your own understanding. In all your ways acknowledge Him, and He will make straight your paths. (Proverbs 3:5–6)

LEARNING TO TRUST AGAIN

Learning to trust again is one of the biggest challenges following divorce. Because you have been hurt, you are more likely to approach new relationships warily as a form of self-protection. When you experience broken trust, you suddenly doubt your judgment. However, trust is about much more than catching someone in a lie; it's about believing that he or she has your best interests at heart.

Learning to trust again is one of the biggest challenges following divorce.

One of the most dangerous obstacles I faced was avoiding transferring my lack of trust onto God. Over time, He showed me that it's impossible to move through any crisis successfully when I fail to trust Him. I had to remind myself daily that He has never broken a promise. Every single promise He made to us in Scripture He has fulfilled and faithfully continues to do so.

We have little difficulty believing in God, but perhaps we hesitate to fully trust Him when people break our trust. After losing so much of what we held dear, it is hard to let go of our own solutions and fully place ourselves in God's hands. But when we trust God and follow His guidance, He will heal our hearts and help us embrace our future.

WHAT THE DEVIL IS REALLY AFTER

We tend to think that the devil is after our happiness, spouse, children, or security. Well, he is. But those are merely distractions to the devil's ultimate goal: to steal your faith. Because without it, it's impossible to please God (Hebrews 11:6).

Paul, a pillar of faith, expressed nearly palpable relief in his final letter: *"I have fought the good fight, I have finished the race, I have kept the faith"* (2 Timothy 4:7).

In the end, we all reach the finish line of this life. As you struggle through divorce, pain, and fear along this journey, the question is, will you keep your faith? Now, that's not the same thing as keeping your salvation. Salvation is a gift from God and not something we can just give back. We receive it by grace through faith, and not by works (Ephesians 2:8).

Faith is our active belief that God is who He says He is and does what He says He will do. During difficult seasons, we may struggle to actively believe that God is good. Or faithful. Or even listens to us. That's when the enemy does his best work to knock the wind out of us. To kick us while we're down. To feed our doubts with fear. For me, that translates into targeting those I love most in this world.

In Hebrews 10:23, faith is translated as "hope": *"Let us hold fast the confession of our hope without wavering, for He who promised is faithful."* "Hope" means confidence, faith, reliance, trust, belief, and assurance—many of which are temporary casualties of divorce. Scripture clearly connects faith, hope, and trust:

During difficult seasons, we may struggle to actively believe that God is good.

Faith is the assurance of things hoped for. (Hebrews 11:1)

Through Him we have also obtained access by faith into this grace in which we stand, and we rejoice in hope of the glory of God. (Romans 5:2)

266

And in His name the Gentiles will hope. (Matthew 12:21)

Those who brush off trust issues do not realize the overarching impact of lost trust. It affects faith and dims hope—at least for a time. Shattered trust alters our beliefs about safety, security, love, and relationships. Consequently, it is vital to reestablish trust. Don't be afraid to ask for what you need—first in prayer, then with others. If you want to form a new relationship based on trust, speak up when something bothers you or you have a question. Searching for answers from God first is key.

SEARCHING TO TRUST AGAIN

In order to truly understand trust once again, I searched Scripture for every occurrence of *trust*. What I discovered is that faith and trust go hand in hand. In fact, the words or concepts of faith, trust, confidence, and belief are sometimes used interchangeably in Scripture:

Abram put *faith* in the Lord. He had *faith* in Yahweh's word.	Abram had *confidence* in the Lord. His *confidence* was in God alone.
Abram *trusted* the Lord. He knew Yahweh to be *trustworthy*.	Abram *believed* the Lord. He *believed* what Yahweh said.

Searching Scripture revealed that each time someone placed their faith and trust in the Lord, God faithfully guided their steps toward Him and a higher purpose. Sometimes the paths God led them down were uncomfortable and even painful, but the paths always led to Him, hope, and a stronger faith. Just look at Abram above (later Abraham). God called Abram out of a comfortable life to a strange land with many challenges, yet God made Abram's offspring more numerous than the stars in the sky.

I don't believe that God calls people out of their marriage covenant, but when we choose that path (or it is chosen for us), God still guides and lights our path toward Him in faith, not away in defeated darkness.

Throughout the Book of Psalms, trust often means to have confidence, to be bold and secure: Psalms 4:5; 9:10; 25:2; 31:14; 33:21. When the psalmists faced difficulties, oppression, or doubt, they met it with the faith to trust God at His word. Reading through the hymns of praise psalms (8, 18, 19, 104, 145, 147) helped refocus my thoughts when I doubted God's plan (which I certainly did on some of the hardest days). God used those psalms to put my mind back on Him instead of my doubts and fears.

For my trust issues, I inhaled and kept revisiting the songs of trust (Psalms 11, 16, 23, 27, 62, 63, 91, 121, 125, and 131). I cannot recommend highly enough that you take the time to read and reread those psalms often when trust issues surface.

God holds you in the palm of His hand, and nothing can snatch you from His iron grip of love.

The beautiful words that God gave the psalmists reaffirmed that I can always trust Him, wholeheartedly and without question.

If you are experiencing a crisis of faith due to trust issues, you can stand on the unwavering truth that God does not abandon you. Even when you struggle, He is with you. His Holy Spirit resides in every believer and acts as His interpreter in our lives, nudging and guiding us back toward Him. The same power that raised Christ from the grave and conquered death lives in you. God holds you in the palm of His hand, and nothing can snatch you from His iron grip of love.

You are never at the devil's mercy. You are at the extraordinary, life-giving mercy and sustaining grace of our Savior, Jesus Christ, which leads to eternal life free from suffering. So if you are experiencing a crisis of faith through your divorce, remember: *"He who is in you is greater than he who is in the world"* (1 John 4:4).

God's love does conquer all. He is our refuge and fortress, so stand firm in the strength of His might, wearing His armor into your daily battle. Because His love wins. Always.

LETTING EXPERIENCE TALK

Several of the people whom I interviewed for this book struggled with trust issues following their divorce. Trust can hit us on many fronts—physical, emotional, and spiritual. Perhaps you will find yourself in their experiences:

> I was scared to trust another man. I was scared to have sex with another man again. I didn't know what to expect or what he would expect from me. —Nicole

> As for relationships, I am very jaded, very untrusting, and very cautious. I want someone to spend time with—to go to a movie, a bike ride, or dinner—but to BE in a relationship? Not sure about that. —Cheryl

> It was very difficult for me to remarry. I was the one with "HELP ME" written on the bottom of my shoes. Trusting and depending on someone else again was the hardest. —Loretta

> The hardest part about remarrying was knowing if I could trust him! How do I know that he's not going to run around on me or beat me like my ex did? How do I know I can trust him? It was then I heard the Lord say to me: "I never asked you to trust him, I asked you to trust Me." That was all I needed to hear. —Jana

LAUGHTER: THE UNEXPECTED CASUALTY OF MISTRUST

Although divorce caused sadness in many ways, trust issues robbed me of genuine laughter for a time. You know, the belly-jiggling, snort-inducing laughter that makes us feel better—*that* laughter.

My dad had a wonderful sense of humor that, thankfully, he passed down to his four daughters. Laughter rang through our home regularly, and it later continued in my own home. Belly laughs usually happened daily without effort. (Seeing the humor in most circumstances can be both a blessing and a curse.)

269

I didn't realize laughter was an unwilling casualty of my trust issues until it dawned on me one day that it had been months since I'd had a good ol' belly laugh. Afterward, I commented that it had been a long time. It was such an odd sensation to rack my brain and try to remember the last time I had genuinely laughed. And it made me profoundly sad.

Eventually, I traced the cause back to mistrust. I don't know about you, but I do not often laugh in a carefree manner around people with whom I am not free to be myself. In withholding trust, I was pulling back my heart from relationships, effectively erasing any carefree feelings.

When you lock your heart away, laughter becomes its cellmate.

It took a long time to talk through my trust issues with Kristin, my counselor, before carefree laughter eventually returned. I was sad that laughter had almost vanished because I couldn't laugh when I was sad. It was a vicious cycle that only prayer and intentionality conquered. Relentlessly, I asked God to restore my trust in those I held dear, and God faithfully answered that prayer with gusto.

I still face trust issues from time to time—especially when it comes to someone whom I perceive to be romantically interested. Even now, I offer this simple prayer each day: *God, give me the wisdom and discernment to trust before my heart rusts.* That may sound silly, but I needed it to rhyme and be silly because it made me laugh. And genuine laughter represented a giant step back toward being open to trust again.

Practical Steps toward Trusting Again

If you're like me, you gravitate toward checklists. In order to get from point A to point B, I need practical steps. Over the past six years, my ability to trust others has slowly returned, thanks to these helpful steps:

1. Pray. Okay, for a Christian, that's a given, but I mean pray to specifically seek God's wisdom and discernment. Only God can repair our broken hearts and trust, so put it in His hands and keep moving forward. God desires to help you make wise decisions—especially in relationships.

2. Challenge mistrustful thoughts. When faced with feelings of mistrust, take a moment to ask yourself whether your lack of trust is due to the other person's actions, your own issues, or both. Do you have all the facts? Could it be a misunderstanding or an honest mistake? As you ask questions and learn the facts, move forward accordingly.

Only God can repair our broken hearts and trust, so put it in His hands and keep moving forward.

3. Trust your instincts. God gave us instincts for a reason. Whether you call it a funny feeling in the pit of your stomach or a check in your spirit, pay attention to red flags. Looking back to my engagement, there were several red flags that my ex-husband exhibited, but I dismissed or excused them all away. Be forthright with your feelings and ask for explanations.

4. Note your reactions. How we react to others deeply affects relationships. If you tend to overreact (like grabbing a verbal bazooka to swat a fly), gain awareness about how your reactions may have a destructive impact on your relationships. Take responsibility for your actions.

5. Listen and learn. Regardless of what you and I feel, we need to be open to listen before jumping to conclusions. Using words and a tone of voice consistently targeted to rebuild trust can make or break that relationship. Learning to trust again takes time, so be courageously persistent.

While trusting makes you vulnerable, choosing not to trust could mean missing out on the joy God desires to give you. God created us for relationships based on both trust and forgiveness. Following divorce, we may move a tad more slowly than others in the trust department, but don't let fear steal your joy and imprison you in anger and hurt.

Conclusion

Let's face it, we all have reasons not to trust due to past hurt, disappointment, and rejection. And if this life has taught us anything, it teaches that there are never guarantees when it comes to relationships.

Asking someone to earn your trust often means asking them to never make a mistake. Well, that's just not realistic. We will get hurt, even by those we hold dear. The only way to trust again is to intentionally walk past fear to extend it.

Yes, you have been hurt before, during, and after the divorce process. You may feel scared and abandoned, but you are not alone.

Trust in the Lord with *all* of your heart.

In that safe place, God mends fragile hearts to nurture long-standing friendships and embrace new relationships.

Pastoral Wisdom

One of my favorite Scripture passages is one Donna used in this chapter.

> Trust in the LORD with all your heart, and do not lean on your own understanding. In all your ways acknowledge Him, and He will make straight your paths. (Proverbs 3:5–6)

We trust God because He is faithful. People, on the other hand, will let us down. To give yourself and your heart to someone requires a leap of faith. But you did that before, and it did not go well. You feel cheated and deceived. Perhaps one of the most difficult things to overcome in life is having your love rejected and your trust betrayed. Can you trust again?

Trust is something that has to be earned. Scripture tells that:

> Bondservants are to be submissive to their own masters in everything; they are to be well-pleasing, not argumentative, not pilfering, but showing all good faith [trustworthiness], so that in everything they may adorn the doctrine of God our Savior. (Titus 2:9–10)

It would be foolish to trust someone who has not shown himself or herself to be trustworthy.

We trust God because He is faithful. People, on the other hand, will let us down.

In John 14:1, Jesus said, *"[Trust] in God, trust also in me."* He was encouraging His disciples—and us—to trust Him. And He had given them reason to do so. He had shown Himself to be trustworthy, and He would give even more reason to trust Him in the days ahead: He was crucified for the sins of the world and rose again to assure us of victory over death. He gave us more than enough reason to trust Him.

The problem is that we cannot be so certain with people. No one is perfect. If you find someone else, he or she will not be perfect. Neither will you. You will disappoint each other. You will let each other down. How can you trust? Take it slow. See if he or she can be trusted in little things:

> Whoever can be trusted with very little can also be trusted with much, and whoever is dishonest with very little will also be dishonest with much. (Luke 16:10; NIV)

While this passage is not speaking specifically about relationships, the principle is the same. Trust needs to be earned. If you see dishonesty in a person, especially in little things, that is a red flag!

If you are going to love again, you will have to trust.

> [Love] always protects, always trusts, always hopes, always perseveres. (1 Corinthians 13:7; NIV)

A crucial element of trust is making yourself vulnerable. It is also what makes trusting someone so hard. You feel exposed and defenseless. So it is important to make sure someone is trustworthy before you make yourself vulnerable. Go slow. Pay close attention. Can this person be trusted?

What reason do you have to trust another person? <u>A big one should be whether or not they have placed their trust in Jesus.</u> If both of you trust Jesus above everything else, you will be able to trust each other. That does not mean you will never make mistakes. It does, however, point both of you to the One who wants to be in the middle of your relationship, reminding you of His love and forgiveness, and encouraging you to love and forgive each other.

COUNSELOR'S CORNER

Trust is a hard one. <u>Once you have been burned, it's really hard to put your hand near the fire again, isn't it?</u> But God doesn't want you to live without the warmth from a fire again, whether that means a future marriage or just the ability to trust again. <u>He certainly doesn't want trust issues to be a barrier between you and Him!</u> You will have to *trust Him* to help you *trust again.*

When it comes to healing trust issues, it goes back to looking at your junk. Are you sick of me telling you that? Well, Donna empathizes with you! Just remember that if she can do it, so can you, with God's help. It will require you to pinpoint exactly what you don't trust. And I don't mean just a man or woman. Go deeper than that:

- What is it that you honestly don't trust?

- Why?

- What emotions are generated?

- What thoughts cause those emotions?

Okay, go ahead and throw the pillow across the room, because you need to go back to (1) the thoughts you have, and thus, (2) the beliefs you have assumed. Are those beliefs at all irrational?

Just because someone broke your trust once, does that mean it will *always* happen? Kinda sounds to me like "overgeneralization," one of those cognitive distortions we talked about in chapter 7 (see the "Counselor's Corner" section). That doesn't dismiss the fact that you have been hurt and your trust has been mangled, but be careful of the thoughts that feed it. You will need to keep your distortion list handy to refer to when buttons get pushed.

As Donna pointed out, listening is pivotal in trust. Not only do you need to listen to yourself but also to what others are truly saying. Are you practicing healthy listening with the person you want to trust? Go back and review listening in chapter 9 on communication.

People often advise to listen to your gut. I can't completely argue with that, but don't fall into black-and-white thinking: (1) my gut is 100 percent right all the time, or (2) my gut is terrible, thus I can't trust myself because look what happened the last time I did! There needs to be a careful balance between gut and paranoia. That is where counseling is vital to work through issues, but so is having a couple of godly friends whom you trust for advice (ironic, isn't it?). Reviewing the chapter on forgiveness is also vital to resolving trust issues within yourself as well as others.

All of this being said, make sure your expectations of others are realistic. Because of your hurt, what do you expect from someone? Deep down, do you honestly expect them to never hurt you? never lie to you? meet your every need? If so, you are setting yourself up for hurt. Such distorted thinking will throw you back into distrust with whiplash speed!

Make sure your expectations of others are realistic.

Remember, you are striving to trust a sinful human being. He or she will never be perfect. Make sure your expectations are at a human level, and your God-size expectations are put on God, who can meet them.

15: Pausing to Breathe, Pray, and Reflect

Trust is one of the many casualties of divorce. It takes prayer, time, and faith to embrace trust again. Take your time walking through the following Bible passages, questions, prayer time, and journaling time before moving to the next chapter.

SCRIPTURE TO READ, MEDITATE ON, AND MEMORIZE

When I am afraid, I put my trust in You. (Psalm 56:3)

Let me hear in the morning of Your steadfast love, for in You I trust. Make me know the way I should go, for to You I lift up my soul. (Psalm 143:8)

He will not let your foot be moved; He who keeps you will not slumber. (Psalm 121:3)

QUESTIONS FOR REFLECTION

Take time to answer these questions from the gut—real and raw. Honesty opens wide the door for God to continue the healing process in your heart.

1. What is at the root of your trust issue? Don't simply name the divorce process in general or your ex-spouse's misbehavior, but narrow it down and get specific. Is it fear? pride? anger?

2. When your trust alarm is triggered, how could you respond in a different way that may help dispel your trust issues?

Pause for Prayer

Regardless of the depth of our trust issues, God promises that when we submit all things to Him, He will bring beauty out of ashes. Take this time to be still before the Lord in prayer.

A—Acknowledge God's sovereignty: Sometimes we dwell on our situation and temporarily forget that God is still in control of everything. Read 1 Chronicles 29:12 aloud with confidence.

C—Confession: Working through trust issues to emerge on the other side healed by God takes time and diligence. Take this time to confess aloud what part of the trust issue you are struggling with most.

T—Thanksgiving: It is hard to express thanks when trust causes us to shrink back. Yet even in the midst of your struggle, God has blessed you with people and/or things for which you owe Him thanks. List three things you are thankful for right now, and thank God for them.

1.

2.

3.

S—Supplication (requests): God promises that when we pray, He faithfully hears us. Identify what you need from Him right now and ask Him in faith to provide it.

Exhaling on the Page

It's never too late to start the journaling process. It is an excellent tool that allows you to see your feelings on paper and begin to connect the dots to discover underlying issues. You may not see the benefit today, but you will one day. Trust Him.

Here are some suggested questions to answer as you journal:

1. What happened today?

2. How do you feel?

277

3. What made you angry or made you grateful?

4. How did someone encourage you today or show kindness?

5. Where did you see God at work in your circumstances today?

You did it! Take a deep breath and exhale slowly. God is with you, dear one. He will NEVER leave you or forsake you. He will see you through each day and every circumstance.

16

You Can Do It!

Self-Care, Establishing Boundaries, and Setting Goals

Your days are numbered. Use them to throw open
the windows of your soul to the sun. If you do not,
the sun will soon set, and you with it.

—Marcus Aurelius

Why do some people seem to be able to move through the emotional and spiritual challenges of divorce quickly, while others seem to get stuck?

It's simple: the first group learned how to set boundaries and goals.

Once your divorce proceedings are finished, your time and future plans are your own (and your children's). Spending time seeking God's guidance about your future is essential to attaining them. Setting boundaries that guard your heart, time, and resources while also setting goals moves you forward.

Following my divorce, I set my heart on becoming an author and speaker to teach people about God and His great love. God has turned that dream into reality, but it required prayer, intentionality, perseverance, and taking leaps of faith into the fog.

Since few people feel like leaping following a divorce, learning how to set appropriate boundaries and goals while continuing important self-care is crucial. This helps to motivate you toward God's plan for your future, which He has already prepared.

Learning how to set appropriate boundaries and goals while continuing important self-care is crucial.

SETTING BOUNDARIES

Whether in a relationship, parenting, or your career, boundaries are essential to embracing a full, healthy life. However, it's a skill that takes diligence and time to learn. Setting boundaries basically means recognizing and embracing your limits.

For example, I determined to wholeheartedly follow God's calling on my life to write. However, I also worked full time, traveled to teach God's Word, and was very active in my congregation. I didn't want to fill every second of every day without leaving some white space in the margin to breathe.

Family and friends may have opinions or suggestions regarding how we should spend our time. In my case, I needed to step back and figure it out through prayer and much thought.

With that in mind and through wise counsel that I intentionally sought, I put the following steps into place to build my boundaries. They may help you as well.

1. Figure out where you stand.

Healthy boundaries cannot be set until we properly identify our spiritual, emotional, and physical limits. Tune in to your feelings to determine what causes you to feel discomfort and resentment. For example, I was perfectly fine with family and friends texting and emailing me to say that they were praying for me. I appreciated it and felt loved.

However, I was very uncomfortable when a well-meaning church member emailed my private prayer request to her entire prayer group without my consent. The group contained people I did not know, and I did not appreciate my laundry being aired to strangers; I felt exposed.

Experiencing discomfort is your first clue that someone may be violating or crossing one of your boundaries. Resentment indicates that someone may be taking advantage of you or not appreciating you. Once you identify your feelings, move to the next step.

2. Be direct.

Some people are not attentive to subtle facial hints or negative body language to discern when they have crossed your boundaries. When someone knowingly or unknowingly steps over that line, don't be afraid to speak up. Gently but firmly, let them know how you feel, and politely ask them to avoid similar behavior in the future.

For example, a kind friend liked to demonstrate her support and love by showering me with fresh fruit and veggies from the local farmers market. She would leave them in baskets on my front porch every other day so that they were there when I got home. It was a wonderful gesture, but she never let me know what she was doing, and she didn't realize that the only time I open my front door is when a visitor knocks.

One day, she asked if I was enjoying the gifts she faithfully deposited on my front porch. I was clueless. She was hurt. Needless to say, weeks later, after cleaning my porch of spoiled, messy produce, I thanked her but asked her directly to communicate better. With no notes on the baskets and no heads-up from her, I would not have known who to thank, even if I had been aware of them.

On a more serious note, if someone consistently asks to know the latest "scoop" about your divorce or its aftermath and it makes you defensive or uncomfortable, be polite but direct in asking him or her to stop asking.

There are many respected resources available if you find that you need to spend extra time learning how to set various types of boundaries for your particular situation. One of the best and most respected resources was co-written by noted Christian psychologist Dr. Henry Cloud: *Boundaries: When to Say Yes, How to Say No, to Take Control of Your Life.* He also wrote several other boundaries books for specific issues.

The important thing is that your boundaries are important. The sooner you start setting and enforcing them, the sooner you will not fall victim to the whims of those around you.

SETTING GOALS

Only after my divorce did I become aware that I had stunk as a goal setter while I was married. Perhaps I felt as if setting my own goals negated the ones that my ex-husband and I might have set together (though we never did).

Following my divorce, I realized I would have significant time alone since we didn't have children. I remember waking up the morning after signing the decree of divorce, dropping beside my bed, and with tears blurring my freckles, I asked God to "fill my time."

I quickly discovered that if I did not set goals, time sifted through my fingers like hourglass sand. Days turned into weeks that turned into months when I felt like I accomplished little. I really did not have a clue about how to set realistic goals, so I read books and blogs that provided much-needed expertise.

Now, after setting goals and successfully achieving them for the past three years, I have narrowed down goal setting to five easy steps that anyone can follow.

1. Start small.

This is especially true if you are a goal-setting novice. Regardless of what they are, focus on three new goals in the beginning. Avoid adding a bunch of detailed subsections under each goal. Keep them simple enough that you can commit them to memory.

2. Make them "SMART."

Using a common acronym, SMART goals include five basic criteria. They must be the following:

Specific: The goals you want to accomplish must be as specific as possible. For instance, one of my SMART goals for 2016 is *"Write an eight-lesson Bible study on the life and ministry of the apostle Peter by May 1, 2016."* A nonspecific version would read: *"Write a Bible study."*

Measurable: The goals you set must contain a measurable result. You want to be able to diligently assign time and resources in order to achieve it. With my goal above, I am able to measure it by my research and writing time. I allotted two hours a day (however that fit into each day) to research and write. I divided the total number of hours I'd need by two and *voilà*! I knew exactly how many days I would need to devote to complete my goal.

Actionable: Effective goals start with an action verb to get us moving, such as *write, walk, finish,* etc. Forms of the verb *be,* such as *am, be,* and *have,* do not motivate us.

Realistic: It takes commitment and diligence to accomplish your goals, but you have to be sure to leave enough white space in the margin of your life for downtime and wiggle room. Effective goals should challenge you, not choke you. Work within a reasonable comfort zone.

Timely: Effective goals include due dates. When do you plan to complete your goal? A goal without a deadline is just a dream. Each goal needs a completion date.

If your goals are "SMART," you stand a far better chance of achieving them.

3. Write them down.

Seeing your goals in black and white is HUGE. Writing down your goals states your intention and serves as a catalyst to get the ball rolling each time you see them.

4. Keep them handy.

In the hecticness of day-to-day life, we need reminders that our goals still exist. You made them for a reason, so they are important and relevant. Each time you see your list of goals, it encourages and inspires you to work toward them with diligence.

5. Tell a friend or two.

As a novice goal setter, it may not be a good idea to tweet them out to the whole world. The key is sharing your goals with a few key people who are committed to walking with you and encouraging you toward success.

Setting your goals is as simple as seeking God's discernment through prayer, settling on a few key goals, writing them down, and getting started. You can do it!

SELF-CARE

One of the most important lessons that I learned in counseling was to begin focusing on myself again. During my married life, my focus was on examining what was best for me and my husband together. At the beginning of my divorced life, my focus turned to minimizing the pain that family and close friends felt over my situation. It had been a long time since I focused solely on me.

At first, it felt selfish. Almost like it was a luxury I couldn't afford. After all, Jesus was all about serving others and meeting their needs first, right? As His follower, I should do likewise. Above all, I should spend my extra time finding new ways to serve, right?

But Jesus also spent significant time alone with His Father. Several times throughout the Gospels, we see Jesus going off to find a quiet place to pray. Yes, He always made time to serve others, but His relationship with the Father was His nonnegotiable core focus. Jesus never asked the disciples to check His calendar to see if He could spare the time away from serving others. He just did it and in so doing, perfectly demonstrates self-care.

Over time, I relearned to do some things that I liked to do . . . just because. I didn't need to justify it to anyone. It doesn't take much effort to fill my calendar every hour of every day, so I actually set appointments for myself to take a break, have fun, walk in the park, or just *be*. I even went so far as to count my calendar entries each week to ensure that time spent working and serving others was equally balanced with personal, self-care time.

During my post-divorce counseling, Kristin never failed to ask if I was eating right, sleeping well, and spending time in prayer and God's Word.

The benefits were astonishing. I discovered newfound energy, peace of mind, and a more positive outlook. I learned that when I put myself and my relationship with God above all else, He provides the joy and stamina to serve Him by serving others.

Self-care is important. Give it a whirl.

You owe it to yourself.

GOD MEETS YOU IN THE DIRT

She stood, trembling, in front of Jesus, standing right in her own dirt as they accused her. Eyes downcast. Shame creeping up red on her face. Fear pounding her chest in waves. Here's how the story went:

> Jesus went to the Mount of Olives. Early in the morning He came again to the temple. All the people came to Him, and He sat down and taught them. The scribes and the Pharisees brought a woman who had been caught in adultery, and placing her in the midst they said to Him, "Teacher, this woman has been caught in the act of adultery. Now in the Law Moses commanded us to stone such women. So what do You say?" (John 8:1–5)

That story causes me to cringe on many levels. But one thing blares loudly: <u>Don't we all have to face our own dirt sooner or later?</u> Sometimes we eat dirt over poor choices. We don't really talk about our divorce, but others find out. Haters yell it from rooftops.

Perhaps we believe that we deserve such treatment. Maybe the woman did as well. Condemned by her actions. Accused by her thoughts. Braced to endure the harsh stones of judgment. But landing in the dirt doesn't

Don't we all have to face our own dirt sooner or later?

mean we have to call it home. The story continues like this:

> Jesus bent down and wrote with His finger on the
> ground. And as they continued to ask Him, He stood
> up and said to them, "Let him who is without sin among
> you be the first to throw a stone at her." And once more
> He bent down and wrote on the ground. (John 8:6–8)

Jesus refused to pick up a stone. And He blatantly challenged those who did. Scripture doesn't tell us where His gaze fell as He uttered those words.

Who would you be in this scenario? Some days, we crumple hard. Other days, we hurl thoughtless stones. But Jesus? He's different:

> But when they heard it, they went away one by one,
> beginning with the older ones, and Jesus was left alone
> with the woman standing before Him. Jesus stood up
> and said to her, "Woman, where are they? Has no one
> condemned you?" She said, "No one, Lord." And Jesus
> said, "Neither do I condemn you; go, and from now on
> sin no more." (John 8:9–11)

The older ones left first. I noticed that for the very first time when rereading these passages. The older ones had lived more of life. They knew how easily we can face-plant in the muck. How consequences can make your chest heave heavily.

Yet . . . Jesus didn't condemn her . . . or you . . . or me. Time and again, Jesus is faithful to pick us up, dust us off, and set us on the right path again. The only thing He asks in return? "Go, and from now on sin no more." In other words, turn away from suffocating, dirt-inviting sin to breathe new life offered by Him.

Jesus is faithful to pick us up, dust us off, and set us on the right path again.

This is a story of hope. Jesus doesn't care what you've done. He doesn't care that you've been divorced. He cares about YOU. And His faithful, loving heart extends strong arms to lift us up. No stones. No condemnation.

And home? It isn't in the dirt. He's preparing mansions for us in heaven.

That, dear friend, is the ultimate goal.

COUNSELOR'S CORNER

Many of us rarely think about boundaries. We simply go about life and handle what comes. We may make goals and plans for certain things, but not very often do we involve our boundary skills. It's usually not until something has slammed us in the face that we even think about a boundary. We usually react and then decide if we felt violated; then maybe we think we actually need to set a boundary.

It's so easy to be reactive instead of proactive. However, that backward approach takes a toll on our emotions and thoughts and brings undue stress. The whole crazy cycle of irrational thoughts starts spinning like the Tilt-A-Whirl at the local carnival. We need to learn to be proactive so we don't become nearly as reactive in situations. Sounds great, doesn't it? "How do we do that?" you ask. Well, let's take a look.

Boundaries are for others, but they're also for you. They are not threats; rather, they give people choices. How people respond to the boundaries you set is their choice, and they are responsible for accepting the consequences of their choice. Remember, there can be both good and bad consequences; our society just happens to think of them as bad.

There are several purposes for setting boundaries that are important to keep in mind when you are considering using them. Here is a list of their healthy purposes:

- They assign responsibility.

- They are for protection, not power.

- They are for respect of self and others.

- They are for motivation.

When you are creating boundaries, there are a few things to remember:

1. **Look again at your motivation.** Is it aimed toward health or getting even? If it's for health, where does the boundary need to be? What and whom is it helping?

2. **Make sure the boundary you set is very clear.** You need to communicate it to others instead of assuming they know. Leave no room for misunderstanding and confusion.

3. **Keep a cause-and-effect relationship in mind when setting a boundary.** If _____ happens, then _____ happens. Again, watch that it's not for manipulation or a threat.

4. **Make sure it's maintainable.** Once you put it up, maintaining it is crucial, or it will be very difficult to set and maintain future boundaries. The individual won't respect it.

Boundaries can be divided into two areas: ourselves and others. We have already discussed in previous chapters the need to put boundaries around ourselves for health and healing. For a quick review, such areas include our thoughts, emotions, and behaviors concerning relationships; communication patterns; listening skills; support system; and sexual integrity.

With regard to setting boundaries for others, we can break that down into the public, kids, and ex-spouse. We are going to include in "public" our family, friends, acquaintances—basically anyone other than our kids and our ex. Donna talked about the importance of being able to stand up for yourself and tell people when they need to step back. Doing so is important for you but also for them. Remember, it's very likely that they do not realize when they are being intrusive, although we all know the Nosy Nellie who just wants the latest juicy gossip. Tell them how they can help, which includes taking a step back.

With your ex and kids, you are focused on making your environment as healthy as possible. It is important to try to be on the same page (or at least in the same chapter) while respecting each other's new separation and individuality. This can be difficult at times, yet it is critical in trying to co-parent.

In closing, remember the purposes for boundaries. If you keep those purposes in mind and use them as a checks-and-balances system, it will make things easier. Setting and maintaining boundaries takes skill and practice.

Read the boundaries book Donna mentioned. Also consider reading the spin-off topical books that those authors have written on boundaries, such as *Boundaries in Marriage, Boundaries with Kids,* and *Boundaries with Teens.* They will help fine-tune your growing skills.

16: Pausing to Breathe, Pray, and Reflect

You are important to God and those who love you. Taking care of yourself and actively planning for your future prepares you to fulfill the plan that God has prepared for your life.

Take your time walking through the following Bible passages, questions, prayer time, and journaling time before moving to the next chapter.

Scripture to Read, Meditate on, and Memorize

Hope in God; for I shall again praise Him, my salvation and my God. (Psalm 43:5)

Your word is a lamp to my feet and a light to my path. (Psalm 119:105)

Let me hear in the morning of Your steadfast love, for in You I trust. Make me know the way I should go, for to You I lift up my soul. (Psalm 143:8)

Questions for Reflection

If you are having difficulty taking proper care of yourself or finding the motivation to set boundaries and goals, pondering and answering these questions may lend valuable insight:

1. What is one thing you've always wanted to do but placed on the back burner?

2. Think of one small step that you can take toward it and give yourself a deadline to take that step.

3. For boundaries, if you have difficulty being direct with people, practice in the mirror. Ask God to bring to mind one person you need to ask to either step back or step up in your life, ask His discernment in determining what you need from that person, then practice in front of the mirror saying those things out loud. This builds your confidence and helps you work on the best grace-filled words to use.

Pause for Prayer

It takes time to adjust to your new life. Many changes and unfamiliar routines can wreak havoc on your mind, body, and soul. Exhale now and be still before the Lord. Let's pray:

A—Acknowledge God's sovereignty: With all the changes in your life right now, it helps to acknowledge that God is still in control of everything. Even your situation. Read Revelation 19:6 aloud with confidence.

C—Confession: Working through divorce and emerging healed by God on the other side takes time and diligence. Take this time to confess to God what you are struggling with most; narrow it down and get specific. He already knows each circumstance, but verbally expressing those feelings ejects them from your heart, mind, and soul so that He can begin the healing process. Please pray aloud to God now.

T—Thanksgiving: It is hard to express thanks when the future is uncertain. Yet, even in the midst of your circumstances, God has blessed you with people and things for which you owe Him thanks. List three things you are thankful for right now, and thank God for them.

1.

2.

3.

S—Supplication (requests): God promises that when we pray, He faithfully hears us. Identify what you need from Him right now, and ask Him in faith to provide it.

EXHALING ON THE PAGE

As you know by now, God uses journaling as another way to release pent-up feelings and allow Him to fill you with His peace that passes all understanding. You may not see the benefits of journaling today, but you will one day. Trust Him.

Here are some suggested questions to answer as you journal:

1. What happened today?

2. How do you feel?

3. What made you angry or made you grateful?

4. How did someone encourage you today or show kindness?

5. Where did you see God at work in your circumstances today?

You did it! Take a deep breath and sit back. God is with you, dear one. He will NEVER leave you or forsake you. He will see you through each day and every circumstance.

17

Breathing the Fresh Air of Freedom and Embracing Your Future

Now faith is the assurance of things hoped for,
the conviction of things not seen.
—Hebrews 11:1

For months or even years now, you have endured the heavy burden of divorce, pain, and brokenness. You run and labor hard to breathe but seldom stop to catch your breath. Here is where we pause to analyze what we have learned and get on our knees before God to ask Him what He holds in our future. We ask Him because He is the one who enables all breath:

> The letters of the name of God in Hebrew . . . are infrequently pronounced Yahweh. But in truth they are inutterable. . . . This Word [YHWH] is the sound of breathing. The holiest name in the world, the Name of our Creator, is the sound of your own breathing.
> —Rabbi Lawrence Kushner

God and His Word represent our very life breath. They are meant to be savored, not gulped before we rush forward to the next item on our to-do list. As you and I look forward into an unknown future, we take a deep breath, inhale His peace, and exhale the world's addiction to speed.

God and His Word represent our very life breath.

You have been through emotional, spiritual, and physical trauma while trying to balance daily life. In this chapter, we will pause to replace our to-do list with His breath of peace-filled life.

So What Does That Look Like?

I embraced my love for traveling. My ex-husband and I traveled, but after the divorce it became a passion. Despite some people's inference that perhaps I was running from life, I discovered that I fully embraced it. I love interacting in different cultures and adventuring into centuries-old castles and cathedrals. It makes me appreciate home that much more.

I also discovered a passion for photography. Although I have always loved exploring nature to behold both the vast and the minute in God's creation, photography forces me to slow my pace and actually see it. To notice the rugged beauty of the Scottish Highlands, the delicate flower petals in Canada's Butchart Gardens, or the endless desert surrounding Jericho. To appreciate the architectural genius of Paris' Notre Dame, the vaulted grandeur of England's Canterbury Cathedral, the fairy-tale splendor of Ludwig's Neuschwanstein Castle in Bavaria, or the intricate carvings in Munich's Theatine Church.

The "we" doesn't exist anymore, so rediscover your individual identity in Christ, which is vital to moving forward.

BE A FRUIT BEARER

You have probably heard the phrase "He (or she) is on fire for God!" Perhaps people have said it about you. But what does that really mean? What does it look like?

Every time I hear that phrase, I pause to look more closely at that person. I read their Facebook posts and Twitter feed. I check out their latest blog post or book. Peruse their website. In a nutshell, I'm looking for fruit.

Scripture says: *"Beware of false prophets, who come to you in sheep's clothing but inwardly are ravenous wolves. You will recognize them by their fruits. Are grapes gathered from thornbushes, or figs from thistles? So, every healthy tree bears good fruit, but the diseased tree bears bad fruit. A healthy tree cannot bear bad fruit, nor can a diseased tree bear good fruit. Every tree that does not bear good fruit is cut down and thrown into the fire. Thus you will recognize them by their fruits"* (Matthew 7:15–20).

We ultimately recognize Jesus followers by their fruit, not their plans. All too often we deem people to be "on fire for God" because of their words. They have big ideas. Lots of enthusiasm. A new project perpetually in the works. But does it ever come to fruition?

I'm blessed to know many talented, sold-out Jesus followers. I don't have to search for their fruit because, figuratively speaking, I can't reach them without wading through the piles of good fruit surrounding them.

Through the power of the Holy Spirit, God enables them to accomplish much for His kingdom. They are involved in mission work, shepherding godly children, dynamic pastoring, or helping those in need. Abundant fruit becomes part of how we identify radical disciples. Yet such a crop costs much.

Prolific fruit bearers have not lived free of difficulties, heart scrapes, or soul blows. They obediently allow God to shape them by pruning weak or diseased branches so that only good fruit comes forth. They surrender their brokenness to God to redeem as fertile ground to plant fruit-producing crops. I trust them to speak truth into my life because they've been in the trenches. Patiently waiting. Studying Scripture. Listening. They recognize and wholeheartedly follow our Savior's voice.

Those are disciples on fire for God. And it's not because they say it, but because we "recognize them by their fruit." They live truly radical, non-lukewarm, Spirit-led lives. That's the kind of disciple I want to be. Every. Single. Day.

Hope from the Voices of Experience

As we near the end of our journey through this book, I would be remiss if I did not leave hope and encouragement as a lasting impression. I asked each person I interviewed what advice he or she would give to you—someone now experiencing divorce—that would help you most. Truly, it's an exceptional list. I pray that their candid words of wisdom, humor, and love lighten your burden and whisper hope and encouragement into your life today:

> Don't go through divorce alone. —Linda K.

> God can make miracles happen! If there is any chance of repair, seek counseling and pray for each other. If not, remember that God is in control. Trust in Him and lay your burdens before Him. Then roll your windows down, take a drive away from the chaos, and blare the praise music! It will make you smile. —Heather

> Don't focus on your spouse's issues. You couldn't change them and you will never change them. Focus on yourself and what is best for your children. —Lisa S.

> God is there. Trust Him even when you don't feel it. —Kathleen

> Read and study your Bible. Make friends with other divorced and single people. Don't talk badly about your ex. Don't rush into a new relationship. Have confidence

in yourself that you are worthy of waiting for a great person to come along before you start dating. —Tina Y.

Don't spend your energy talking badly about your ex—it only serves to prolong the pain, and it does no good for the children. Look for God's blessings because when we see His blessings, it is very hard to be mean, angry, resentful, or victimized. An attitude of gratitude really helps. —Carolyn

You are not alone—whether from friends, family, or your heavenly Father. You are not abnormal. Don't fall into the pit of despair. Discover things about yourself and your life that God has given you to make a difference in others' lives. Don't focus on one point of misery in your own. Drink adult beverages with friends. Laugh. Sing. Smile. This world is temporary. —Loren

Pray continually for your ex-spouse, your family, wisdom, and grace. Ask for forgiveness, and forgive. —Nancy

This too shall pass. Keep your focus on Jesus. Find Scriptures that sing to your heart and read them out loud over and over. Keep good, God-fearing friends around and lean on them when you need to. —Gertrude

Don't lose sight of yourself. You are important; you are valued. Your worth is not with that other person. You are strong and you are loved. God WILL NOT leave you. He's got your best interests in mind. You may not see it right now, but He's got plans for you, and you will be fine. —Cheryl

This too shall pass. Keep your focus on Jesus.

Divorce has permanently altered my story and is a part of my past, but it does not have to determine how I view my future. —Kole

Trust God. Be in His Word and worship. Fellowship with other Christians. Keep busy. Be involved in making a difference in someone or something. —Marguerite

If there's physical or mental abuse, GET OUT NOW. If not, seek counseling. Try to make it work. If your spouse doesn't want to fix it—get out. The Lord is there to help you through whatever you're going through. —Janetta

Don't judge your divorced parents, friends, and neighbors. Extend grace to them. —Tim

God's love for you is not based on your circumstances. He loves you the same the day you were born, the day you got married, and the day you divorced. —Linda P.

REMEMBER: JESUS WINS

Sometimes I wonder if the bends and twists on this road of life can break things. As we slip behind the wheel of life, you and I need to know this one thing to face tomorrow: **Jesus wins**.

This journey zigzags and spirals, but what keeps us from face-planting in a ditch is just that: **Jesus wins**.

We stagger toward Easter morning whiplashed, bruised, and broken—desperately needing God's resurrection promise. Our hearts suffer in this fallen world—but what can scare us when we know **Jesus wins?**

When chaos shatters tranquility and we need peace like a river, God buckles us into His indestructible resurrection truth that no matter how dizzily the road blurs our vision, **Jesus wins**.

God's love for you is not based on your circumstances.

It means we can risk it all to share the hope of salvation, because when we surrender the driver's seat to Jesus, we can let go and rest in His amazing grace. He lovingly navigates those hairpin turns when hurt skids us sideways on two wheels.

He stands beside us in the debris to offer the ultimate CPR of hope: *"For God so loved the world, that He gave His only Son, that whoever believes in Him should not perish but have eternal life"* (John 3:16).

We suffer relationship rollovers, yet we experience healing in this: Christ repurposes pain for His gain to use what we thought was wreckage for His glory.

Life's darkest moments could send us careening headlong into a tree of fear—to give up and not allow the power of His healing and forgiveness to shine bright. Instead, His Word provides strength and assurance that this road leads precisely to one life-changing truth that buckles us in safe and sound: **JESUS WINS.**

And because He lives, we can face tomorrow.

17: Pausing to Breathe, Pray, and Reflect

Despite divorce, you are still breathing, which means that God is not done with you yet. Each day is a gift from Him to operate in His strength as you put the past behind you and embrace this new path in your life.

One final time, walk through the following Bible passages, questions, prayer time, and journaling time before we finish our journey through this book together.

Scripture to Read, Meditate on, and Memorize

For the gifts and the calling of God are irrevocable.
(Romans 11:29)

The LORD your God is in your midst, a mighty one who will save; He will rejoice over you with gladness; He will quiet you by His love; He will exult over you with loud singing. (Zephaniah 3:17)

I am with you and will keep you wherever you go.
(Genesis 28:15)

Those who look to Him are radiant, and their faces shall never be ashamed. (Psalm 34:5)

Questions for Reflection

We have covered a lot of ground in this book, including how to forgive, how to deal with grief and anger, and the importance of godly counseling, true friends, and our faith family. We learned about communication skills, dealing with loneliness, survival skills for the holidays, and a new world of dating, among other things. We looked at how to trust again, set boundaries and goals, and embrace the future. Now, take time to answer these questions:

1. Which chapter(s) did you find most helpful in your current stage of divorce or post-divorce? Why?

2. What invaluable tools have you learned that you can begin putting into practice?

3. How has this book affected how you perceive your future?

PAUSE FOR PRAYER

Once more, bow before the Lord in prayer. Day by day, hour by hour, He continues to restore you and heal your heart. He never abandons you, and He promises to make you new. Let's pray:

A—Acknowledge God's sovereignty: God remains in control of everything and every day. Read Psalm 139 aloud with confidence.

C—Confession: Some days will still present challenges. Perhaps today was one of those days. Take this time to confess those feelings to God and allow Him to eject them from your heart, mind, and soul so that He can begin the healing process. Please pray aloud to God now.

T—Thanksgiving: God continues to bless you every single day. Although you may not see each blessing, God still provides them. List three things you are thankful for right now, and thank God for them.

1.

2.

3.

S—Supplication (requests): God promises that when we pray, He faithfully hears us. As we close our journey together, identify what you need most from Him right now, and ask Him in faith to provide it for you.

EXHALING ON THE PAGE

I pray that you have discovered the benefits of journaling, as I did during my divorce. I hope that you continue to journal so that one day you can look back on the words you wrote and see where God faithfully provided exactly what you needed each step of the way.

Here are some suggested questions to answer as you journal:

1. What happened today?

2. How do you feel?

3. What made you angry or made you grateful?

4. How did someone encourage you today or show kindness?

5. Where did you see God at work in your circumstances today?

You did it! Take a deep breath and exhale slowly. Even though our journey together has come to an end, God's journey with you lasts into eternity. I pray that you embrace your new future and the plans God has for you. They are always for your good and His glory.

Acknowledgments

Throughout the two-year process of writing this book, I have been blessed beyond measure by many friends who faithfully walked this journey with me. What originally started as a labor of obedience morphed into a labor of love. My family, church, and countless friends held my hands, prayed relentlessly, and wiped my tears as I faced divorce and its aftermath. This book never would have come to fruition without their love and support.

Although I cannot thank everyone by name, I must thank Kristin Niekerk and Doug Dommer for grabbing my hand and holding me tight to God's foundation as the storm of discovery and divorce raged. You were Psalm 18:16–17 in the flesh. I love you.

To my BFF, Luanne, thank you for listening, praying without ceasing, letting me cry ugly, and margarita outings. Truly, "two are better than one." You always knew what I needed. Jesus shines ridiculously bright through you, dear friend. I love you.

To my Salem small group, worship team, and church, thank you for your gifts of encouragement and perspective to teach me what God's grace and love feel like in real time.

To Rev. Tim Niekerk, Rev. Wayne Graumann, and Rev. John Heckmann, thank you for your relentless encouragement and prayers when I could not find the words. I hold you and our friendships in the highest esteem.

To my family, thank you for knowing when to drag me out of the house during my divorce and when to let me rest after it. Your love, support, and humorous interruptions solidified the fact that I am crazy blessed to have the best family on the planet. I love you!

To the expert consultants, Rev. Mike Mattil and Kristin Niekerk, thank you for enriching my life and this book far beyond every expectation. It is a humble privilege to serve Jesus alongside you.

To my editor, Peggy Kuethe, my heartfelt thanks. Your wise counsel helped me find the right words to convey the message that filled my heart. Thank you for providing the breathing room and structure to express it. You are a rare and wonderful treasure.

To the incredible team at Concordia Publishing House—Loren, Elizabeth, and Lindsey, to name three—my deepest gratitude for letting me dream with you.

To my friend and attorney, Kathy Terry, thank you for walking me through the legal process of divorce with such grace, wisdom, and compassion.

To my ex-husband, thank you for the years we were married and the lessons I learned. You have my forgiveness and best wishes for your future.

To the dozens of people who granted interviews for this book, thank you for your bravery to dig into past pain to provide an avenue of hope for those experiencing divorce.

I am especially thankful to my literary agent and friend, Rachelle Gardner. Thank you for believing in me and for all of the wonderful things you are.

But most of all, to my Lord and Savior, Jesus Christ, thank You for forgiveness, grace, the gift of faith, Your everlasting love, and for rescuing my life from the pit. Your Word breathes life into my soul and anchors me every hour. I cannot even imagine seeing You face-to-face one day. I shall be absolutely undone on that glorious day. *Soli Deo Gloria.* To You alone.

Expert Consultants

———

The ultimate goal of *Without This Ring* is to walk people who are experiencing the trauma of divorce toward complete healing in Christ. I have experienced divorce, and I sought professional Christian counseling and pastoral wisdom to get through the process whole and at peace again. To that end, I have asked and been granted permission to share guidance from two expert consultants who weighed in on each chapter of this book from professional points of view.

Rev. Michael J. Mattil: An avid student of God's Word and a gifted teacher of Scripture, Mike has been an LCMS ordained minister for more than thirty years. He received his associate of arts degree from Concordia Junior College in 1978 and earned a bachelor of science degree in education from Concordia University, Nebraska, in 1980. Afterward, he attended Concordia Seminary in St. Louis, Missouri, and received his master of divinity degree in 1984.

Mike has served as pastor of Grace Lutheran Church in Denison, Texas, since 1988. As a pastor and counselor for more than three decades, Mike is uniquely qualified to offer invaluable wisdom, experience, and scriptural insight to help those walking through the pain and trauma of divorce.

I have known this gifted man of God and his wife, Cheryl, since we began serving in the Lutheran Women's Missionary League together in the Texas District in 2004, and I consider them dear friends. Sitting under Mike's gifted teaching for over a decade, witnessing his contagious love for Jesus and his commitment to reaching the lost and hurting with God's grace, mercy, and love, I have trusted him to offer solid, godly wisdom from Scripture that has enriched this book beyond measure.

Kristin L. Niekerk, MS, LPC: Kristin received her bachelor of arts degree in psychology from Concordia University Wisconsin and a master of science degree in educational psychology/community counseling from University of Wisconsin—Milwaukee.

As a licensed psychotherapist in both Texas and Wisconsin, Kristin has specialized in treating eating and weight disorders for over a decade. A lifelong Christian and a pastor's wife, Kristin approaches treatment with a focus on spirituality as the foundation of physical and emotional wellness. She founded Pathway Counseling Services in Tomball, Texas (www.pathwaycounselingservices.com).

Kristin is the wife of Rev. Timothy Niekerk, an LCMS ordained minister serving as the senior pastor at Salem Lutheran Church in Tomball, Texas. With great love, tenderness, and grace, Kristin counseled and worked with me for more than a year to sift through the painful issues and scars following my divorce. Time and time again, she pointed me to God, our healer. Her professional counseling experience provided indispensable depth and insight that are invaluable to the heart of this book.

References

American Heritage Dictionary, The. 3rd ed. Boston: Houghton Mifflin, 1992. See esp. p. 331.

Augustine of Hippo, quote on hope. Accessed January 13, 2016. www.goodreads.com/quotes/107417-hope-has-two-beautiful-daughters-their-names-are-anger-and.

Ch. 5 (no specific quotation) Axelrod, Julie. "The 5 Stages of Loss and Grief." Published November 4, 2006. Accessed November 20, 2015. psychcentral.com/lib/the-5-stages-of-loss-and-grief/.

Beckhom, Nancy. Interviewed and quoted by permission.

P. 268 (no specific quotation) "The Bible Book by Book: Psalms." Accessed December 28, 2015. biblehub.com/psalms/.

Blendermann, Loretta. Interviewed and quoted by permission.

Burns, Samantha. Interviewed and quoted by permission.

Carter, Rev. Timothy R. Interviewed and quoted by permission.

Pp. 62–63 Carter, Rev. Timothy R. *The Executioner's Redemption.* St. Louis: Concordia Publishing House, 2016. See esp. pp. 5, 28.

Christman, Marguerite. Interviewed and quoted by permission.

Cross, John R. *By This Name.* Alberta: GoodSeed® International, 2014. See esp. pp. 119–120.

Dommer, Rev. Doug. "Deadly Games: Time to Party," sermon at Salem Lutheran Church, Tomball, Texas. August 16, 2015. Accessed August 19, 2015. vimeo.com/136523497.

Drake-Tornga, Jana. Interviewed and quoted by permission.

Elsey, Carolyn. Interviewed and quoted by permission.

P. 72 Franklin, Benjamin, quote on anger. Accessed January 13, 2016. www.goodreads.com/quotes/62435-whatever-is-begun-in-anger-ends-in-shame.

Giovanetti, Bill. Quoted by permission.

Guest, Tina. Quoted by permission.

Hamil, Cheryl. Interviewed and quoted by permission.

Henderson, Jeff. "The Forgiveness App," sermon at Northpoint Community Church. March 20, 2011. Accessed June 2, 2015. northpoint.org/messages/life_apps/the-forgiveness-app/.

Holbrook, Cindy. "After Divorce: Why It's OK to Be Angry at Your Ex." *Huffington Post*. Published June 27, 2013. Accessed November 9, 2015. www.huffingtonpost.com/2013/06/27/after-divorce-angry-at-yo_n_3399259.html.

Humplik, Doris. Quoted by permission.

Hyatt, Michael. "The Beginner's Guide to Goal Setting" blog post on MichaelHyatt.com. June 14, 2013. Accessed January 4, 2016. michaelhyatt.com/goal-setting.html.

James, Jeanette. Interviewed and quoted by permission.

Kozar, Linda. Interviewed and quoted by permission.

Kromberg, Jennifer, PsyD. "The 5 Stages of Grieving the End of a Relationship," blog post on *Psychology Today*. September 11, 2013. Accessed November 20, 2015. www.psychologytoday.com/blog/inside-out/201309/the-5-stages-grieving-the-end-relationship.

P. 294 Kushner, Rabbi Lawrence, quote on the name of God in Hebrew. Accessed January 13, 2016. www.goodreads.com/author/quotes/14244358._Rabbi_Lawrence_Kushner.

Lee, Whitney. Interviewed and quoted by permission.

Messmer, Janetta. Interviewed and quoted by permission.

Meyers, Tiffany. Interviewed and quoted by permission.

Miller, Matthew. Interviewed and quoted by permission.

P. 152 Paden, Linda. Interviewed and quoted by permission.

Pawlitz, Loren. Interviewed and quoted by permission.

P. 72 Peale, Norman Vincent, quote on anger. Accessed January 13, 2016. www.goodreads.com/quotes/163748-be-so-strong-that-nothing-can-disturb-your-peace-of.

Piper, John. "What is a 'Root of Bitterness'?" article posted at www.desiringgod.org. April 1, 1997. Accessed November 11, 2015. www.desiringgod.org/articles/what-is-a-root-of-bitterness.

Rogers, Dr. Adrian. "The Root of Bitterness," article posted at www.oneplace.com. Accessed November 11, 2015. www.oneplace.com/ministries/love-worth-finding/read/articles/root-of-bitterness-8599.html.

Stanley, Andy. "Nothing But," sermon at Northpoint Community Church. September 8, 2013. Accessed June 2, 2015. northpoint.org/messages/starting-point-series/nothing-but/.

P. 249 Stanley, Andy. "The New Rules of Love, Sex & Dating," sermon series at Northpoint Community Church. May 2011. Accessed May 2011. northpoint.org/messages/starting-point-series/nothing-but/.

Stetler, Lisa. Interviewed and quoted by permission.

Tartakovsky, Margarita. "10 Ways to Build and Preserve Better Boundaries." *Psych Central.* 2015. Accessed on January 3, 2016. psychcentral.com/lib/10-way-to-build-and-preserve-better-boundaries/.

Urick, Louise. Interviewed and quoted by permission.

Y'Barbo-Turner, Kathleen. Interviewed and quoted by permission.

Yagow, Tina. Interviewed and quoted by permission.